# Language and Bilingualism

# Language and Bilingualism

## More Tests of Tests

John W. Oller, Jr.

with the assistance of Steve Chesarek and
Robert Scott

Lewisburg
Bucknell University Press
London and Toronto: Associated University Presses

Associated University Presses
440 Forsgate Drive
Cranbury, NJ 08512

Associated University Presses
25 Sicilian Avenue
London WC1A 2QH, England

Associated University Presses
P.O. Box 39, Clarkson Pstl. Stn.
Mississauga, Ontario,
L5J 3X9 Canada

The paper used in this publication meets the requirements of the American National Standard for Permanence of Paper for Printed Library Materials Z39.48-1984.

**Library of Congress Cataloging-in Publication Data**

Oller, John W., Jr.
    Language and bilingualism : more tests of tests / by John W. Oller, Jr. : with the assistance of Steve Chesarek and Robert Scott.
        p.   cm.
    Includes bibliographical references and index.
    ISBN 0-8387-5210-1 (alk. paper)
    1. Language and languages--ability testing. 2. English language--Study and teaching--Foreign speakers. 3. Bilingualism in children.
I. Chesarek, Steve. II. Scott, Robert. III. Title.
P53.4.O45  1991
418'.0076--dc20

90-55874
CIP

Printed in the United States of America

# Foreword

Language proficiency as a factor in the whole school curriculum remains a topic of considerable importance and concern not only to educators and testers, but to school-goers in general. The publication in 1978 of *Language in Education: Testing the Tests* was indicative of the intrinsic interest the topic holds for educators. That book demonstrated that a substantial amount of the variance observed in a variety of educational and psychological tests is common to language tests. It assumed that there is such a thing as general language proficiency and found evidence to support the thesis that such a factor markedly impacts performance on a wide variety of other kinds of tests.

Many questions, however, were left open by that earlier work. One of them was the relation between primary and non-primary language proficiency. Is it true in bilingual or multilingual children that the child's stronger language, the primary language, is the better indicator of performance on educational tests that are supposed to be free of language influence, such as performance batteries or non-verbal IQ tests? Also, are educational tests in English more susceptible to influence from proficiency in English than are so-called performance and non-verbal tests? The former book scarcely addressed these more specific questions, nor will this one resolve them. However, it is hoped that this volume will accomplish three objectives: (1) improve upon the statistical methods of the earlier work; (2) deepen theoretical understanding of the issues; and (3) broaden the data base. For instance, three Native American groups in addition to Hopis, namely, Crows, Choctaws, and Navajos, are reported on here more extensively than before and additional data are provided for Spanish/English bilinguals as well. Further, a good deal of data are provided concerning the new wave of competency testing (as an exit or graduation criterion) at the secondary level.

It is good to continue to examine the validity of educational tests in a critical fashion. Of course, this includes the ones devised by teachers and researchers as well as commercially produced standardized tests. While the evidence may warrant somewhat more confidence in certain kinds of tests aimed at language proficiency than in tests intended to measure almost any other educational construct, it is the objective in this book to maintain a critical view of language tests along with the rest. On the other hand, associated with a fairly general skepticism about the validity of tests, is a certain hopefulness that some of the discouraging claims (notably those of Arthur Jensen, 1969, 1980) about the impossibility of substantially improving IQ scores or related school performances may have been based on inappropriate interpretations

of test scores, especially scores on what are called "intelligence measures". Although I, for one, never intended to question the *existence* of
intelligence, nor even to assert that "language proficiency and intelligence are virtually equivalent" (contrary to Boyle, 1987, p. 277), I *have*
questioned the validity of many of the tests that purport to measure
"intelligence"--especially if taken to mean "innate capacity". However,
attention has not been limited to intelligence tests, nor is it here. Also
considered are a number of achievement batteries as well as competency
tests, and certain widely used tests of language skills that are somewhat
surface-oriented.

It is asked: isn't it possible that many so-called "intelligence",
"achievement", and "competency" tests (and to some extent even "personality" inventories) may measure proficiency in the examinee's
primary language in some cases more than they measure the constructs
indicated in their labels? Moreover, sustaining earlier research with
language tests per se, evidence is provided showing that surface-oriented
language tests (those focussing on phonology and morphology) generally
have less reliability and less validity than deeper, more pragmatic tests.
Finally, a solid theoretical basis is proposed for the hypothesis that
intelligence itself is a kind of semiotic or representational capacity (cf.
Oller, 1989a). This idea has its roots deep in the philosophy of Charles
Sanders Peirce [1839-1914], and more recently, Albert Einstein, and
John Dewey (Oller, 1989b). Since language, especially one's primary
or best developed language, represents the most powerful and most
general semiotic system for nearly all normal human beings, it follows
that primary language abilities will play a central role in all sorts of
abstract representational tasks. It is in this refined sense that the
hypothesis that intelligence may have a kind of abstract semiotic (even
a sort of deep linguistic) basis has, it would seem, its greatest
plausibility and theoretical strength.

The discerning reader will see immediately that this is not a
statistical argument. It cannot be made to depend on any sort of
statistical reasoning. However, it does have certain consequences in
terms of educational testing, and these consequences lead to certain
statistically testable hypotheses. Some of those as well as the theory
itself are explored here somewhat more deeply than in the 1978 volume.
It would have been good to have been able to work with confirmatory
factoring rather than the classical exploratory approach, but because
of the way the data were collected by the various contributors this was
hardly feasible. At any rate, it is hoped that careful readers will see
that there is yet much to be learned from the classical factoring approach in relation to the questions posed here and especially with the
specific populations of subjects studied.

John W. Oller, Jr.
July 1, 1990

# Acknowledgments

There were a number of collaborators in earlier stages of this work who deserve special mention. Chief among them were Paul and Virginia Streiff who have explicitly asked not to be included as co-authors. Nevertheless, their contribution in the data collection stages of the work was indispensable and is gratefully acknowledged. In addition a number of people at the University of Texas at San Antonio were also involved in data collection: these included John Ball, Virginia Berk, Sandra Di Quinzio, Armando Ibarra, Anne Krueger, and Joyce Osborn. Co-authors, Robert Scott and Steve Chesarek are also gratefully acknowledged.

More importantly still, perhaps, are the several subject populations who participated in various stages of the research by taking one or more of the tests investigated here. The greatest debt of thanks is owed to them, and in a broader sense to all the students in classrooms, and others outside the classroom, who were ever asked to submit their talents, skills, knowledge, and abilities to whatever scrutiny may be afforded by educational or other mental tests.

It should be clear from the outset that in this book, as in the one with Perkins in 1978, the research questions are focussed not on the subject populations per se, *but on the tests themselves.* The key issue remains the same now as it was more than a decade ago: *to what extent are the tests measuring what they purport to measure?* As far as the research in this book is concerned, therefore, it is the tests that are being tested (not the speakers of Choctaw, Crow, Hopi, Navajo, Spanish, and/or English). It is hoped that such research attention, addressed to tests rather than subject populations, will help all school-goers, but especially those of enriched multilingual and multicultural heritage, to get a more valid, more equitable, and fairer education. To that end, this book is dedicated. May it serve in a small way as a statement in honor of the various groups of subjects whose performance proves the benefits of having more than one language system through which to view the experience that both defines us as members of one or more communities and richly marks us as culturally distinct.

# Contents

Foreword . . . . . . . . . . . . . . . . . . . . . . . . . . . . . . iii
Acknowledgments . . . . . . . . . . . . . . . . . . . . . . . . . . v

**Part I:** **Background and Theory** . . . . . . . . . . . . . . . 1

Chapter 1 Introduction . . . . . . . . . . . . . . . . . . . . . . . 3
Chapter 2 Intelligence as Semiosis . . . . . . . . . . . . . . . . . 11
Chapter 3 Intelligence, Semiosis, and Biology . . . . . . . . . . 31
Chapter 4 Intelligence Test Items . . . . . . . . . . . . . . . . . 49

**Part II:** **Monolinguals and ESL Adults** . . . . . . . . . . . 61

Chapter 5 Competency and Monolinguals at the Secondary
 Level . . . . . . . . . . . . . . . . . . . . . . . . . . . . . . . 63
Chapter 6 Competency Scores and English Proficiency of Adult
 ESL Students . . . . . . . . . . . . . . . . . . . . . . . . . . 75
Chapter 7 Non-Verbal Intelligence and English Proficiency of
 Adult ESL Students . . . . . . . . . . . . . . . . . . . . . . 85

**Part III:** **English Proficiency and Achievement of
 Bilingual Children** . . . . . . . . . . . . . . . . . . . . 93

Chapter 8 Language, Achievement, and Non-Verbal Intelligence
 Tests of Bilingual Children (with Steve Chesarek)
 . . . . . . . . . . . . . . . . . . . . . . . . . . . . . . . . . . 95
Chapter 9 Language and Achievement of Hopi-English
 Bilinguals, Grades 2-6 . . . . . . . . . . . . . . . . . . . 113
Chapter 10 Language and Achievement of Navajo-English
 Bilinguals at Grades 3-9 . . . . . . . . . . . . . . . . . . 125

**Part IV:** **Achievement and Bilingualism** . . . . . . . . . . 141

Chapter 11 Language and Achievement of Choctaw-English
 Bilinguals in Kindergarten (with Robert Scott) . . . 143
Chapter 12 Language and Achievement of Spanish-English
 Bilinguals, Grades 3-5 . . . . . . . . . . . . . . . . . . . 148

References . . . . . . . . . . . . . . . . . . . . . . . . . . . . . . 163
Tests, Manuals, and Reports . . . . . . . . . . . . . . . . . . . 171
Index . . . . . . . . . . . . . . . . . . . . . . . . . . . . . . . . . 172

# List of Tables

*CHART 5.1* The "Content-by-Skills Matrix: Examples of Tasks" from the *Adult Performance Level Program (User's Guide*, n. d., p. 1) . . . . . . . . . . . . . . . . . . . . . . . . . . . . . . . . . . 66

*TABLE 5.1* APL *Survey* Means, Totals Possible, Standard Deviations, and KR-20 Reliabilities Adjusted to Full-Length Tests, N = 2853 . . . . . . . . . . . . . . . . . . . . . . . . . . . . . . . . . . . . 70

*TABLE 5.2* APL *Survey* Intercorrelations among Content Area Subscales (Form AS1), N = 2853 . . . . . . . . . . . . . . . . 71

*TABLE 5.3* APL *Survey* Intercorrelations among Skill Area Subscales (Form AS1), N = 2853 . . . . . . . . . . . . . . . . . . 72

*TABLE 5.4* Principal Factor Solutions (with iterations) for Content and Skill Areas on the APL Survey (Form AS1), N = 2853 . . . . . . . . . . . . . . . . . . . . . . . . . . . . . . . . . . 72

*TABLE 5.5* Specificities and Error Terms for the Subscales of the APL *Survey* (Form AS1), N = 2853 . . . . . . . . . . . . . . 73

*TABLE 6.1* Means, Standard Deviations, and KR-21 Reliabilities for the *English Comprehension Level* and Subscores on the *Tests of Adult Basic Education*, Form E, N = 172 . . . . 79

*TABLE 6.2* Means, Standard Deviations, and KR-21 Reliabilities for the *English Comprehension Level* and Subscores on the *Tests of Adult Basic Education*, Form M, N = 187 . . . . 79

*TABLE 6.3* Means, Standard Deviations, and KR-21 Reliabilities for the *English Comprehension Level* and Subscores on the *Tests of Adult Basic Education*, Form D, N = 486 . . . . 80

*TABLE 6.4* Correlations between the Total Score on the *English Comprehension Level* and the Subscores on the *Tests of Adult Basic Education*, Form E, N = 172 . . . . . . . . . . . 80

*TABLE 6.5* Correlations between the Total Score on the *English Comprehension Level* and the Subscores on the *Tests of Adult Basic Education*, Form M, N = 187 . . . . . . . . . . 81

*TABLE 6.6* Correlations between the Total Score on the *English Comprehension Level* and the Subscores on the *Tests of Adult Basic Education*, Form D, N = 486 . . . . . . . . . . 81

*TABLE 6.7* Principal Factor Solution with Iterations for the *English Comprehension Level* and the Subscores on the *Tests of Adult Basic Education*, Form E, N = 172 . . . . . 82

*TABLE 6.8* Principal Factor Solution with Iterations for the *English Comprehension Level* and the Subscores on the *Tests of Adult Basic Education*, Form M, N = 187 . . . . . 82

*TABLE 6.9* Principal Factor Solution with Iterations (Varimax Rotation) for the *English Comprehension Level* and the Subscores on the *Tests of Adult Basic Education*, Form D, N = 486 . . . . . . . . . . . . . . . . . . . . . . . . . . . . . . . . . . 83

*TABLE 6.10* Estimates of Specificity and Error for the *English*

*Comprehension Level* and the Subscores on the *Tests of Adult Basic Education*, Forms E (N =172), M (N =187), and D (N = 486) .......................... 83

TABLE *7.1* Means, Standard Deviations, and KR-21 Reliabilities for the *English Comprehension Level*, a Multiple Choice Cloze Test, a Standard Cloze Test, and the *Test of Non-Verbal Reasoning*, N = 72 ...................... 89

TABLE *7.2* Correlations between the *English Comprehension Level*, a Multiple Choice Cloze Test, a Standard Cloze Test, and the *Test of Non-Verbal Reasoning*, N = 72 .......... 89

TABLE *7.3* Principal Factor Solution with Iterations for the *English Comprehension Level*, a Multiple Choice Cloze Test, a Standard Cloze Test, and the *Test of Non-Verbal Reasoning*, N = 72 ............................ 90

TABLE *7.4* Reliabilities, Communalities, Specificities, and Error Estimates for Scores on the *English Comprehension Level*, a Multiple Choice Cloze Test, a Standard Cloze Test, and the *Test of Non-Verbal Reasoning*, N = 72 .......... 91

TABLE *8.1* Means, Number of Cases, Standard Deviations, and Estimated Reliabilities for the *Peabody Individual Achievement Tests*, the *Raven's Progressive Matrices*, the *Peabody Picture Vocabulary Test*, and Portions of the *Revised Illinois Test of Psycholinguistic Abilities*: First and Second Graders at Crow Agency in 1971-72, N > 72 < 79 ..... 105

TABLE *8.2* Means, Number of Cases, Standard Deviations, and Estimated Reliabilities for the *Peabody Individual Achievement Tests*, the *Raven's Progressive Matrices*, the *Peabody Picture Vocabulary Test*, and Portions of the *Revised Illinois Test of Psycholinguistic Abilities*: First and Second Graders at Crow Agency in 1972-73, N > 68 < 74 ..... 106

TABLE *8.3* Means, Number of Cases, Standard Deviations, and Estimated Reliabilities for the *Peabody Individual Achievement Tests*, *Cattell's Culture Fair Intelligence Tests*, Scale 2, Forms A and B, the *Peabody Picture Vocabulary Test*, the Auditory Vocal Association Test from the *Revised ITPA*, and the *Bellugi Syntax Measure*: Third Graders at Crow Agency in 1972-73, N > 21 < 25 .............. 107

TABLE *8.4* Intercorrelations for the *Peabody Individual Achievement Tests*, the Raven Progressive Matrices, the *Peabody Picture Vocabulary Test*, and Portions of the *Revised Illinois Test of Psycholinguistic Abilities*: First and Second Graders at Crow Agency in 1971-72, N > 72 < 79 .......... 107

TABLE *8.5* Intercorrelations for the *Peabody Individual Achievement Tests*, the Raven Progressive Matrices, the *Peabody Picture Vocabulary Test*, and Portions of the *Revised Illinois Test of Psycholinguistic Abilities*: First and Second Graders at Crow Agency in 1972-73, N > 68 < 74 .......... 108

TABLE *8.6* Intercorrelations for the *Peabody Individual Achieve-*

ment Tests, *Cattell's Culture Fair Intelligence Tests*, Scale 2, Forms A and B, the *Peabody Picture Vocabulary Test*, the Auditory Vocal Association Test (from the *ITPA*), and the *Bellugi Syntax Measure*: Third Graders at Crow Agency in 1972-73, N > 22 < 25 ................ 108

TABLE *8.7* Principal Factor Analysis with Iterations (Varimax Rotation) for the *Peabody Individual Achievement Tests*, the *Raven Progressive Matrices*, the *Peabody Picture Vocabulary Test*, and Portions of the *Revised Illinois Test of Psycholinguistic Abilities*: First and Second Graders at Crow Agency in 1971-72, N > 72 < 79 ............ 109

TABLE *8.8* Principal Factor Analysis with Iterations (Varimax Rotation) for the *Peabody Individual Achievement Tests*, the *Raven Progressive Matrices*, the *Peabody Picture Vocabulary Test*, and Portions of the *Revised Illinois Test of Psycholinguistic Abilities*: First and Second Graders at Crow Agency in 1972-73, N > 68 < 74 ............ 110

TABLE *8.9* Principal Factor Analysis with Iterations (Varimax Rotation) for Intercorrelations for the *Peabody Individual Achievement Tests*, *Cattell's Culture Fair Intelligence Tests*, Scale 2, Forms A and B, the *Peabody Picture Vocabulary Test*, the Auditory-Vocal Association Test (from the *ITPA*), and the *Bellugi Syntax Measure*: Third Graders at Crow Agency in 1972-73, N > 22 < 25 ................ 111

TABLE *8.10* Estimates of Specificity and Error for the *Peabody Individual Achievement Tests*, *Cattell's Culture Fair Intelligence Tests*, Scale 2, Forms A and B, *Raven's Progressive Matrices*, the *Peabody Picture Vocabulary Test*, the *Illinois Test of Psycholinguistic Abilities*, *Cattell's Culture Fair Intelligence Tests*, Scale 2, Forms A and B, and the *Bellugi Syntax Measure* ........................ 112

TABLE *9.1* Dominance Ratings by Grade Level for Hopi-English Bilinguals in Northern Arizona ............. 116

TABLE *9.2* Fluency Ratings in English and Hopi ......... 117

TABLE *9.3* Means, Standard Deviations, and Reliabilities for Cloze, Subjective Ratings, and the *California Achievement Tests* ............................... 117

TABLE *9.4* Correlations between Cloze, Subjective Ratings, and the California Achievement Tests for Grade 3 at Hopi, N = 15 ................................... 118

TABLE *9.5* Correlations between Cloze, Subjective Ratings, and the *California Achievement Tests* for Grade 4 at Hopi, N = 19 ................................ 118

TABLE *9.6* Correlations between Cloze, Subjective Ratings, and the *California Achievement Tests* for Grade 5 at Hopi, N = 10 ................................ 119

TABLE *9.7* Correlations between Cloze, Subjective Ratings, and the *California Achievement Tests* for Grade 6 at Hopi, N = 15 . . . . . . . . . . . . . . . . . . . . . . . . . . . . . . . . . 119

TABLE *9.8* Principal Factor Analysis with Iterations (Varimax Rotation) for Cloze, Subjective Ratings, and the *California Achievement Tests*: Third Graders at Hopi 1978-79, N = 15 . . . . . . . . . . . . . . . . . . . . . . . . . . . . . . . 120

TABLE *9.9* Principal Factor Analysis with Iterations (Varimax Rotation) for Cloze, Subjective Ratings, and the *California Achievement Tests*: Fourth Graders at Hopi 1978-79, N = 19 . . . . . . . . . . . . . . . . . . . . . . . . . . . . . 121

TABLE *9.10* Principal Factor Analysis with Iterations (Varimax Rotation) for Cloze, Subjective Ratings, and the *California Achievement Tests*: Fifth Graders at Hopi 1978-79, N = 10 . . . . . . . . . . . . . . . . . . . . . . . . . . . . . . . 122

TABLE *9.11* Principal Factor Analysis with Iterations (Varimax Rotation) for Cloze, Subjective Ratings, and the *California Achievement Tests*: Sixth Graders at Hopi 1978-79, N = 15 . . . . . . . . . . . . . . . . . . . . . . . . . . . . : 123

TABLE *9.12* Estimates of Specificity and Error for Cloze, Subjective Ratings, and the *California Achievement Tests* . . . . 124

TABLE *10.1* Language Dominance in Navajo and English as Judged by Teachers, N = 181 . . . . . . . . . . . . . . . . 126

TABLE *10.2* Means and Standard Deviations for Grades 3 to 9 at Rock Point on the *Comprehensive Tests of Basic Skills* and Written Cloze Tests . . . . . . . . . . . . . . . . . . . . . . 128

TABLE *10.3* Correlations between a Cloze Test, and the Various Parts of the *Comprehensive Tests of Basic Skills* for Grade 3 at Rock Point, N = 30 . . . . . . . . . . . . . . . . . . . . . . 129

TABLE *10.4* Correlations between a Cloze Test, and the Various Parts of the *Comprehensive Tests of Basic Skills* for Grade 4 at Rock Point, N > 22 < 28 . . . . . . . . . . . . . . . . . . 130

TABLE *10.5* Correlations between a Cloze Test, and the Various Parts of the *Comprehensive Tests of Basic Skills* for Grade 5 at Rock Point, N > 21 < 24 . . . . . . . . . . . . . . . . . . 130

TABLE *10.6* Correlations between a Cloze Test, and the Various Parts of the *Comprehensive Tests of Basic Skills* for Grade 6 at Rock Point, N > 36 < 40 . . . . . . . . . . . . . . . . . . 131

TABLE *10.7* Correlations between a Cloze Test, and the Various Parts of the *Comprehensive Tests of Basic Skills* for Grade 7 at Rock Point, N > 18 < 23 . . . . . . . . . . . . . . . . . . 131

TABLE *10.8* Correlations between a Cloze Test, and the Various Parts of the *Comprehensive Tests of Basic Skills* for Grade 8 at Rock Point, N > 20 < 23 . . . . . . . . . . . . . . . . . . 132

TABLE *10.9* Correlations between a Cloze Test, and the Various Parts of the *Comprehensive Tests of Basic Skills* for Grade 9 at Rock Point, N > 14 < 18 . . . . . . . . . . . . . . . . . 132

TABLE *10.10* Principal Factor Analysis with Iterations (Varimax Rotation) for a Cloze Test and the *Comprehensive Tests*

*of Basic Skills*: Third Graders at Rock Point in 1978-79,
N = 30 . . . . . . . . . . . . . . . . . . . . . . . . . . . . . . . . 133
*TABLE 10.11* Principal Factor Analysis with Iterations (Varimax
Rotation) for a Cloze Test and the *Comprehensive Tests
of Basic Skills*: Fourth Graders at Rock Point in 1978-
79, N > 22 < 28 . . . . . . . . . . . . . . . . . . . . . . . . . 133
*TABLE 10.12* Principal Factor Analysis with Iterations (Varimax
Rotation) for a Cloze Test and the *Comprehensive Tests
of Basic Skills* Fifth Graders at Rock Point in 1978-79, N
> 21 < 24 . . . . . . . . . . . . . . . . . . . . . . . . . . . . . 134
*TABLE 10.13* Principal Factor Analysis with Iterations (Varimax
Rotation) for a Cloze Test and the *Comprehensive Tests
of Basic Skills*: Sixth Graders at Rock Point in 1978-79,
N > 36 < 40 . . . . . . . . . . . . . . . . . . . . . . . . . . . . 134
*TABLE 10.14* Principal Factor Analysis with Iterations (Varimax
Rotation) for a Cloze Test and the *Comprehensive Tests
of Basic Skills*: Seventh Graders at Rock Point in 1978-
79, N > 18 < 23 . . . . . . . . . . . . . . . . . . . . . . . . . 135
*TABLE 10.15* Principal Factor Analysis with Iterations (Varimax
Rotation) for a Cloze Test and the *Comprehensive Tests
of Basic Skills*: Eighth Graders at Rock Point in 1978-
79, N > 20 < 23 . . . . . . . . . . . . . . . . . . . . . . . . . 135
*TABLE 10.16* Principal Factor Analysis with Iterations (Varimax
Rotation) for a Cloze Test and the *Comprehensive Tests
of Basic Skills*: Ninth Graders at Rock Point in 1978-79,
N > 14 < 18 . . . . . . . . . . . . . . . . . . . . . . . . . . . . 136
*TABLE 10.17* Specificities and Error Terms for Grades 3 to 9 at
Rock Point on the *Comprehensive Tests of Basic Skills* and
Written Cloze Tests . . . . . . . . . . . . . . . . . . . . . . . 137
*TABLE 11.1* Means and Standard Deviations on the *Metropolitan
Readiness Test* and Selected Predictor Measures: 1976
Sample, N = 32 . . . . . . . . . . . . . . . . . . . . . . . . . . 146
*TABLE 12.1* Dominance Ratings by Grade Level for Spanish-Eng-
lish Bilinguals in San Antonio, Texas, N = 70 . . . . . . . 149
*TABLE 12.2* Fluency Ratings in English and Spanish . . . . . . . 149
*TABLE 12.3* Means, Standard Deviations, and Reliabilities for
Grades 3, 4, and 5 in a San Antonio Inner City School on
English and Spanish Cloze Scores, Dominance and Fluency
Ratings, the *Language Assessment Scales*, and the *Metropol-
itan Achievement Tests* . . . . . . . . . . . . . . . . . . . . . 154
*TABLE 12.4* Correlations between English and Spanish Cloze
Tests, the *Language Assessment Scales*, and Three Com-
posite Scores from the *Metropolitan Achievement Tests* . . 155
*TABLE 12.5* Correlations between Spanish and English Cloze
Tests, Fluency Ratings, and the *Metropolitan Achievement
Tests* for a Sample of Spanish and English Bilinguals in
San Antonio at Grade 3, N > 18 < 23 . . . . . . . . . . . . 156

TABLE *12.6* Correlations between Spanish and English Cloze Tests, Fluency Ratings, and the *Metropolitan Achievement Tests* for a Sample of Spanish and English Bilinguals in San Antonio at Grade 4, N > 21 < 24 . . . . . . . . . . . . . 157

TABLE *12.7* Correlations between Spanish and English Cloze Tests, Fluency Ratings, and the *Metropolitan Achievement Tests* for a Sample of Spanish and English Bilinguals in San Antonio at Grade 5, N > 23 < 26 . . . . . . . . . . . . . 157

TABLE *12.8* Principal Factor Analysis with Iterations (Varimax Rotation) for Spanish and English Cloze Tests, Ratings of Spanish and English Fluency, and the *Metropolitan Achievement Tests* for a Sample of Spanish and English Bilinguals in San Antonio at Grade 3, N > 18 < 24 . . . . . . . . . . . 158

TABLE *12.9* Principal Factor Analysis with Iterations (Unrotated Solution) for Spanish and English Cloze Tests, Ratings of Spanish and English Fluency, and the *Metropolitan Achievement Tests* for a Sample of Spanish and English Bilinguals in San Antonio at Grade 4, N > 22 < 24 . . . . 159

TABLE *12.10* Principal Factor Analysis with Iterations (Unrotated Solution) for Spanish and English Cloze Tests, Ratings of Spanish and English Fluency, and the *Metropolitan Achievement Tests* for a Sample of Spanish and English Bilinguals in San Antonio at Grade 5, N > 23 < 26 . . . . 160

TABLE *12.11* Specificities and Error Terms on Spanish and English Cloze Tests, Fluency Scales, and the *Metropolitan Achievement Tests* . . . . . . . . . . . . . . . . . . . . . . . . 161

## List of Figures

FIGURE 2.1. PRAGMATIC MAPPING. . . . . . . . . . . . . . . . . . 13

FIGURE 2.2. DIFFERENT KINDS OF SEMIOTIC CAPACITIES. . . . . . 13

FIGURE 2.3 A MODULAR INFORMATION PROCESSING EXPANSION OF THE PRAGMATIC MAPPING PROCESS. . . . . . . . . . . . . 18

FIGURE 2.4. LANGUAGE PROFICIENCY IN TERMS OF DOMAINS OF GRAMMAR. . . . . . . . . . . . . . . . . . . . . . . . . . . . 28

FIGURE 2.5. LANGUAGE PROFICIENCY IN TERMS OF SKILLS. . . . . 28

FIGURE 4.1. ITEMS FROM "AN INTRODUCTION TO **IPAT** ... ". . . . 52

ILLUSTRATION 8.1. ITEM 9, *PIAT* MATHEMATICS. . . . . . . . . . 96

Illustration 8.2. ITEM 25, *PIAT* READING COMPREHENSION. . . 97

ILLUSTRATION 8.3. ITEM 74, *PIAT* SPELLING. . . . . . . . . . . . 98

ILLUSTRATION 8.4. ITEM 93, *PPVT*. . . . . . . . . . . . . . . . . . 100

ILLUSTRATION 8.5. A PATTERN FROM *RAVEN'S MATRICES*. . . . . . 101

ILLUSTRATION 8.6. A MATRIX FROM *RAVEN'S MATRICES*. . . . . . 102

# Part I: Background and Theory

# Chapter 1
# Introduction

This book considers the role of language as a factor in educational practice in general, but more particularly in educational or mental tests. As such, it is both sequel and update to *Language in Education: Testing the Tests* published by Newbury House in 1978. Another pair of books dealing with some of the same subject matter were *Issues in Language Testing Research* (Oller, 1983b) and *Research in Language Testing* (Oller and Perkins, 1980). The positions staked out in Chapter 22 of the *Issues* book especially are updated here and carried somewhat further. The central question remains: what part does language proficiency play in education in general, and more particularly, in educational or other mental tests?

In the earlier volume, Oller and Perkins along with their collaborators, Gunnarsson, Stump, and V. Streiff, asked, what if the variance in many educational and mental tests were largely due to proficiency in the primary language of the test taker? At that time, all of the contributors to that book assumed a positive answer to this question. We contended that language proficiency probably is a major factor in nearly all psychological and educational tests. However, the research reported in that volume was regarded as controversial at best.

Two main counter arguments were advanced and more than one study was put forward (e.g., see Boyle, 1987 and his references) to try to refute either our theoretical position or our research methods or both. Interestingly, however, the counter arguments offered (e.g., Farhady, 1983, Carroll, 1983, Vollmer and Sang, 1983, and Boyle, 1987) seemed to contradict each other. Before going further, those arguments must be considered carefully.

On the one hand, it was claimed that the importance of a general factor of language proficiency was already apparent and did not merit further attention. In this case, the intent was, it would seem, to trivialize the whole issue. On the other hand, it was argued that the importance of the language factor in previous research (especially in Oller and Perkins, 1978, and 1980) was exaggerated and inflated artefactually by inappropriate statistical methods. Interestingly, it can hardly be both ways. If the first argument were correct, the second would have no effect. A method that demonstrates what is already admitted to be correct is, at least that far, *ipso facto* correct. On the other hand, if the statistical methods were adjusted as recommended, in particular, that is, where principal components analysis was replaced by classical principal factor analysis, the critics merely defined a secondary position by saying that the result, though true, was trivial.

3

Both of these arguments are answered here. The first is best answered on theoretical grounds (Chapter 2 below) which show that there is simply no way to trivialize the central role of language in human representational systems. This point was argued by Ferdinand de Saussure (see Oller, 1989b) and was developed more fully by C. S. Peirce than by any other scholar. Later, following Peirce, John Dewey, and even Albert Einstein developed the point in a similar vein. More recently, advances in biology and the brain sciences have given additional theoretical support to the view that deep language-like representational systems are critical to all aspects of biological organization and neurological functioning (a point developed in Chapter 3 below).

The second argument is answered by additional evidence drawn from studies that remove the critical statistical weaknesses pointed up in reference to the earlier work (Chapters 5-12). In sum, the first counter-argument is disposed of on the basis of a hierarchical semiotic theory that shows semiotic representation to be the sine qua non of intelligence in general, and the second counter-argument is disposed of by showing that the hypothesized relationship between language proficiency and other tests persists when the statistical weaknesses of principal components analysis are removed.

On the side of statistical method, the main argument has been that principal components analysis, which was used in much of the earlier work, inflated the apparent strength of the hypothesized general language factor (Farhady, 1983, Vollmer and Sang, 1983, Carroll, 1983a, 1983b). Would the language factor in educational tests remain strong if this error were corrected? It should be noted that Carroll (1983a) admitted that it would (for confirming evidence see Boldt, 1989, and Oltman, Stricker, and Barrows, 1990), yet, apparently for other reasons, Carroll continued to argue that the importance of such a factor was overdrawn.

Farhady and others argued that classical factor analysis should be applied rather than principal components analysis. Both methods begin with a square correlation matrix; that is, a matrix consisting of all the intercorrelations between a given set of measures. However, they handle the elements on the diagonal somewhat differently. In the initial square correlation matrix, the diagonal elements consist of the correlations between each test and itself. Or, alternatively, they may be viewed as the total variance in each test (since by definition each measure correlates perfectly with itself). The diagonal elements, therefore, of the raw correlation matrix are arbitrarily defined as unities.

In classical factoring, the elements on the diagonal are replaced with estimates of common variance; that is, instead of using all of the variance in each test, the variance which is not shared by two or more tests is discarded at the outset. In this way, the error variance is eliminated along with any variance that is entirely specific to a single measure. By contrast, the principal components method, works with unities (that is all of the variance in each test) on the diagonal and thus distributes error variance and specific variance to the factor(s) which it subsequently derives. This is generally recognized as undesirable. The only case where it makes no difference is when the specific variance and the error variance are negligibly small in all of the tests input to the analysis. This rarely occurs in actual situations.

Therefore, the analyses presented here all use the classical factoring approach. As noted earlier, it would have been desirable to have been able to apply the more powerful confirmatory factoring methods advocated by Purcell (1983) and Bachman and Palmer (1981, 1982), but since the designs employed did not permit this in most cases, for the sake of consistency, wherever factoring methods are required, in this book, classical factoring is used.

While earlier work (especially that reported in *Language in Education: Testing the Tests*) was concerned with the content of tests themselves (Gunnarsson, 1978), the performances they required (Streiff, 1983, and especially Chapter 4 in this volume), or the variance generated by them (Stump, 1978; Oller, 1976a; Oller and Hinofotis, 1980), here equal interest is afforded the crucial question of what abilities actually underlie test performances and mental behavior in general. The latter issue, it would seem is inferentially linked to the former questions, but is nonetheless distinct from them. On the one hand, there are questions about what the tests are capable of measuring, and on the other, there is the question of what abilities exist to be measured. It can be seen that these questions are logically distinguishable.

To determine what the tests are measuring, in addition to theoretical reasoning and content analysis of the tests, at some point empirical methods will be required to examine the variance produced by those tests. To determine what abilities exist, however, the more fundamental issue, is largely a matter of theory construction. The former class of problems generally fall under the *test validity question* and the latter *the competence question*. Of course, this is not to say that it is desirable to deal with either to the neglect of the other as, it would seem, some have (cf. Boyle, 1987). To the contrary, it seems necessary to recognize as inevitable the interaction between theories of competence and hypothesized explanations for the variance generated by tests.

Boyle, for instance, has posited one construct after another while admitting the lack of any comprehensive theory to relate them coherently. Yet just such a theory is what is indispensably required (cf. Cummins, 1981, 1984, 1986, 1989, and Krashen, 1982, 1985). Boyle asserts that "reasoning" is a "subset" of "intelligence" and yet is distinct from the deep semiotic ability posited by Oller (1983a). Yet he admits, after appealing to certain authorities, notably Sternberg (1982, p. 285), that "psychologists disagree considerably about the extent to which the factor associated with reasoning can be usefully subdivided" (Boyle, 1987, p. 279). He cites several different theories suggesting as many as sixteen and as few as three highly overlapping reasoning factors. He offers no attempt to resolve the differences nor to suggest whether they are valid or merely different ways of viewing the phenomena of interest.

While Boyle alludes to the hierarchical model first broached by Oller (1983a) following Peirce and Dewey, his interpretation of it differs from what was intended. Perhaps this is owing to the fact that the model derives from a rather different theory of inferential reasoning than the various ideas about it referred to by Boyle. The model aims to capsulize some of the thinking of C. S. Peirce, who is widely regarded as America's greatest logician (and also a scientist on a level with Leibnitz in scope and quality of work; see Nagel, 1959). Peirce insisted that semiosis, or symbolization, *is* inferential reasoning and vice versa. He demonstrated logically that there are three distinct kinds of inference (or representational capacity)--deductive, inductive, and abductive. Roughly speaking deduction involves reasoning from given rules (general propositions) to specific cases; induction involves the use of specific cases to justify general rules; and abduction involves the association of a subject (any subject) with a predicate (any predicate). These he proved with mathematical rigor could not be reduced to any simpler system. However, Peirce also showed with the same rigorous logic that all ordinary reasoning *is* a manifestation of representational capacity. The hierarchical model based on Peirce's theory (Oller, 1983a; 1989a) and the testable hypotheses that follow from it, however, are passed over by Boyle in favor of a simpler interpretation: he says the model equates general intelligence with primary language proficiency and with non-primary language proficiency. Neither of these equations, however, follows from the hierarchy which was proposed specifically to distinguish general semiotic capacity from more specialized types and at the same time to show how they are all interrelated (more about this in Chapter 2).

Boyle proposed, then, to test his version of the theory by showing that certain tasks involving "inductive reasoning" (as he defines it) produce variance that is distinguishable from language proficiency. Incidentally, according to a Peircean perspective it is easy to see that the tests of "inductive reasoning" used by Boyle involve chiefly what Peirce called abduction and also, to some extent, deduction. However, Boyle does not even attempt to test primary language ability (though his tests of "inductive reasoning" cannot fail to do so in some measure) but rather tests 205 speakers of Cantonese, not in Cantonese (their primary language), but in English. Subsequently he finds that "reasoning ability" is distinguishable (by classical factor analysis with a varimax rotation procedure) from proficiency in English as a non-primary language as acquired by Cantonese speakers. No doubt the conclusion, though inexplicitly stated, is correct on the whole, but if it is construed to bear on the hierarchical model supposedly in question (Oller, 1983a; elaborated in 1989a), it only supports that model (see Chapter 2 below).

In the present book, both the theory and the research base for it are expanded in several ways. On the *test validity question* additional instruments, populations, and language backgrounds are examined. On the *competence question* a couple of possibilities are considered: is language proficiency (primary or non-primary) important only to the sorts of surface processing which are obviously involved in understanding test directions and verbally presented items? Or, is language proficiency also important to performances thought of as "non-verbal" (especially see Chapter 4 on this latter possibility)? The data base is also extended with respect to the more complex case of bilingual populations. Does a general factor on tests that use English reflect mainly English proficiency? Or to what extent and under what circumstances does the other language of bilingual subjects also enter the picture? (Incidentally, these same questions apply with additional force in the case of multi-linguals with more than two languages.) To what extent can language proficiency be separated from the other constructs that educators often wish to measure? Or, under what conditions can it be confidently assumed that intelligence, achievement, and competency (not to mention personality) tests are really measuring what they purport to measure?

It seems that answers to these questions and others that stem from them are crucial to educators who have the difficult and weighty (even onerous) responsibility for selecting, administering, and interpreting tests. This book is certainly not the first to be concerned with these matters and it is not expected to be the last. Foreshadowing some of the concerns addressed here, Wesman (1968) pointed out that many tests which go by different names and which purport to measure quite different constructs may actually measure similar abilities to a great extent. Doesn't any such observation draw the validity of many tests into question? Doesn't it also suggest that many popular theories of human abilities may need revision? Would it surprise anyone if many of the posited constructs of human intelligence, for example, should have to be modified? Wouldn't it in fact be far more surprising if many of the current conceptions (those in this book not exempted by any means) did *not* turn out to need significant revision?

In any case, this book is offered as an update of previous work on this topic (especially Oller and Perkins, 1978), and it is hoped that it will contribute toward developing somewhat more plausible answers to some of the intriguing mysteries of the relation between human language abilities, other representational capacities, and intelligence. Of equal importance is the goal of contributing to a more cautious and less dogmatic interpretation of educational and psychological tests.

The book is divided, somewhat roughly and arbitrarily, into four parts. Part I, consisting of Chapters 1-4, overviews the book and intro-duces its theory and methods. Chapter 2 is a revised and expanded version of a paper that appeared first in the December 1981 issue of the journal *Language Learning*. It is a speculative treatment of the in-terrelationship between language proficiency (primary and non-prima-ry), and other semiotic abilities, with what Spearman loosely called "general" intelligence. Among other things, it asks to what extent prim-ary language ability can be identified with the deepest of cognitive capacities? (On this question also see Streiff, 1983.)

It may be asserted that Chapters 2-4, therefore, are primarily concerned with *the competence question*. As a tentative answer to this question a semiotic hierarchy is proposed in which the development of the primary language plays a central role. The notion that intelligence is based in a deep language-like system is refined: it is supposed that the principal basis of such a system is a general semiotic capacity whose elements are believed to be the underlying semantic/syntactic basis of propositional meanings. These, together with the three sorts of inferential reasoning posited by Peirce (deduction, induction, and abduction--see above), are hypothesized to underlie the whole scope of intelligence. Distinctions, however, are made between three subordinate semiotic systems which include but are not limited to (i) linguistic, (ii) kinesic (not "kinetic" as in Boyle's misquote, 1987, p. 278), and (iii) sensory-motor systems. Each of these subordinate systems branches into more particular representational systems each of which supertends particular representational sequences in experience (called "texts", where this term is used in broad sense to include all sorts of discourse: see Chapter 2 below). Evidence supporting the model is discussed in Chapters 2-4.

All of the remaining parts of the book deal mainly with *the test validity question*. They are divided depending roughly on the type of populations or tests studied. Part III, consisting of Chapters 5-7 deals with adult monolingual speakers of English and with adult students of English as a second language.

Chapter 5 deals specifically with what has been called "competency" testing. "Competency" tests supposedly assess what a person will be able to do with school-acquired skills outside of the classroom in what is often, somewhat naively, called "the real world" (as if the classroom itself were in some other world, or were itself unreal). The development of such tests was motivated by certain objections that were raised from time to time about both intelligence tests and achievement tests. For instance, in his 1921 critique of the *Stanford-Binet Intelligence Scale*, Thorndike insisted that little or no confidence could be placed in such a test as a predictor of performance in ordinary life-tasks such as machine maintenance, crop harvesting, buying and selling, and the like. Competency tests in general were a response to this criticism, and the *Adult Performance-Level Survey* served as the basis of the most widely used competency tests in the United States. All such tests are intended to address more "life-like" tasks than traditional IQ or achievement tests.

In Chapter 5, the question posed is how much common variance underlies the several parts of that inventory? And it is asked to what extent the determined communality can be attributed to proficiency in English (which happens to be the language of the test). Passing this test or one like it is now required of most graduating seniors in the United States. This fact makes the investigation of the character of the test both in terms of its content and the variance that it generates a high priority for psychometricians.

In Chapter 6, for which the assistance of Virginia Berk and Virginia Streiff is acknowledged, competency tests are still in focus, but the subject samples are drawn from a population of students of English as a second language at the Defense Language Institute in San Antonio, Texas. The competency tests used were the *Tests of Adult Basic Education* (forms D, M, and E). Again the major questions asked were the same as in Chapter 5: how much common variance underlies the various subscales (in this case, the parts of the *Tests of Adult Basic Education*)? And, to what extent can this communality be attributed to proficiency in English?

Chapter 7, with the acknowledged assistance of V. Streiff, Krueger, Berk, Di Quinzio, Ball, and Osborn, again deals with students at the Defense Language Institute, but shifts attention to a rather different type of test. Instead of competency tests, it is so-called "non-verbal" intelligence tests which are drawn into focus. In many ways, the examination of such instruments would seem to be the most crucial assessment of tests aimed at non-language skills. If non-verbal IQ tests, are shown to contain a substantial component of language proficiency, then wouldn't many other tests necessarily be implicated *a fortiori*? (Also, see the analysis of "non-verbal" IQ test items given in Chapter 4 below.)

In Part III, Chapters 8-10, attention is shifted from adults to children (elementary and middle school) and from monolinguals and ESL learners to bilingual populations. Steve Chesarek, co-author on Chapter 8, was the one who actually collected the data at Crow Agency in Montana. The children tested included first, second, and third graders. The *Peabody Individual Achievement Test*, the *Illinois Test of Psycholinguistic Abilities*, the *Peabody Picture Vocabulary Test*, the *Bellugi Syntax Test*, *Raven's Progressive Matrices*, and *Cattell's Culture-Fair Intelligence Tests* (Scale 2, Forms A and B) were among the instruments examined. The questions were much as before: to what extent can common variance be demonstrated for all of the tests? And, can this communality be reasonably attributed to an English language factor?

Chapter 9 is also concerned with bilingual children. In this case the sample is drawn from a population of Hopi children in Arizona. The study reported is largely a replication of Streiff (1978) which appeared as Chapter 6 in *Language in Education: Testing the Tests*. As in that study, the *California Achievement Tests* were used along with a written cloze test. However, there were some differences. In this study it was not possible to use an oral cloze test, but teacher ratings of dominance and fluency in English and Hopi were added to the analysis.

Chapter 10 may round out the overall picture some by helping to fill in the gap between children and adults. This study, completed with the collaboration of Paul Streiff, examines the language factor in tests of Navajo-English bilinguals ranging from grades three through nine. The design was essentially similar to that of Chapter 9. A written cloze test was used along with the various subscores on the *Comprehensive Tests of Basic Skills*. A new feature in this study was the opportunity to examine the changing pattern of the factors obtained across various grade levels.

Part IV, Chapters 11-12, addresses the important additional question of the role of the native language (Choctaw or Spanish, in the samples studied) as distinct from that of the secondary language (English in both cases). In Chapter 11, whose principal author is Robert Scott, a rather different approach is employed. The subject population again consists of bilingual children, in this instance, Choctaw-English bilinguals at the kindergarten level. But this time it was possible to obtain scores in the *native* language (Choctaw). The crucial question was whether the relationship of proficiency in the primary language with achievement scores on tests relying exclusively on English would be similar to what was observed in the other cases. In all of the earlier instances, of course, language proficiency scores per se were only available in English. Therefore, Scott's collaborative effort made it possible to gain some insight into the possible role of proficiency in the native and, in this case, the stronger language of the bilingual children who were tested.

Chapter 12, completed with the help of V. Streiff and Armando Ibarra, deals with much the same question as Chapter 11 but in somewhat greater depth. Here, however, a population of Spanish-English bilingual children, somewhat older than Scott's kindergartner's, was employed. They ranged from grades three through five. It was also possible to get some data on an additional achievement test battery, namely, the *Metropolitan Achievement Tests*, and on a more discrete oriented language test than used in previous studies. In this case, it was possible to compare the predictive validity of teacher judgments and a cloze test against the widely used *Language Assessment Scales* developed by DeAvila and his associates.

## CONCLUSION

It is believed that the evidence contained in subsequent chapters will provide additional support for the thesis that language is an important factor in many mental measures commonly used in education. Moreover, it seems possible that language may play a deep role in intelligence itself and, therefore, in all mental abilities. The key to understanding the hypothesized relationships between such factors, however, is a more adequate theoretical conception. Such a conception is attempted in the sequel, Chapter 2.

# Chapter 2
## Intelligence as Semiosis

A theory of semiosis is proposed which integrates linguistic, kinesic (gestural), and sensory-motor systems.[1] Without such an integration it will be impossible to explain the fact that we can talk about what we see, or visualize what someone else talks about. Or, what amounts to the same thing, we can often imagine sensory-motor representations (e.g., what it feels like to pull a pair of old wooden oars). We may also convert such representations to linguistic and/or gestural ones. Such examples show that the traditionally almost unrelated theories of sensory-motor, kinesic, and linguistic systems are inadequate to explain the integration of experience into a more or less coherent and whole fabric. To support the general idea three sources of evidence are marshalled: general theoretical considerations (in this chapter), biological arguments (Chapter 3), and logical analysis of intelligence test items (Chapter 4). Here, in this chapter, some general claims about intelligence are examined, and some corollary hypotheses are offered which follow from the idea that intelligence is semiosis. This thesis is called "the semiotic hypothesis".

### SOME GENERAL THEORETICAL CLAIMS ABOUT INTELLIGENCE

The germ of the relation between language and intellect is capsulized by Albert Einstein (1941) in the following remarks about language and thinking:

---

[1]This chapter, and the two that follow, are based on work done in large measure during academic 1979-80 and in 1986-87, in each case while Oller was on sabbatical leave from the Department of Linguistics at the University of New Mexico. The material contained here served as the basis for several lectures including the Annual Rocky Mountain TESOL Conference in Denver, Colorado, September 1980; the New York ESOL and Bilingual Education Association in October 1980; the Ontario Institute for Studies in Education in February 1981; New Mexico State University in Las Cruces, April 1981; and the fourth Hugo J. Mueller Lecture in April 1981 at the American University in Washington, D. C.. Two previous drafts of the argument have appeared: the first in *Language Learning* (1981) under the title "Language as Intelligence?" and a more recent version has appeared in *Language and Experience: Classic Pragmatism* (Oller, 1989b). Versions of the argument have also been prepared for inclusion in a book to appear (probably in 1990) under the Multilingual Matters imprint edited by Lilliam Malavé and George Blanco, and in a volume entitled *Non-Biased Assessment of Limited English Proficient Special Education Students* (Hamayan and Damico, in press). Thanks are due Mark Clarke and John Haskell for their comments and encouragement concerning earlier drafts of the discussion contained here. Other readers or listeners who helped to shape the final product (but who cannot be held responsible for it) included Jack S. Damico, G. Richard Tucker, Mary Ann Hood, Frank Smith, and Helga Delisle.

11

. . . Everything depends on the degree to which words and word-combinations correspond to the world of impression.

What is it that brings about such an intimate connection between language and thinking? Is there no thinking without the use of language, namely in concepts and concept-combinations for which words need not necessarily come to mind? Has not everyone of us struggled for words although the connection between "things" was already clear?

We might be inclined to attribute to the act of thinking complete independence from language if the individual formed or were able to form his concepts without the verbal guidance of his environment. Yet most likely the mental shape of an individual growing up under such conditions would be very poor. Thus we may conclude that the mental development of the individual and his way of forming concepts depend to a high degree upon language (1941, in Oller 1989b p. 62).

Peirce and Saussure, presumably for similar reasons, agreed in this assessment. Both of them contended that language is the canonical semiotic medium and that by the systematic study of it we should be able to optimize our understanding of representational ("semeiotic", Peirce's spelling of the term, or "semiological", Saussure's preference) processes in general. More recently Noam Chomsky has urged the same program. He wrote in 1972:

One would expect that human language should directly reflect the characteristics of human intellectual capacities (p. ix).

PRAGMATIC MAPPING

Figures 2.1-2.3 elaborate on the central theme of the semiotic hypothesis. Figure 2.1 pictures the primary representational problem as outlined in the above remarks by Einstein, and more fully by Peirce in the nineteenth century (see their contributions in Oller, 1989b). On the left hand side of the diagram the raw uninterpreted facts of experience are pictured. On the right hand side representations of them. The question for a theory of intellect is how the connection between the two realms is accomplished. This, in a nutshell, is the pragmatic mapping problem. It is construed, by the semiotic hypothesis as the primary problem of intelligence.

THE GULF

Einstein described pragmatic mapping and defined the "gulf" as shown in the following lines:

. . . the concepts which arise in our thought and in our linguistic expressions are all--when viewed logically--the free creations of thought which cannot inductively be

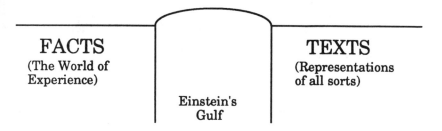

FIGURE 2.1.  PRAGMATIC MAPPING.

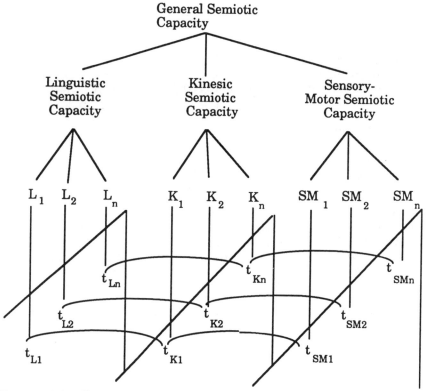

FIGURE 2.2.  DIFFERENT KINDS OF SEMIOTIC CAPACITIES.

gained from sense experiences. This is not so easily noticed only because we have the habit of combining certain concepts and conceptual relations (propositions) so definitely with certain sense experiences that we do not become conscious of the gulf--logically unbridgeable--which separates the world of sensory experiences from the world of concepts and propositions (1944, in Oller 1989b, p. 25).[2]

## THREE KINDS OF REPRESENTATIONAL CAPACITIES

Figure 2.2 elaborates on the model by proposing a hierarchy of three distinct kinds of representational capacities: linguistic, kinesic, and sensory-motor. Clearly, the language capacity is fully abstract and may be used to represent any imaginable, or even unimaginable idea whatever. (We may at least speak of the unimaginably fantastic.) The kinesic, gestural, sort of representation is intermediate. It is conventional and arbitrary to some extent, but may also involve iconic (analogical) elements. For instance, a brandished fist suggests, more or less iconically, the act of punching someone. However, it may by convention acquire a rather different meaning--e.g., as a sign of solidarity or brotherhood.

Or consider the fact that Americans and most western Europeans in pointing to themselves aim roughly at their own sternum with the right index finger or (for males especially) the thumb of the right hand. Japanese, however, point to themselves by touching or pointing toward their nose with the right index finger. Each of these gestures has its conventional aspects as well as its universal basis in the ego-reference point. The latter is not a mere convention since it is physiologically impossible for a perceiver to have any other primary reference point. (Without the notion of one's own self, it would be impossible to credit any other self with existence or to differentiate one from the other; see Peirce, in Moore, et al., 1984, pp. 201ff.)

Sensory-motor representations on the other hand are more or less directly, and iconically, related to the facts of experience. A person skiing down a mountain not only represents the terrain ahead in a continuous flow of images, but must also represent at some level body postures and internal commands for motor adjustments turning and relating body and skis to accommodate the changing slope.[3] Such a person feels (i.e., represents in sensory-motor fashion) the skis, the movements, the slope, the snow, etc.

As Peirce showed, sensory-motor representations are analogues, copies, or *icons* of the facts they represent, and as such they are degenerate. If we look away from an object, its image quickly fades. Details are lost or may be wrongly reconstructed in the mental picture.

Kinesic representations are similar to sensory-motor ones in their iconic aspect, though kinesic representations often contain an even more

---

[2]Readers familiar with Chomsky's work will not fail to see the profound similarity between what Einstein says here and what Chomsky has said many times elsewhere.

[3]This example is a reinterpretation of an argument proposed by John Searle in a public lecture at the University of New Mexico in 1984 and in personal communication. Searle, in effect, denied that any representation per se is involved in the act of a person skiing down a mountain.

salient conventional element. Further, when it comes to kinesic representations that point out or index objects for attention, namely, *indexes*, a kind of sign distinct from an icon, another kind of degeneracy enters the system. However, first consider the conventionality of indexes: English speakers, for instance, are apt to point with the "index" finger to call attention to an object or event. Navajos achieve the same purpose by extending the lower lip. The difference between these forms shows the conventional side of indexes. Second, consider the fact that all indexes are, as Peirce argued, reactionally degenerate. The interlocutor or person addressed may single out the wrong object or event for attention and not the one intended.

## LINGUISTIC SYMBOLS: THE "RELATIVELY GENUINE GENUS"

Linguistic representations by contrast usually achieve a higher level of abstraction and a closer approximation to validity. While they always involve indexes (such as pronouns or nominals) to the extent that they are synthetic in character (i.e., to the extent that they inform us about actual experience), and sometimes they involve icons as well (e.g., a sentence which includes a stretching of the word "huge" to indicate something really "huuuuuuuuuuuuuge"), much of their meaning is quite abstract and does not point to or picture anything in the world of experience directly at all.

For instance, the word "dog" may involve reference to a particular dog in experience, or it may be used as a more or less pure abstraction to call to mind what dogs have in common or what we know of them in general, apart from any particular instance (e.g., such general information as the claim that "a dog is a man's best friend" and the like). It follows that linguistic forms that depend on sensory-motor representations of non-linguistic states of affairs (e.g., factual or fictional contexts), or that appeal to indexical or deictic relations (e.g., pointing or naming or referring) involve the same kinds of degeneracy as do icons and indexes in general.

However, purely abstract semantic/syntactic relations (e.g., the subject predicate relation per se, or the semantic distinction between dogs and cats) do not involve any such degeneracy. They enjoy a greater independence and freedom from direct connections to objects in experience that must be represented in some way by the other degenerate representational forms, i.e., by icons (e.g., sensory-motor images) and indexes (some method of singling out or pointing which effectively distinguishes one object from another). For this reason, Peirce called purely abstract representations, of the sort found in general propositions (e.g., "Men are mortal"), *symbols*, as contrasted with icons and indexes.

Analytic or pure syntactic/semantic propositions do not involve either qualitative or reactional degeneracy per se. For example, the Aristotelian proposition that "Men are mortal" does not necessarily involve any indexical or iconic representation at all. It is an abstract universal proposition. It does involve English conventions in this form, but could as easily have been expressed in Greek, or Navajo, or American Sign Language. Or, it could simply be represented in a pure semantic form, in abstract concepts, without the words of any particular language. In this latter sense, and for these reasons, Peirce defined *symbols* as contrasted with icons and indexes, as the "relatively genuine genus".

To the extent that symbols can be separated from their conventional aspect, i.e., from a particular acquired grammar, e.g., that of English, or Spanish, or Choctaw, etc., they are known absolutely, as Peirce demonstrated, and they are valid in an unassailable sense. However, the validity would be an inconsequential and empty sort unless the symbols were related to particular elements of experience. If this is done, plenty of opportunity for error arises, and symbolization as a process, in ordinary experience, becomes a risky venture again.

SUBORDINATE TERMS: PARTICULAR SYSTEMS AND THEIR TEXTS

So much for the three general headings under the overall intellectual ability termed GENERAL SEMIOTIC CAPACITY in Figure 2.2. It remains to explain the terms subordinate to each of these. Under LINGUISTIC CAPACITY, an ability that is believed to be innate and species specific to human beings, come terms that correspond to the grammars of particular language systems, $L_1$, $L_2$, through $L_n$. These systems, to the extent they are not already specified by innate knowledge of universal grammar, must be acquired if they are to be known at all. Each in its turn corresponds to a class of textual (i.e., sequentially or structurally arranged) representations in experience, $t_{L1}$, $t_{L2}$, through $t_{Ln}$. These terms stand for the texts, for instance, that conform to one's primary language, or second language, and so forth.

The same sort of hierarchical arrangement is hypothesized under the KINESIC SEMIOTIC CAPACITY. It too is must involve a substantial innate element though it is not entirely species specific to human beings. Again, the universal kinesic capacity dominates (or branches into) a plurality (or at least a potential plurality) of subordinate acquired systems. Each of these subordinate systems dominates a class of texts or representational forms in experience, and these tend to be loosely tied to linguistic texts. For example, English speakers are apt to accompany the statement that a certain person is about "so tall" with a corresponding gesture, palm down, hand extended. A Latin American Spanish-speaker by contrast uses a very different gesture for the same meaning.

More importantly, research shows that the sequence of gestures is delicately coordinated with the sequence of linguistic forms and meanings. According to research by Condon and Ogston (1971) this is true not only of the speaker but also of the audience to such an extent that their body movements appear to be under the control of one and the same puppeteer.

The case for SENSORY-MOTOR CAPACITY, if anything, is stronger. There is no question that much of our ability to perceive the world and our body as part of it, must be innate (cf. T. G. R. Bower, 1971, 1974; also the Chomsky and Piaget debate in Piatelli-Palmarini, 1980 and comments from the other participants). However, every normal person operates in ordinary experience by so many routines and patterns that it would be impossible to estimate how many distinct sensory-motor systems an ordinary individual possesses. There are sensory-motor programs for almost every imaginable aspect of routine experience, chewing gum, brushing your teeth, grooming in general, dressing, tying your shoes, driving a car, riding a bicycle, playing basketball, going to class, giving a talk, writing a letter, typing one, talking on the phone, etc., etc. And each of these routines is divisible into subroutines.

To the extent that such programs can be made explicit as rule governed systems, they are like the grammars of natural languages. They also have their own sensory-motor texts, $t_{SM1}$, $t_{SM2}$, and so forth. For instance, our ability to recognize a game of basketball and to distinguish it from a tennis match, or to distinguish either of these from a boxing match, is dependent in part on our knowledge of the corresponding sensory-motor systems. But none of these knowledge systems is the same as an actual game of basketball, or tennis, or a particular boxing match. Yet, the general rule-systems underlying the particular manifest forms ($t_{SM}$'s in Figure 2.2) are at least as distinct from each other as are the diverse "textual" manifestations. Sensory-motor texts, in their turn, are also coordinated in ordinary experience in delicately articulate ways with kinesic and linguistic texts.

## PRAGMATIC MAPPING AS INFORMATION PROCESSING

Yet another way of viewing the same pragmatic process of linking texts with the facts of experience is given in Figure 2.3. The focal element in this diagram is consciousness or immediate awareness. The question addressed is how information from the senses is processed via the kinds of grammatical structure that are supplied by the various semiotic systems--linguistic, kinesic, and sensory-motor. The idea is that the determination of the meaning of texts is chiefly a matter of relating them via representational capacity with the facts of experience and vice versa. As new texts or representations are processed, they are fed into short-term memory and some of them from there into a longer-term memory. Consciousness and memory, together, interact with semiotic systems so as to modify them. Presumably, this is the basis for the acquisition of the conventional aspects of semiotic systems.

## EVIDENCE SUPPORTING THE THEORY

Empirical evidence in favor of the theory is abundant. Here the points to be covered in greater detail below are summarized. First, the theory gives a plausible explanation of our ability to translate information from one semiotic system into another. Second, the proposed model provides a heuristically appealing basis for the common distinctions made between such cognitive processes as experiencing

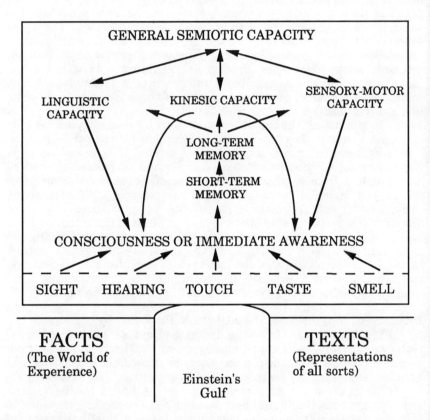

FIGURE 2.3 A MODULAR INFORMATION PROCESSING EXPANSION OF THE PRAGMATIC MAPPING PROCESS.

something versus remembering it versus recalling the memory, and so on. Third, systems are shown to be related in ways that correspond to what is known from research. Fourth, the special case of the interaction between primary and non-primary languages is explained in a straightforward way. And, fifth, seven intuitively appealing hypotheses concerning which there is some consensus are incorporated without difficulty. Each of the foregoing sources of evidence is discussed:

### GENERAL SEMIOTIC CAPACITY

How can we be sure that there must be a general semiotic capacity allowing intertranslatability of representations across the various semiotic systems? The chief evidence for this aspect of the model is that we can usually work up in our imagination appropriate sensory-motor representations in response to a narrative, for instance, told by someone else. Similarly, an observer of a boxing match is apt to become involved in the action by dodging punches, bobbing and weaving. Or, more commonly still, we grimace in response to someone else's discomfort. Each of these commonplace phenomena demonstrate the undeniable intertranslatability of at least some representations across a diversity of semiotic systems.

Clearly there must be an intimate connection between the several representational systems hypothesized. Unless there were some deeper abstract semiotic representation of meaning, it would, presumably, be impossible for us to talk about what we see, or to imagine appropriate sensory-motor images of what we, or someone else, may describe.

We can also paraphrase meanings that have been expressed in a certain surface form by putting them into other surface forms that give more or less the same result. For instance, the statement that "Men are mortal" may be paraphrased by saying that "All humanity must ultimately face death" or that "Mortality is a trait of human beings", etc. Translation across distinct language systems, e.g., "Los hombres son mortales" or "La mortalidad es una de las cualidades de los hombres", or translation into any language or other form that can be imagined, is ample evidence in favor of a general factor of semiotic capacity. Apart from such a general capacity, such translations (even quite imperfect ones) would be inexplicable.

## DESIRABLE THEORETICAL DISTINCTIONS SUSTAINED

The model under consideration also enables us to make certain distinctions that are, it would seem, critical to any theory of intellect that aims for explanatory adequacy (cf. Chomsky, 1965). For instance, we may distinguish innate from acquired knowledge. Innate knowledge is that which is present before any experience occurs, or which is triggered by experience and matures more or less automatically and somewhat independently of experience.

The difference between innate and acquired knowledge can be seen in all three of the semiotic systems proposed to underlie the general semiotic capacity. For instance, universal aspects of linguistic capacity which could not be acquired from experience but are in fact prerequisite to it would have to include such things as the subject-predicate relation, as well as the capacity for negation, conjunction, and disjunction of propositional meanings.

Universal aspects of kinesic systems would include such things as smiles, laughter, tears, and cries of joy or pain. Universal aspects of sensory-motor capacity would include the intimate association of the senses as demonstrated in the work of T. G. R. Bower (1971, 1974). It would extend to the physiological character of the senses and their tuning to facts external to the organism. All of these things, it would seem, are prerequisite to any explanation of the common experiences shared by human beings across the vast range of cultures and backgrounds our diverse experiences afford.

## RELATIONSHIP BETWEEN SYSTEMS EXPLAINED

Each of the universal systems of knowledge (and no claim is made as to the completeness of the ones postulated, only their necessity) though distinct, is related to the others through the domination of the general capacity, and each also subordinates one or more particular systems that are acquired and are to some extent conventional in character. For example, the acquisition of the primary language at once fleshes out the universal aspects of language that are realized in that system and at the same time results in the addition of conventional features that are unique to the primary language. Much the same will be true in the acquisition of the kinesic system that accompanies the first language.

Even sensory-motor systems have their noteworthy conventional aspects. For instance, to take a trivial but suitable case for the sake of illustration, in one culture it is customary for automobiles to drive on the right hand side of a roadway while in another motorists stay to the left. If it is hypothesized that conventional aspects of the various semiotic systems in question must be acquired, this sort of acquired knowledge will be distinguished from innate knowledge to the extent that the former is a product of experience involving the senses. It is suggested that information from the sensory-motor system passes to consciousness where the sensory-motor texts (i.e., sequences of sensory-motor images) are interpreted. As they are understood, and just to that extent, they are passed through various stages of memory more or less distant from consciousness. The depth of the comprehension in question will determine the degree of impact on semiotic systems. It is hypothesized that the acquisition of grammar is a process of comprehending a particular kind of texts so as to develop the sort of intuitive feel which constitutes knowledge of a language. By this reckoning, the acquisition of a particular grammar is a process of comprehending texts in that language at a sufficient depth so as to acquire the conventional aspects of the grammatical system.

## PRIMARY AND NON-PRIMARY LANGUAGE ACQUISITION RELATED

Contrary to a lot of recent speculation about non-primary language acquisition (e.g. Gregg, 1985, 1988, and his references), the theory under consideration hypothesizes that non-primary language acquisition will proceed in a manner much like primary language acquisition except for the fact that acquisition of a second language will benefit greatly (and suffer minor interferences from) the prior acquisition of the first language (Asher and Price, 1967; Asher and Garcia, 1969). Similarly, the acquisition of a third language will benefit (mainly and suffer a little) from the first and second, and so on.

The fact that non-primary language acquisition usually falls short of the mark achieved in primary language acquisition (Gregg, 1988), it is supposed, should be explained not by positing a radical difference in the physiology (Scovel, 1988) or even the internal strategies of the person involved in one or the other task (Selinker, 1972), but by noting the radical differences across the two cases in access to target language texts and the relative motivations to comprehend and produce them (Brown, 1973; Schumann, 1975, 1986; Vigil and Oller, 1976).

In the primary language situation, the person doing the acquisition is under incredible community pressure to conform to the norms of the primary-language. A child who persists in nonconformities will be ostracized or punished while the one who succeeds in overcoming them will be rewarded by all the privileges of membership in a community.

For any one other than a child acquiring a non-primary language, no similar pressures or rewards are likely to be experienced (cf. Brown, 1973; Schumann, 1975, 1986; Vigil and Oller, 1976; etc.). Exceptional cases, where non-primary language acquisition succeeds in fairly dramatic ways are precisely those cases where access to target language texts and susceptibility to pressures and rewards are both provided for. For instance, the person who marries across language boundaries and then moves to the country where the non-primary language predominates is far more apt to achieve native-like ability in the non-primary language than someone who merely takes a college course in that language. In fact, it seems reasonable to suppose, along the lines of Vigil and Oller (1976), that continuing progress toward native competence in any language is much more a function of internally defined motives and sensitivities than it is a function of methods of teaching or modes of exposure. Clearly access to pragmatically rich and meaningful texts in the target language is requisite, but insufficient by itself. Motivation to conform to the conventions of the target language system is also required.

CONSENSUAL HYPOTHESES INCORPORATED

The hierarchical model under consideration not only supports the kinds of theoretical distinctions that are required in practice, e.g., the distinction between innate and acquired knowledge, consciousness and memory, memory and grammatical knowledge, grammar and text, text and comprehension, comprehension and production, primary and non-primary language acquisition, etc., but it also suggests some fairly explicit hypotheses about relationships within the proposed hierarchy that are immanently susceptible to empirical testing.

1. ROLE OF THE PRIMARY LANGUAGE IN INTELLIGENCE

Since linguistic representations are the most abstract ones in the model it follows that the primary language is the most likely basis for the development of general semiotic capacity. It has often been observed that mathematics as a kind of reasoning is parasitic and derivative inasmuch as it is entirely dependent upon language (Peirce, in Hartshorne and Weiss, 1931-1935; Lotz, 1951; Church, 1951; Russell,

1919). Einstein alluded to the closeness of the relationship between language development and cognitive growth in general in the remarks quoted above (see page 12). It was a point developed further by Vygotsky (1934, n. d.), Piaget (1947), Luria and Yudovich (1959) and Luria (1961, 1973).

Empirical evidence may be seen in the remarkable accomplishments of deaf children with hearing parents. In cases where the children, for whatever reasons, are deprived of access to visual sign language they face a language acquisition problem far more difficult than that of the hearing child. Such children, it seems, face special cognitive difficulties that only the acquisition of a fully developed language system will enable them to overcome. Typically this is accomplished through a natural visual-manual sign system such as American Sign Language (cf. Lane, 1984, 1988; Wilcox, 1988). Deaf children deprived of this opportunity and forced to acquire speech directly are placed at a serious disadvantage (Lane, 1988). The difficulties they face in cognitive development across the board are predicted by the hierarchical model under consideration. It follows that if children are denied access to a full and rich primary language system, they will suffer consequences of this lack throughout the cognitive hierarchy and especially in areas that depend on communication, e.g., social development.

Moreover, children who acquire some ASL and are then taught Signed English (SE), an artificial system invented by hearing persons to correspond to English lexicon, syntax, and so forth, are apparently in the position of persons trying to acquire a second language system. In this instance, however, the system is artificial and bizarre in a variety of ways. For instance, in theory SE gives equal emphasis to stressed and unstressed morphological and lexical elements. In this respect, and others, it is somewhat like Morse Code. Unlike ASL, SE is a fully dependent system. Therefore, when deaf children de-emphasize or omit redundancies of English structure, e.g., the "-ing" of present progressives and the like, they are making natural modifications in surface forms of signed texts that would conform to more normal expectations about universal grammar. For evidence that deaf children do this in SE, see Kretschmer (in press).

## 2. TRANSFER AND INTERFERENCE PREDICTED

Another hypothesis that is suggested by the theory under consideration is that neighboring elements of the hierarchy are more apt to influence each other than distant ones. For example, we might expect the primary language to have greater impact on second language acquisition than third. The second similarly would be expected to influence the third, and so on. Again, experience of polyglots bears this out. Typically, "padding" (a term from Newmark, 1966, i.e., the use of known language forms in place of target language forms) is more often from the most recently acquired language rather than from any other.

Following out the same idea, transfer in general would be expected to occur from the more developed systems to less developed ones. For example, the primary language would be expected to influence a non-primary language rather than the reverse. The situation would be altered in favor of the non-primary language at just the point where the person in question achieved greater proficiency in the non-primary system. However, at just that point, the non-primary system would be promoted to the status of the primary system and the former primary system would presumably be demoted to a secondary status.

### 3. INPUT HYPOTHESIS VINDICATED

Another consequence of the postulated hierarchy is that distinct representational systems provide the means in some cases for comprehending what would otherwise be incomprehensible. For instance, a discourse in a target language that might be entirely incomprehensible if one had to rely on knowledge of that particular language alone can be made comprehensible if one has access to a translation provided in some other semiotic system. In normal language acquisition, e.g., primary language acquisition, as has often been pointed out (Macnamara, 1973, 1982) meanings of surface forms are often contextually obvious when those forms are being acquired (Krashen, 1985). The child first understands the context, e.g., by representing it in a comprehensible sensory-motor form, and subsequently becomes able to understand the utterances associated with the context. In non-primary language acquisition, wherever it succeeds, a similar scaffolding is often provided. It may be presented in some dramatization, in a film, or it may be presented through a translation, literally, into a language that the subject already knows.

By this line of reasoning, Krashen's input hypothesis (Krashen, 1985) is in part vindicated (Oller, 1988). The input hypothesis in its most basic form says simply that language acquisition progresses as the acquirer comprehends texts that are a little beyond his or her current level of development in the target language. Spolsky (1985, 1988) and Gregg (1985, 1988) have contended that the input hypothesis is either false or trivially true. If it means we must understand what is beyond our understanding, it is false. If it means merely that we must comprehend in order to learn, it is trivially true. However, the theory we are advocating here disposes of both of these interpretations. We do indeed understand representations (target language texts) beyond our reach in one system (namely the target language) by appealing to representations in another semiotic system. The one provides an interpretation of the other. Therefore, because of the intertranslatability of semiotic representations, the input hypothesis remains viable.

### 4. THE THRESHOLD HYPOTHESIS INCORPORATED

Cummins (1976) proposed the threshold hypothesis, an idea that relates to the impact of bilingualism, or more specifically adding a second language, on cognitive development. Subsequently (see Cummins, 1984, pp. 107-108) he modified his hypothesis and extended it. The threshold hypothesis suggests that the child's starting level of proficiency in one or both languages may be an important mediating variable in avoiding a burden in becoming bilingual or in benefitting from bilingualism once achieved. There are actually two thresholds being proposed.

On the low end, it is claimed that a child may have to achieve a certain minimal level of proficiency in one or both languages in order to avoid deficits. In other words, if the child falls below threshold in both languages, presumably it will be difficult or even impossible for that child to benefit from instruction in either language. Further, it follows that a child who has not acquired threshold level in the primary language will only receive an unnecessary additional burden by being instructed in a second language. Therefore, the lower threshold is presumably important in the determination of when instruction might be beneficially introduced in a non-primary language.

At the other end of the scale, a high threshold is also posited. In order for a bilingual child to experience the expected benefits of bilingualism, e.g., greater ability to appreciate and utilize symbols and greater "metalinguistic awareness", i.e., ability to appreciate the arbitrariness and conventionality of linguistic symbols, the child must have surpassed the high threshold presumably in one or both languages.

Admittedly, the idea of one or more thresholds is loosely stated, but the research seems to support it (Cummins and Mulcahy, 1978; Duncan and DeAvila, 1979; Hakuta and Diaz, 1984; Kessler and Quinn, 1980). In fact, as Hakuta (1986; also see Lambert, 1975, and his references) has shown, there is a long history of debate concerning the deleterious versus beneficial effects of bilingualism. Until relatively recent years the argument tended to be based more on partisan interests than on evidence or sound thinking. Formerly, especially in the U. S. there was a widespread prejudice against "bilingualism" based on research showing that minority language children got low scores on IQ tests. It scarcely occurred to the persons interpreting the research that the IQ tests were mainly measures of English language proficiency--something that the minorities in question had not yet had the opportunity to acquire.

Our main point here, however, is that the hierarchical model under consideration explains the available evidence concerning the threshold hypothesis and provides a convenient framework within which to understand the interrelationships of semiotic systems in general. Within a hierarchical model, the threshold hypothesis can be incorporated and elaborated in terms of transfer and interference (see 2 above in this section), and in terms of a more explicit theory of the role of language proficiency in relation to cognition in general. Bilingualism and indeed multilingualism deserve special consideration since they are bound to play a central role in the education of minorities. Moreover, the elaboration suggested by the theory under consideration is compatible, it is claimed, with the course that Cummins followed in the CALP/BICS distinction.

## 5. THE CALP/BICS DISTINCTION ACCOMMODATED

In response to consideration of the possibility of a general language proficiency factor, Cummins hypothesized a distinction between what he called cognitive academic language proficiency (CALP) and basic interpersonal communicative skills (BICS). This idea was appealing because most any educator who has dealt with bilingual or multilingual contexts has observed ample evidence in its favor.

A child who gets along satisfactorily on the playground, where cognitive demands are presumably lessened by the immediacy of physical and social context, may encounter difficulty in the classroom when it comes to reading, writing, solving word and math problems, and in general interacting on a more abstract level. The child may have adequate BICS without sufficient CALP. Cummins (1983c) clarified that he did not intend to argue that the two kinds of ability were unrelated, but rather that they were apt to appear as such at the surface. To illustrate he adapted an "iceberg" model (from Shuy 1978, 1981) where the two visible points, CALP and BICS, were clearly distinct, but were joined below the surface in what he called "common underlying proficiency" (cf. Cummins, 1984, p. 143).

There was a further implication that the two kinds of ability might be developed in somewhat different contexts and perhaps using distinct strategies. Cummins (1983c) quoted David Olson (1977) who said:

> . . . language development is not simply a matter of progressively elaborating the oral mother tongue as a means of sharing intentions. The developmental hypothesis offered here is that the ability to assign meaning to the sentence per se [as in a written text], independent of its nonlinguistic context, is achieved only well into the school years (p. 275, cited by Cummins 1983c, p. 116; Oller's interpolation).

What Cummins and Olson apparently intend to emphasize is the more abstract inference required to link up a written text with its author's intended meanings than is required in the case of an interactive discourse in the here and now. The latter, presumably the typical context of the exercise of BICS, is less cognitively demanding, *ceteris paribus*, than the former, a typical context for the use of CALP. From the point of view of the model proposed here, the main differences have to do with the presence or absence of sensory-motor icons and kinesically supported indexes. Where CALP is in focus, presumably fewer icons and kinesic supports are available.

Within the more elaborate Peircean perspective proposed here, Olson's phrase "independent of its nonlinguistic context" might be reformulated as "without firsthand [iconic and gesturally supported indexical] access to its nonlinguistic context". This, it is suggested, does no violence to Olson's intention, nor Cummins application of the idea in reference to CALP. However, it is a necessary modification if Peirce's foundational claim that all interpretation is translation from one form of semiotic representation to another.[4] This sort of translation is not viciously circular only because sensory-motor representations enable the investment of all other sorts of representation with material (non-empty) content.

However, strictly speaking, there is no such thing as a meaningful "sentence" without a "nonlinguistic" context. With that in mind, it is assumed that Olson and Cummins might accept as a friendly amendment to their ideas the interpretation that CALP (or in Olson's case, literacy) requires a larger inferential leap from the perceptible form of a representation (a written text in the case under consideration) and an appropriate interpretation that associates it with experiential context. Failing this, it might be argued that a representation which has no inferential relation to any experiential context whatever is necessarily meaningless. It would be entirely uninterpretable (cf. Einstein, 1944, in Oller, 1989b, p. 25, paragraph 3.13; and Peirce, pp. 99-105 in Oller, 1989b).

How then can the CALP/BICS dichotomy be understood within the proposed hierarchical model? The overlapping part of the iceberg beneath the surface would be explained in part as the general factor of language proficiency which incorporates whatever aspects of general intelligence are necessary to that proficiency. For BICS, also, it is clear that the utilization of both sensory-motor information and linguistically coded representations simultaneously would require a pragmatic linking that could only be accomplished by access to general semiotic ability. However, with BICS, sensory-motor and kinesic texts are immediately accessible to aid the pragmatic linkage of linguistic texts with facts in experience.

In the exercise of CALP, on the other hand, say in reading an unillustrated text, e.g., that which appears on this page, any necessary sensory-motor representations would have to be supplied by the reader. This is a more difficult semiotic task. It requires a higher degree of inference based on a more abstract semiotic system, namely a linguistic one, from which the sensory-motor type images must be inferred where they are needed. The move from graphological representations to a more abstract linguistic form is already a difficult inferential process (reading), and the absence of sensory-motor images or kinesic indexes that might

---

[4]Roman Jakobson (1980) commented on this aspect of Peircean theory saying that "the translation of a sign into another system of signs" as a definition of the process of interpretation was "one of the most felicitous, brilliant ideas which general linguistics and semiotics gained from the American thinker" (p. 35). This foundational aspect of Peirce's approach to semiotics was dependent on the rigorously logical claim that every perception, comprehension, or thought is a representation, and that interpretations are always and only representations of representations. Jakobson says, "How many fruitless discussions about mentalism and antimentalism could be avoided if one approached the notion of meaning in terms of translation, which no mentalist and no behaviorist could reject" (p. 35). Of course, it is important to realize that the standard use of the term "translation" involves a gross narrowing of the term as it is understood in Peircean theory. Still, the usual meaning of the term does not distort Peirce's intention if the narrowness be removed.

give some clue concerning reference, deixis, and the whole pragmatic mapping process involves another complex of inferences.

Thus, CALP, with its special emphasis on literacy and abstract reasoning would presumably require the development of reading and writing skills in the primary or some non-primary language. Whereas BICS might benefit indirectly from such a development, literacy and specialized abstract reasoning skills, e.g., ability to do arithmetic leading on to higher mathematical skills, would not be necessary to BICS. To this extent, BICS and CALP are usefully distinguishable which suggests an important amplification of Cummins's threshold hypothesis--one that he has commented on (Cummins, 1984, p. 117).

The initial distinction between "surface fluency" and "conceptual-linguistic knowledge" Cummins attributes to Skutnabb-Kangas and Toukomaa (1976). They, no doubt, were influenced by the distinction between "surface" structure and "deep" structure from Chomskyan linguistics. At any rate, it seemed clear that a child might develop quite a lot of routine facility with greetings, leave-takings, playground games, and the like, and still fall short of the level of language proficiency and concept development necessary to reading, writing, and doing arithmetic. Therefore, a child might appear to be doing quite well in conversation but fail as a reader (Olson, 1977).

The low threshold for language skill, then, might be construed as a completely general requirement applying as much to monolinguals as to multilinguals. Presumably this same notion was what another generation of specialists in another paradigm meant by "readiness". The higher threshold too would have a more general interpretation in this context. Presumably "metalinguistic awareness" is merely another way of referring to what an earlier generation of psychologists and educators called "learning to learn" or "talking about talk", etc.

Finally, there is also a parallel with the traditional distinction between "language disorders" and "learning disabilities" where the former have been defined more in terms of surface language problems (sometimes even speech difficulties per se) and the latter in terms of deeper conceptual difficulties--"neurological" deficits (see Coles, 1978; Cummins, 1986) or, more recently, "inefficiencies" (Swanson, 1988). Damico (1985) has argued that traditional tests of language disorders have tended to focus on surface forms of language (also see Damico, Oller, and Storey, 1983) while definitions of learning disabilities have been put forward, to the extent they have been offered at all, in terms of deeper conceptual problems. Again, something like the BICS/CALP distinction appears. It is a virtue of the proposed model, or so it is claimed, that it can accommodate such distinctions in intuitively appealing ways.

## 6. MULTIPLE MODELS OF LANGUAGE PROFICIENCY

One of the most difficult things to see about language proficiency is that it may be conceptualized in a considerable variety of different but mutually compatible ways. For instance, language proficiency may be though of in terms of the various components of grammar that constitute it in theory, or it may be thought of in terms of the traditional skills. What is difficult to see is that these are not incompatible ways of viewing language--merely different ways--and there are many others.

If attention is focussed on primary language ability as represented in Figure 2.2 above, that portion of the diagram might be amplified

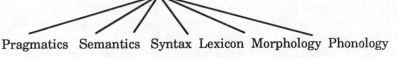

Language (Li)

Pragmatics  Semantics  Syntax  Lexicon  Morphology  Phonology

FIGURE 2.4. LANGUAGE PROFICIENCY IN TERMS OF DOMAINS OF GRAMMAR.

as shown in Figures 2.4 or 2.5. In Figure 2.4, language proficiency is seen as divisible, more or less, into domains of grammar. Pragmatics may be defined as pertaining to those aspects of meaning that have to do with actual, particular, concrete contexts of experience. Semantics embraces those aspects of meaning that are virtual, universal, or abstract. Syntax is concerned with the sequential or simultaneous arrangement of categories of grammar into texts. Lexicon comprises those inventories of elements that are acquired as whole units, e.g., words, idioms, pat phrases, verbal routines, and the like. Morphology in English is a question of inflections, e.g., pluralization, tense and number marking on verbs, etc., and derivations, e.g., adding a morpheme to make a verb of an adjective, e.g., "real" plus "-ize" to get "realize", and so forth. Phonology is a matter of determining the surface forms of phonemes, syllables, lexical items, and larger units of structure.

Figure 2.5 shows a similar breakdown with reference to skills such as listening, speaking, reading, writing, and verbal thinking. It may be argued without risk of contradiction that such hypothetical domains of structure, or distinct skills, are as valid as the theories upon which they are based. However, such divisions can never be finally determined anymore than Immanuel Kant could determine once for all the ultimate categories of reason. As Peirce, Einstein, and others have shown, such categories are intrinsically arbitrary and cannot be finally fixed or completely determined by any amount of empirical research (see especially Einstein, 1941, 1944, and the papers by Peirce in Oller,

Language (Li)

Listening  Speaking  Signing  Interpreting  Reading  Writing  Thinking

FIGURE 2.5. LANGUAGE PROFICIENCY IN TERMS OF SKILLS.

1989b). While it may be possible to fix upper and lower limits within which the simplicity/complexity of the model must fall, its specifics will apparently always retain a substantial arbitrariness nonetheless.

For instance, there is no conceivable argument that would prove either of the componential breakdowns of Figure 2.4 or 2.5 to be intrinsically superior to the other, except for some identified purpose or other. For one purpose, one model might be preferred, for some other purpose, the other. In yet other cases, both sets of distinctions will be required. What is more, many other componential models may be conceived. For example, modes of processing (productive versus receptive) may be distinguished, modalities of processing (articulatory/auditory versus visual/manual), stages of processing (consciousness, short-term, long-term memory), etc. In principle, there exists an indefinite variety of componential models. Within the proposed hierarchy, this fact can be construed as a natural outcome of different ways of combining and/or parsing up various of the proposed elements.

### 7. RELATION OF BILINGUALISM TO INTELLIGENCE

While it was long maintained that cognitive development may be hindered by becoming bilingual, the evidence clearly points in the other direction (cf. Hakuta and Diaz, 1984; Cummins, 1983a, 1983b, 1984, 1986, 1989; Hakuta, 1986). Dabbling in non-primary language acquisition may have little or no impact on intellect, but the acquisition of a second, third, or fourth language to a substantial degree of proficiency is apt to result in significant, though modest, cognitive gains. In particular, the evidence suggests that bilinguals achieve some kinds of flexibility in reasoning and a capacity to appreciate certain abstract relations that might remain outside the reach of monolinguals. This result (see the research cited above with reference to the "threshold" hypothesis), is predicted on the basis of the hierarchy under consideration.

Moreover, as in the case of the threshold hypothesis, a more general hypothesis is suggested. If bilingualism contributes to mental growth only after some threshold is passed, it follows that simply attaining proficiency in one's primary or native language must be important to normal mental maturation. Further, if language is a window through which researchers may get a fairly clear look at the mind, a thesis Chomsky has been promoting, it follows that the development of language proficiency must be linked to normal cognitive development. Putting this hypothesis in its most general form (cf. Oller, 1986) following Peirce, Einstein (see the quote above on page 12), Dewey, Piaget, Vygotsky, and others as noted above, it may be predicted that the normal development of deep semiotic abilities depends largely on the development of the primary language.

While it may be possible for deep semiotic abilities to be developed to a high degree with reference to some other manifest form, say, sensory-motor representations, or kinesic forms, since true linguistic symbols achieve a more complete level of logical abstractness and conventional arbitrariness, it seems likely that in normal human beings language development in all of its diversity is the fulcrum on which intellect attains its greatest leverage. It also follows that language abilities will tend toward the center of any definition of human exceptionalities ranging from giftedness in all its varieties to disabilities of all types.

Cummins (1986) writes:

> Historically, assessment has played the role of legitimizing the disabling of minority students. In some cases assessment itself may play the primary role, but more often it has been used to locate the 'problem' within the minority student . . . (p. 29).

This process may not have been intentional, but the effect has been summed up by Chase (1977) in a single phrase. He called it "the biologizing of social problems" (cf. Coles, 1978, for concurrence).

Not to deny the fact that some children may indeed have genuine "neurological" or other "deficits" or even "abnormalities", Cummins still contends that the medical "diagnosis/prescription" paradigm has seduced a whole generation of educators and clinicians, and that in many cases children from minority language backgrounds have been ludicrously over-represented in deficit categories (e.g., see Ortiz and Yates, 1983). This over-representation, or misdiagnosis, can be explained as the result of failing to distinguish acquired second language abilities, in many cases, from deeper semiotic capacities (cf. Damico, Oller, and Storey, 1983).

CONCLUSION

According to the proposed hierarchy of semiotic abilities, intelligence is the capacity for semiosis or representation. Of the three different subordinate semiotic capacities--linguistic, kinesic, and sensory-motor--linguistic capacity seems to be the only one that achieves sufficient independence and abstraction in order to provide a ground for developing a full and rich, general semiotic capacity. This development is expected to take place chiefly, though certainly not exclusively, in the primary language. Since icons are qualitatively degenerate, and indexes are reactionally degenerate, it follows that symbols (of an abstract and general linguistic sort, or the equivalent in some other conceptual system) are the only suitable basis for the full expression and development of semiotic powers. In the following chapter the semiotic definition of intelligence is extended to the general scope of biology and genetics.

# Chapter 3
# Intelligence, Semiosis, and Biology

While social problems should not be "biologized", biology is increasingly a semiotic science, and semiotics an increasingly biological one. In fact, biology affords perhaps the strongest empirical basis for the general theme that semiotic abilities are the essence of intelligence. Nearly half a century ago, in the preface to his treatise on *The Psychology of Intelligence* (completed about 1942 and published in 1947), Jean Piaget wrote:

> Every definition of intelligence comes sooner or later to lean on biology or logic (p. 3).

Above logic has already been leaned on heavily, and now we come to lean on biology. In Chapter 4, we will return to logic with an analysis of the kinds of things logically required by items that typify tests aimed at measuring various aspects of intelligence.

## ADAPTABILITY AND INFERENCE

As regards biology, perhaps the primary characteristic to be associated with intelligence is *adaptability*. The latter can be defined in terms of the capacity of an organism to "assimilate" (in Piaget's term) its environment to itself and to "accommodate" itself to the environment wherever change is needed and the environment itself is unyielding. This biological perspective contrasts with the logical one, which emphasizes inference and reason, only with respect to the more obvious interactive character of the biological definition: both adaptability and inference require representation. Furthermore, inference is a far more interactive affair than at first meets the eye. Therefore, the arguments from logic and biology in favor of a semiotic model of intellect are more similar than they might appear at the beginning.

The capacity to reason or make inferences has long been associated almost exclusively with *homo sapiens*. To the extent that this exclusivity is empirically justified, the argument from inference is already a biological one. Inference, the capacity to reason, is apparently man's special (if not unique) gift which sets him apart from the other creatures. This is obvious and well-known. However, what has not been discussed much in the literature concerning either language or intelligence, is that both biological organization itself and man's capacities of reason are dependent on the kinds of structures typified in natural language systems--especially in propositional forms linked together to form sequentially structured and meaningful discourse. Biological as well as other types of logical discourse presuppose operations linking subjects and predicates, negation, conjunction, modification, and the like.

31

NEITHER SPEECH NOR PROFICIENCY IN A LANGUAGE

Some readers may wish to ask at this point, "Are you saying that intelligence can be equated with speech?" Absolutely not. Since every system of speech, other than mere animalistic vocal gestures, is based on a particular grammar of some language system, it is clear that speech itself is narrower and more specific than the deep, abstract, and entirely general system of semiotics to which appeal is made. In the hierarchy under consideration, speech per se is a far more superficial function than what might be called deep "intelligence" or "general semiotic capacity". In fact, it is certain that intelligence can never be equated with proficiency in any *particular* language, though it must, logically speaking, be developed largely in terms of *some* particular language. Still, intelligence is not the same as proficiency in a particular language any more than semiotic capacity is the same as proficiency in Lithuanian (or any other particular language).

Rather, it is hypothesized that intelligence in its deepest and most universal sense is logically dependent on, and in fact indistinguishable from, semiotic or representational capacity. However, it must be kept in mind that semiosis is deeper than any particular language in precisely the same way that any given language per se is deeper than speech (i.e., texts uttered in that language).

Before going further, it is necessary to dispose of the idea that language may be equated with speech. This idea has sometimes been popularized by authors of texts for introductory courses on linguistics. Usually, it is expressed in the form of a caveat that "language is primarily spoken" rather than "written" or something else. The motivation for this claim seems clear enough but the claim itself results in the misleading impression that language is essentially speech. At least since Saussure, there have been good arguments against any such equivalence. His distinction between *langue* and *parole* (which parallels but is not identical with Chomsky's distinction between competence and performance) makes this clear. If the incorrect equivalence of language and speech is disposed of, many of the objections to the hypothesized relationship of semiosis and intelligence are done away with at the same time.

While speech may be the most salient manifestation of language, just as physical appearance is the most obvious manifestation of personality, it can no more be said that language is merely speech than that personality is merely clothing, hair style, and body-type. Though it is difficult to argue that these things are independent of personality just as it is absurd to claim that meaningful speech in any language is independent of intelligence. Perhaps the best proof that language is not mere speech is the fact that there are other manifestations of language. There are, for example, the signing systems of the deaf. While some of these, it is true, are derived from existing spoken languages, most apparently are not (cf. Wilcox, 1988). They constitute, therefore, a completely separate language category. Nor can we neglect the kinesic or gestural systems of hearing persons. Both the sign systems of deafness and kinesic systems in general (though the latter much less richly) manifest meanings with propositional complexities. Further, these gestural systems do so every bit as vividly and deliberately in many cases as the speech of any particular language.

Consider the gestural mechanisms employed by infants to effect the communication of abstract propositional meanings prior to the onset of speech. For instance, an infant may indicate wanting to be picked up by raising the arms and looking up into the face of an adult. Such a gesture clearly has propositional complexity. It takes account of the potential agency of the adult in picking up the child, as well as the object-status of the child as recipient of the action (or patient of the understood verb). At a still higher level, such a communicative act implicitly takes note of the present state of affairs and the goal-state of being held by the adult. Or consider the case of an infant indicating in no uncertain terms that she wants no more of a certain bowl of food which is being spooned into her mouth by an adult. This act implicitly involves the propositional operation of negation.

Or, what about the case of an infant (still not talking much: Stephen David Oller at about fourteen months) who succeeds, mainly through gestures, in letting you know that he wants you to remove more of the peel from the banana that he is munching on. In such a case as this, we can discern a whole series of propositionally complex intended meanings which are conjoined in highly constrained ways. There is the plan to eat the rest of the banana; the state of affairs that blocks progress (the peel being as it is); an implicit noting of the fact that the nearby adult can remedy the undesirable state of affairs and restore progress toward the goal of eating the rest of the banana. When the child arrives at the stage of presenting the half-eaten banana to the adult in order to get the adult to remove some more of the peel, a complex propositional plan is being carried out. The plan itself presupposes a semiotic system with considerable propositional complexity. This is especially remarkable and pertinent to the argument in cases where no adequately sequentialized syllabic speech system is yet present. The child may complain vocally, but not in any intelligible speech forms.

As seen above, another proof that language is more than any particular system of speech is translation or paraphrase. Both depend on the fact that the surface forms of speech can be altered while propositional meanings remain more or less constant. There is no need to offer a further example because the ubiquitous fact of the possibility of translating (or paraphrasing, which is merely a special case) defeats any possible counter to the claim that language is deeper than mere speech.

## WHAT'S A PROPOSITION?

A crucial term in all of the foregoing is "proposition". A question that must be addressed at some point is just how such a thing might be defined. This is a difficult requirement to meet because the term "proposition" is like the terms "number" or "set" in mathematics, or "line" and "point" in geometry. "Proposition" is a necessary primitive term, and, therefore, a fully satisfactory definition cannot be provided but must rather be assumed in advance. Nevertheless, an idea can be given that will roughly parallel the loose and non-technical sort of description that mathematicians give of the term "set" (which, for example, is said to be "an abstract collection of objects" or something of this sort). To do so, the subject is approached through the back door by inverting the old school definition of a "sentence": "that which expresses a complete thought". By inverting this definition, a rough definition of a "proposition" is obtained : *a thought which can be expressed in a sentence.*

This is a crude definition, but it is serviceable. Like any other primitive term, the meaning of "proposition" can only be made quite explicit in within the scope of the broader theoretical perspective of which it forms a part (just as "line" and "point" are defined in geometry by their relations to each other and to other terms; notably spatio-temporal ones as Einstein stressed). Much can be said about the structure of propositions, their causal relationships in discourse, and the like, but as Peirce noted at about the turn of the century, there is no such thing as a truly simple (atomic) proposition.

There are only propositions which are linked in complex ways with other propositions through inference. This can be seen easily by examining any proposition that might be thought to be simple. It will turn out to consist, at a bare minimum, of an understood subject and some predicate. However, it is necessary in order to determine what a proposition means to differentiate its subject from others that might have been selected, and the same will hold for the predicate. Once these possibilities are explored fully it will turn out that it is impossible in principle for there to be a proposition that is quite simple since any given proposition will necessarily entail implicit or explicit reference to a plurality of others (other subjects and other predicates). This is already a sufficient proof that there can be no simple propositions. However, there is yet another that is also irrefragable.

To the extent that any proposition can be said to be non-empty from the material point of view, that is, to the extent that it can be said to be meaningful in human experience, it must be connected with experience inferentially. Once that connection is made, the whole continuum of experience and the space-time universe to which it is related are called into consideration and it cannot rationally be argued that the proposition is simple. Therefore, no meaningful proposition is simple.

## NOT SPEECH BUT SEMIOSIS: THE POWER TO REPRESENT

At the same time, symbolization is a pre-requisite to any sort of knowledge and is the only means we have of understanding our

experience or whatever world(s) in which we suppose it occurs. John
Dewey, following Peirce, put the argument as follows:

> . . . symbolization is a necessary condition of all inquiry
> and of all knowledge, instead of being a linguistic expression
> of something already known which needs symbols only for
> the purposes of convenient recall and communication (John
> Dewey, 1938, p. 263).

Language, in the most general sense of the term, or better,
semiosis, inevitably plays the central role in all of our knowledge of
experience and the universe. This has long been recognized. The Pen-
tateuch says the universe came into being in response to the utterance
of God. This teaching is capsulized in the Greek account by the proposition that "in the beginning was the word". The Russian genius,
Vygotsky (1934) adjusted this proposition by quoting Faust who said
that "in the beginning was the deed"[5]. Vygotsky elaborated by saying
that "the word is the end of development, crowning the deed". A few
months later, he died never dreaming that his remarks would be tested
in scarcely three decades by one of the most remarkable advances in
the history of science--the discovery of the genetic code.

## LANGUAGE (OR SEMIOSIS) AS A GENERAL TERM

It is not a new idea that "language" (or better, "semiosis") can
be regarded as a thoroughly abstract and general term. From such a
point of view, it is possible to say that the word is both the beginning,
middle, and end of development. While it may be true that mature
expression of human capacity for language may indeed be the crowning
evidence of intelligent action, deeds without plans can hardly be termed
intelligent at all. If there were no semiotic system in which to formulate
a plan, or some other sort of conception, there could be no intelligent
action at all. Therefore, intelligence is a problem of symbolization from
start to finish.

Interestingly, John Dewey understood "language" in the broad
sense of "semiosis" or representational capacity, a sense in which it has
been used in various discussion pertaining to the general content of
this book (Oller, 1981, 1983a, 1989a, Streiff, 1983). Dewey saw "language" as properly applied to all modes of conventional semiotic representation. He wrote:

> Language in its widest sense--that is, including all means
> of communication such as, for example, monuments, rituals,
> and formalized arts--is the medium in which culture exists
> and through which it is transmitted. Phenomena that are
> not recorded cannot be even discussed. Language is the
> record that perpetuates occurrences and renders them
> amenable to public consideration. On the other hand, ideas
> or meanings that exist *only* [his italics] in symbols that

---

[5]Faust, a character of Goethe, sold his soul to the Devil in exchange for knowledge
and power.

are not communicable are fantastic beyond imagination (1938, p. 20).

Moreover, Dewey contended that actions themselves are governed by a kind of grammatical system--a fact generally unappreciated in the classical logic of philosophers not to mention modern-day psychologists, linguists, and language teachers:

> The authors of the classic logic did not recognize that tools constitute a kind of language which is in more compelling connection with things of nature than are words, nor that the syntax of operations [actions; or Vygotsky's "deeds"] provides a model for the scheme of ordered knowledge more exacting that of spoken and written language (1938, p. 94).

In other words, actions are governed by a kind of grammar that is more rigorous and unyielding than the grammars of natural language systems such as English, Spanish, Hopi, Crow, Navajo, Choctaw, etc.

For example, to test Dewey's claim, consider the order of events necessary to start your car: it is necessary to first have the keys before you get in the car (or else go back to get them); to insert the right key in the ignition; etc. Or take any physical routine whatever and think it through in terms of the sequence of specific acts required to perform it. The sequence will turn out to be far less flexible than the order of words and phrases that are possible to describe the same events, or to misrepresent them. Misrepresentation on the side of the events themselves is not possible to the same degree; not at least if we are ever to get the car started.

In fact, though Dewey could not have known it since he died in 1952, even life itself would be shown to be based in a "language" system in the broadest sense of the term "language". A better term, perhaps, would be "semiotic" system--which achieves the same level of generality without running counter to so many associations with particular speech systems. The point is that the biological or genetic code *is* a semiotic system par excellence and, it would seem, is as close as science has yet approached to the basis of all living things. In short, the code itself may be construed as the microcosmic basis of intelligence itself.

## THE BIOLOGICAL LANGUAGE

In a classic textbook on the subject, titled *The Genetic Code*, Carl Woese (1967, p. 4) wrote about the "vocabulary" which the cell uses "to construct messages in nucleic acid language"--messages which are then "translated into amino acid language by means of a dictionary or codebook". He said that every living cell uses "a tape-reading process in the synthesis of protein". He even went so far as to suggest that "the cell can be considered as consisting of a collection of genetic tapes"-- that the cell itself *is* a collection of tapes realized as certain complex linear molecules. Indeed, he said that the DNA molecule itself is not merely a long string of tapes, but a whole "library" of them. Carl Sagan (1978) estimated that a single human DNA molecule consists of roughly 500 million words of text--each DNA text, a unique library, that is quite perfectly replicated and deposited in every single cell of each unique organism. (More recent research on the human genome upped the figure to three billion words; according to a Nova special aired on the Public Broadcasting Service, April 1990.)

Another biologist, Brian Clark (1977), wrote that the discovery and partial deciphering of the genetic code was one of the most significant scientific advances in the twentieth century. It is owing to the genetic library of life-discourses, according to Clark and other biologists, that species have hereditary continuity. In fact, this library of texts, biological words strung together in meaningful ways, ultimately directs all of the processes required for sustaining life and provides the foundation for all intelligent biological action.

Therefore, contrary to Vygotsky's claim, the meaningful arrangement of biological words into genetic texts must, it would seem, predate the existence of living organisms in order to make possible that existence and thus the various activities of life. Deeds, in this sense, cannot predate words--at least not in the sense of semiosis as defined in the present discussion.

It was realized with the discovery of DNA in the early 1950s that proteins were genetic products rather than genetic materials in the raw. With the discovery of DNA, an almost unbelievably complex polymer (cf. Denton, 1986), began the search for its relationship to the proteins. The key to the pragmatic linkage between the two was the genetic code. Interestingly, this code, once it began to be understood, proved to be the basis of all living things. The genetic code is, apparently, a universal system governing all biological organisms. The code is as rigidly followed in the construction of an amoeba as in the making of a human being. Even viruses, which are possibly derivative corruptions, it seems, fall within the scope of the same biological system.

In fact, research has demonstrated that even minute changes in the system as a whole would be lethal not just to some, but apparently to all living species (Hinegardner and Engelberg, 1963, 1964). The genetic code appears to be an exceedingly articulate system in an improbable and delicate ecological balance (cf. Hoyle, 1983).

However, the approach of this discussion is not merely to look into the cell for clues concerning the character of intelligence. It is to examine the analogical linkage of the genetic texts contained within living cells to the very character of those cells themselves, as well as the differentiation and integration of those cells into complex organisms, their development into various organs, and, ultimately, their organization in the human brain. In other words, the argument for the proposition that intelligence is based on words appeals to a remarkable hierarchy of languages beginning with the genetic code per se and extending through various intermediate levels of organization to the point where human intelligence becomes able to relate purely abstract linguistic structures to experience of the physical world in such a way as to make sense of both the structures themselves and of experience.

At every discernible point along the way, at every link in the hierarchy, we see analogies of the pragmatic mapping process whereby it is possible for any normal human being to create utterances which are somehow appropriate to the facts of not only that person's experience, but to some extent, those of the common experience of all human beings. The process of pragmatic mapping, viewed at the level of normal human discourse, is an active, intelligent, articulate linking of signs (meaningful semiotic elements--words, phrases, clauses, etc.) with facts of experience. This linking, in all cases it would seem, depends on certain types of grammatical relations. For instance, such a linking depends on an infinitely rich set of subject-predicate relations (both dependent and independent; subordinate and superordinate), as well as negations of such relations, conjunctions of them, and other complications of all of the foregoing.

If these grammatical relations did not exist prior to any given event in experience, it would be impossible (apparently) to conceptualize or represent the experience of any event as humans in fact are able to do. As the philosopher Kant [1724-1804] and other rationalists before and since have argued, if it were not possible to represent events, it would be impossible to experience them at all (Kant, 1783). Or as John Dewey put it in 1938, that which cannot be represented in communicable symbols is "fantastic beyond imagination". That is to say, experience itself, or any kind of knowing whatsoever, depends on representation. Consciousness presupposes a rich ability to utilize conceptual relations between abstract categories. Or, putting the matter in different words, intelligence presupposes semiotic capacity--the ability to represent meanings. All of which implies grammatical complexity from the outset.

In fact, the genetic code itself appears to be a kind of grammar which governs the construction of certain kinds of texts. Apparently, the code sets limits to the kinds of strings of biological words that will turn out to be well-formed texts--ones that define viable organisms. For any given species, for instance, the shape, size, functions, and metabolic processes are pre-determined by the arrangement of genetic-words in the biological text that specifies the character of the type of organism in question.

The biological material is passed from parent to offspring in reproduction and thus ensures the continuity of the species. Within any given text, or library of texts specifying the character of a given organism, there are marks of punctuation indicating how given segments of the string are to be read. From DNA molecules, interpretations are generated (transfer RNA molecules) together with instructions (ribosomal RNA) about how to manufacture proteins, and even instructions (messenger RNA) about how to interpret the instructions (e.g., how to set up the protein manufacturing plant, the ribosome, at the outset). Even now, as work in genetics progresses apace, the detailed character of this grammatical structuring is just beginning to be understood (cf. Denton, 1986).

Not only is the structure of biological organisms programmed into the code, but in a dimly understood manner, the genetic library of texts that determines any given species also provides for certain regulatory processes (e.g., metabolism) and sets limits to what a given organism can be. The structure of any given cell is determined more or less directly by a particular arrangement of proteins which are built from amino acids according to detailed instructions coming from the DNA. The proteins themselves, then, perform a regulatory function in their own right as governors of metabolic processes of various sorts (cf. Clark, 1977, and Woese, 1967), e.g., insulin as an enabler for glucose to be converted to energy in muscle cells.

Since DNA is a more or less linear text (though with some overlapping portions as in a dialogue, as will be seen below) which specifies the character of an organism, the linguistic analogy fits. Even proteins are more or less linear in surface structure, though, again, like the elements of a text, their parts (which consist of other proteins) often lead lives of their own (having multiple functions), which again suggests the aptness of the textual analogy. However, the biological argument for intelligence as having a propositional, textual, grammatical character does not end with the systematic translation of DNA language into protein language. On the contrary, the mystery only begins to unravel there.

When we progress from the structure within a given cell, the substructure of the single cell, to interactions between cells, we find additional evidence for the semiotic (word-like or language-like, textual) basis of intelligence. For example, consider the behavior of a single-celled organism such as an amoeba. Take, for instance, the amoeba's response to light or heat. When exposed to light above a certain threshold, the amoeba will flee into its medium until its comfort level is restored.[6]

How is this possible? In some way, the amoeba must represent (or take notice of) the fact that brightness (or heat) is making it uncomfortable. Then, in some manner, it must internally issue an order to its protoplasm to move until it is out of the light (or heat). This order then is executed until some previously defined equilibrium is restored. All of this activity requires taking account of states of affairs external to the amoeba itself triggering operations which will tend to bring about some different state of affairs. Is this sort of activity intelligent? Perhaps so, perhaps not. Everything depends on the definition of intelligence.

It is certain, however, that the amoeba's behavior does involve a kind of complexity which can only be accounted for by appealing to the sorts of propositional relations previously mentioned--subject-predicate relations, together with such constructive operations as superordination, subordination, negation, and conjunction. The whole process,

---

[6]This example and much of its development here is based on a conversation with Robert Scott, one of the collaborators on this book, which took place in 1978 on the way to the Dulles Airport near Washington, D.C.

implicit in the amoeba's tropic behavior, is even discourse-like: "It's getting uncomfortable here. I'd better move. Okay, I'm moving. Ah! That's better. I'll quit moving now." To the extent that such propositional complexities (regardless what molecular or other form they may take) are involved in the amoeba's behavior, then, it might be said that the behavior in question is intelligent. Moreover, and more to the point of this discussion, this elaboration of the amoeba's behavior may help, I think, to illustrate the sort of thing that intelligence is.

While pondering these ideas some years ago, it was interesting to discover that the famed inventor of the precursor of our modern intelligence tests, the biologist-turned-psychologist, Alfred Binet, had discussed much the same constellation of problems before the turn of the century, and had come to somewhat the same conclusion about the behavior of single-celled organisms as is suggested for consideration here--that they demonstrate a surprising degree of propositionally complex intelligence.

Clear back in 1888 Binet had written a charming treatise whose English translation was entitled *The Psychic Life of Micro-Organisms.* Actually the book was originally published in French, and the title, *La Vie Psychique* . . . would no doubt have been better translated as *The Mental Life* . . . , or perhaps even, *The Cognitive Experience of Micro-Organisms.*

Binet contended that all ciliated infusoria (single-celled protozoans with oar-like appendages, such as Paramecium Aurelius) could be frightened by placing a drop of acetic acid in the organism's medium. If this were done under a microscope, the organisms, Binet wrote, would be seen to flee in all directions "like a flock of frightened sheep" (1888, p. vi). He claimed, therefore, that such organisms could be said to demonstrate the seemingly advanced state of mind called "fear"--along with other psychological traits.

In addition, Binet argued that such organisms could be shown to demonstrate intelligent behaviors such as hunting for a particular type of prey, memory of the way out of a certain type of enclosure, planning for the future as demonstrated by preparing a perfectly suited housing for an offspring, courtship behavior including the game of hard-to-get, and other mental behaviors commonly believed to occur only in higher species.

Of course, the point here is not merely to praise the mental skills of an amoeba, but to argue quite simply that considerable propositional complexities are involved in any activities of the sort demonstrated by Binet. He himself observed that somehow the behavior of a single-celled organism was controlled by the powers contained within its nucleus, which he described as "an essential factor in the cell's vitality" (1888, p. 100). Beyond this, he wondered by what mechanism certain internal states of the organism were set in correspondence with states external to the organism. In his view,

> what would be necessary to explain, is how and in consequence of what mechanism of structure, one form of molecu-

lar movement, corresponding to a given excitation, is followed by a certain other form of molecular movement corresponding to an act likewise determined (1888, p. 65).

A similar problem arises in any attempt to explain the manner in which cells in a more complex multicellular organism are able to know their respective functions--or how they are able to communicate with each other. In fact, an analog of this problem arises in the world of single cells that have special, short-lived, functions. For example, consider a male sperm cell. How does it know its objective of uniting with a female egg cell, and how does it know when to stop looking and start uniting? Regarding this feat, Binet quoted contemporary biologist, Balbiani, who said,

> I believe that the spermatozoids do not move about blindly, but . . . act in obedience to a kind of inner impulsion, to a sort of volition which directs them to a definite object (1888, p. 78).

Or, how does a cell of a developing embryo know whether it is to be part of a hand, or eye, or ear, or whatever? Or, how do cells know their proper functions when in fact so many functions are metabolically and otherwise differentiated?

In a popular article, Lewis Wolpert a decade ago noted that there had already been widespread speculation among microbiologists and embryologists about whether "cells have complex conversations with each other during development" (1978, p. 157). Regardless of the answer to that question, he concluded that "a large number of experiments indicate that most patterns arise as the result of cell-to-cell interaction" (1978, p. 64). The mystery is, what kinds of physico-chemical mechanisms are employed in this process. For the most part, biologists (not to mention the rest of us) remain somewhat in the dark (again, cf. Denton, 1986).

Still, there is evidence that communication both within and between the cells of complex organisms is extensive. Further, it is clear that the genetic basis of life and its relationship to the basic protein building blocks is essentially one of design and governance. Apparently the system is anything but haphazard and chaotic. To illustrate this point consider the following remarks from microbiologist, Michael Denton, 1986:

> Viewed down a light microscope at a magnification of some several hundred times, such as would have been possible in Darwin's time [and Binet's too], a living cell is a relatively disappointing spectacle appearing only as an ever-changing and apparently disordered pattern of blobs and particles which, under the influence of unseen turbulent forces, are continually tossed haphazardly in all directions. To grasp the reality of life as it has been revealed by molecular biology, we must magnify a cell a thousand million times until it is twenty kilometers in diameter and resembles a giant airship large enough to cover a great city like London or New York. What we would then see

would be an object of unparalleled complexity and adaptive design. On the surface of the cell we would see millions of openings, like the port holes of a vast space ship, opening and closing to allow a continual stream of materials to flow in and out. If we were to enter one of these openings we would find ourselves in a world of supreme technology and bewildering complexity. We would see endless highly organized corridors and conduits branching in every direction away from the perimeter of the cell, some leading to the central memory bank in the nucleus and others to assembly plants and processing units. The nucleus itself would be a vast spherical chamber more than a kilometer in diameter, resembling a geodesic dome inside of which we would see, all neatly stacked together in ordered arrays, the miles of coiled chains of the DNA molecules. A huge range of products and raw materials would shuttle along all the manifold conduits in a highly ordered fashion to and from all the various assembly plants in the outer regions of the cell (1986, p. 328).

Leaping over the middle ground between the micro-cosmic world of DNA to the organic complexities of a human being, we discover that the most complex organ known to science, a human brain, may also best be described in linguistic terms. We have already seen that the grammatical complexity of a cell is substantial, but by comparison to a single living cell, the complexity of the human brain is awe-inspiring. Michael Denton (1986, p. 330) writes:

An individual cell is nothing when compared with a system like the mammalian brain. The human brain consists of about ten thousand million nerve cells. Each nerve cell puts out somewhere in the region of between ten thousand and one hundred thousand connecting fibers by which it makes contact with other nerve cells in the brain. Altogether the total number of connections in the human brain approaches $10^{15}$ or a thousand million million . . . . Imagine an area about half the size of the USA (one million square miles) covered in a forest of trees containing ten thousand trees per square mile. If each tree contained one hundred thousand leaves the total number of leaves in the forest would be . . . equivalent to the number of connections in the human brain!

The semiotic metaphor with reference to brain studies was canonized in the book, *Languages of the Brain*, by Karl Pribram in 1971--a person referred to a few years later in *Psychology Today* as "the Magellan of brain science". Another brain scientist, distinguished Oxford professor, J. Z. Young, extended the language metaphor still further:

To understand the language of the brain it is necessary to know how the nerve cells combine, like letters or the phones of speech, to produce units that have meaning, like

words. . . . If grammar is the system that regulates the
. . . use of language, we might say that the brain operates
as sort of metalanguage with a metagrammar, which
regulates the . . . conduct of life, including speech (1978,
p. 46).

Furthermore, the brain does not merely function in the control
of mental behaviors, though nonspecialists often tend to see it as if it
were limited to that role. In much the way that DNA controls
organismic development at the micro-level, the brain (indeed the whole
central nervous system) seems to play a crucial role in the global
architecture and construction of the entire body at the macro-level.
Lenneberg (1967) cited the research of Critchley (1955) showing that
damage to either of the parietal lobes in infancy results in stunting
of the corresponding body parts on the opposite side. Moreover,
Lenneberg argued that mere "disuse" is an insufficient explanation of
this stunting since it is apparent in pre-natal stages. Thus, muscular
and skeletal development seem to be under the control of the developing
central nervous system in much the way that cell architecture and
metabolism fall under the control of DNA.

Summing up and extending the whole thesis of this discussion,
it might be argued that the genetic code sets limits and also specifies
the underlying possibilities for living organisms. Particular expressions
(interpretations) of that grammatical control mechanism or governance
system are realized in the DNA molecules that specify particular living
organisms. However, the DNA molecules themselves, in like manner,
constitute a kind of grammar governing the development of proteins.
The latter, in their turn, and again in a similar manner, seem to
constitute grammatical systems in their own right, and in like manner,
also control a whole constellation of factors (cf. Woese, 1967 and Clark,
1977) including cell architecture, metabolism, defense, etc. Skipping the
intermediate ground of embryology and the differentiation of distinct
organs in complex life-forms, we come to the advanced complexity of
mammalian nervous systems including the brains of human beings.
Here, again, we see a sort of grammatical governance relationship--
both to physical development and mental behavior.

Thus, from the DNA upward, biological development is somewhat
like the cascading network of propositional relationships in a text--
that is, it is a network of relationships of subordination and
superordination, of implication, presupposition, and association. However,
when we examine more closely the increasingly complex developments
of the upward cascade in the case of biology, each step seems quite
miraculous in its own right. Also, from the lowest level upward, what
charms the linguist in us (if there is one), is that there is a surprising
text-like quality from start to finish. Michael Denton comments on the
densely packed information system which is apparently unpacked in
a cascading series during biological maturation. For instance, concerning
proteins, Denton comments that

the breakdown products of proteins [are used] to perform all sorts of functions often quite unrelated to the function of the "mother" protein. Thus, many protein functions are compacted into an original molecule. The process begins by the synthesis of the original protein which, after performing its function, is broken down in the cell into two smaller proteins, each of which perform two further functions. These two proteins are again broken down into still smaller proteins capable of yet further functions. The device is somewhat analogous to having a whole tool kit compacted within the first tool we require to initiate a particular operation; and when the initial operation is complete, the tool breaks down into the next two tools required for the operation, and so on until the operation is complete (1986, p. 337).

The whole process appears to depend on the sort of multi-layered hierarchical structuring that is characteristic of natural language systems, and of texts expressed in natural languages, except for the fact that the wisdom of the biological solution with respect to functions served by particular proteins cannot be fully appreciated until the anticipatory character of each component step in the process is understood.

Another sort of textual compacting is observed in interpretations of DNA so as to produce more proteins than are theoretically possible to derive from a single linear sequence. This is accomplished, in Denton's own words, "by a mechanism of wonderful ingenuity" (1986, p. 336), by simply parsing the same structure in a variety of ways so as to produce a considerable variety of interpretations (proteins, in this case). Just as the sequence of letters "n-o-w-h-e-r-e" may be read as "now here" or "no where" the same sequence of DNA words may provide for the synthesis of different proteins on different readings.

However, in order for the process to work as efficiently as it does, there must be internal marks of punctuation, or instructions about how distinct parsings are to be achieved. Denton writes:

Overlapping genes are not the only recently discovered ingenious device for compacting information with great economy into DNA sequences. DNA does not consist entirely of genes containing encoded messages for the specification of proteins; a considerable proportion is involved in control purposes, switching off and on different genes at different times and in different cells. This was considered, again by analogy with human information retrieval systems such as might be used in a library or filing system or computer, to be positioned adjacent to, but separate from, the genes under its control. There was some empirical support for this very logical view, but once more, as in the case of overlapping genes, biological design turned out to be far more clever than was suspected, for it has now been found that many sequences of DNA which perform the crucial control functions related to information retrieval are situated not adjacent to the genes which they control but actually embedded within the genes themselves (1986, p. 337).

While Denton sees "no strict analogy in our own technology" for such "compacting devices", it might be argued that the processes he describes are not unlike the embedding of structure within structure within structure, and so forth, which is so characteristic of the grammar of natural language systems.

Is it possible that the cascading network observed in forward gear with reference to the physical growth and development of biological organisms (moving apparently uphill through increasing levels of complexity) is merely observed in reverse motion with reference to psychological development and language acquisition (moving apparently downhill by fixing and fleshing out innate categories with reference to particular experiences)? This is a possibility to which we return momentarily. Let it be noted here only that the direction of movement may be somewhat incidental: the innateness or pre-programmed aspect of both processes may be their more important quality (just as Chomsky, Fodor, and others have been arguing; cf. Piatelli-Palmarini, 1980, and the contributions by both Chomsky and Fodor included there).

With that in mind, the shared mystery of both embryological development (including perhaps the problem of speciation and phyla) and psychological maturation may be, as Denton's arguments together with those of Chomsky, Fodor, and others (cf. Piatelli-Palmarini, 1980) seem to imply, a single problem of design. As intractable a problem as it may seem, the principal issue would seem to be to find a way to characterize the text-like interrelatedness, the connectedness, of the entire continuum of development ranging from inert matter through the full spectrum of biological order. We need, not merely "a theory of learning", but a better articulated "theory of evolution" in the broadest possible sense of the latter term.

In fact, part of the embryological aspect of the problem, as Denton points out, can be construed as suggested by Von Neumann (1966) as a question about automata: namely, how to design one capable of self-replication. Von Neumann, according to Denton saw the problem as consisting of three parts: (1) information storage; (2) duplication of the stored information; and (3) self-replication--i.e., setting up the information in such a form that it will fully specify the means for it's own duplication. These are scarcely trivial engineering problems, and yet all of them are solved in the design of living organisms. Denton comments:

> So efficient is the mechanism of information storage and so elegant the mechanism of duplication of this remarkable molecule that it is hard to escape the feeling that the DNA molecule may be the one and only perfect solution to the twin problems of information storage and duplication for self-replicating automata.

The solution to the problem of the automatic factory lies in the ribosome. Basically, the ribosome is a collection of some fifty or so large molecules, mainly proteins, which fit tightly together. Altogether the ribosome consists of a highly organized structure of more than one million atoms which can synthesize any protein that it is instructed to make by the DNA, including the particular proteins which compromise [sic, apparently "comprise" is intended] its own structure--so the ribosome can construct itself (1986, p. 337-8).

The sheer difficulty of the engineering problems that are perfectly solved in the ribosome defies the imagination. Denton writes:

It is astonishing to think that this remarkable piece of machinery, which possesses the ultimate capacity to construct every living thing that ever existed on Earth, from a giant redwood to the human brain, can construct all its own components in a matter of minutes and weigh less than $10^{-16}$ grams. It is of the order of several thousand million million times smaller than the smallest piece of functional machinery ever constructed by man (1986, p. 338).

But is the mechanistic analogy appropriate? Denton replies:

In every direction the biochemist gazes as he journeys through this weird molecular labyrinth, he sees devices and appliances reminiscent of our own twentieth-century world of advanced technology. In the atomic fabric of life we have found a reflection of our own technology. We have seen a world as artificial as our own and as familiar as if we had held up a mirror to our own machines (1986, p. 340).

Inevitably, therefore, as astronomer Johannes Kepler [1571-1630] (who correctly predicted the elliptical orbit of the planets) and others have often observed, design implies a designer. The story is told that Kepler had built a model of the solar system which elicited an exchange with an atheistic acquaintance. Upon seeing Kepler's model, the man said, "It's beautiful, who built it?"

"No one," Kepler said with a twinkle, "It just happened" (Naismith, 1962, p. 7).

While few moderns may be willing to embrace the full force of its teleological implications, the existence of design is a fundamental fact of science. It can no longer be construed, at least not in the ninth decade of the twentieth century (if ever it could have been), as an argument based on some dope-smoking ritual of some long outmoded superstition--the opiate of the poor, ignorant, oppressed masses. As Denton says, far from being an *a priori* argument as often argued in modern intellectual circles,

the inference to design is purely *a posteriori* induction based on a ruthlessly consistent application of the logic of analogy.

The conclusion may have religious implications, but it does not depend on religious presuppositions (1986, p. 341.

## CONCLUSION

Biology, more particularly the genetic code, supports the thesis that the organization found in living things is provided for in a semiotic system of elegant design. The idea the life depends on such a system is no longer mere speculation. It is the central empirical finding of twentieth century biology. Moreover, it lends support, albeit indirectly, to the thesis that intelligence itself has the character most typified in natural language systems. While the support, as noted, is indirect, even indirect support from a foundation of bedrock granite can be substantial. In the following chapter a logical analysis of intelligence test items is considered. The upshot of that discussion bears directly, then, on the issues dealt with throughout the rest of the book.

# Chapter 4
# Intelligence Test Items

Harry Jerison, UCLA neuroscientist, once remarked that "language and language-related performances are inevitably dominant in most human performances" (1977, p. 59). He was writing, of course, from the vantage point of biology, and more specifically, brain science. However, it is possible to seek evidence for or against his claim through study of human performance on tests. The fact that verbal and non-verbal test scores are substantially correlated has been known for a long time. The existence of such a correlation is no surprise, therefore, to anyone who has considered the research evidence. For instance, by 1931 Stephenson (as cited by Spearman and Jones, 1950) had obtained a correlation of .82 between eight verbal tests and eight non-verbal tests used with 1,037 subjects. More recently, psychometricians have succeeded in rather deliberately reducing this correlation, and increasing the amount of specific variance attributable to the distinct constructs believed by many to underlie verbal and non-verbal tasks. (In recent years, the term "performance" has sometimes been preferred over the term "nonverbal".) Still the term "general intelligence" persists against all efforts to purge it. In this chapter the question is asked: just what kinds of specific abilities might that general factor consist of?

## THE EMERGENCE OF "*g*"

Kaufman (1979, p. 113) reports figures on the various verbal and performance subscales of the *Revised Wechsler Intelligence Scale for Children (WISC-R)* showing substantial specificities in each of the subscores of that battery. The mean specificity observed for the performance (i.e., "non-verbal") portions was .33 while for the "verbal" parts it was .29. However, Kaufman also found that a common underlying factor, a general factor or "g", could account for an average of 47% of the variance in the verbal tasks and 32% of that in the non-verbal ones. (The number of cases for these estimates was approximately 1,100.)

Thus, after decades of research attempting generally to reduce to a minimum the correlation between verbal and non-verbal tasks, there still remains a substantial communality between the two categories. Kaufman (1979), Carroll (1983a), Upshur and Homburg (1983), Clifford (1981) and others caution against overinterpreting this common factor. For instance, Kaufman writes:

> The notion of *g* must be thought of as the global ability underlying a conventional intelligence test . . . but not as a theoretical construct underlying human intellect (p. 110).

The point behind his cautionary observation is that the concept of "general" intelligence has sometimes been associated with almost magical qualities and a mystique that has probably been misleading. For instance, Arthur Jensen (1969, 1973, 1980) has pressed this general factor right into the genes of human beings and insists that about 80% of it is determined by heredity. However, Carroll (1983b) has challenged Jensen's definition of the general factor and argues that in some cases where Jensen claims to have found a general factor, there actually is none.

Nevertheless, the evidence that there exists a general factor in the variance generated by numerous and diverse mental tests, including at least *some* of the non-verbal sort (see Chapters 7 and 8 below) seems secure even after the cautions recommended by Kaufman, Carroll and others are taken into consideration. There certainly appear to be cases where such a factor can be identified using appropriate statistical procedures (see Carroll, 1983a, Farhady, 1983, Boldt, 1989, and Oltman, Stricker, and Barrows, 1990).

While Kaufman's interpretation of the general factor underlying the various parts of the *WISC-R* can scarcely be faulted for being too daring, it might be asked if it isn't over-conservative. The question, it seems, ought to be: how can the general factor that has been shown to underlie many mental tests *best* be explained? It seems unsatisfactory to label this factor as "general intelligence" and then turn around and define "general intelligence" as "what intelligence tests measure" (see Jensen, 1969, p. 8, and also 1973, 1980). Isn't Jensen traveling in a vicious circle in this definition?

On the other hand, is the counter argument that the general factor is merely a trivial statistical artefact logically defensible? Wouldn't it make more sense to seek a non-trivial, and non-circular explanation? Of course, it is desirable not only to understand the general factor or whatever tasks or procedures may be common to intelligence or performance batteries, but also to understand in what ways such tasks are distinct.

### CONTENT ANALYSIS

Quite apart from the evidence from psychometric studies per se, an analysis of the tasks in so-called "intelligence" tests would seem to have substantial bearing on the determination of what intelligence tests measure. One empirical approach would be to go to the test-takers themselves and get them to introspect about how they are able to solve the problems in the tests. Roth (1978) used this approach. It is an admirable method. However, it can be supplemented by a method that directly analyzes the tasks set by test items. Test-takers may not always know or be able to tell us just how they solve (or attempt to solve) mental problems, though, in some cases careful analysis may solve these mysteries.

Therefore, a supplementary method which may increase the overall reliability of the findings is a purely logical analysis of the tasks that are included in certain so-called "intelligence" tests. The purpose of such an analysis would be to hypothesize just what basic mental operations *must* be involved in the solution of commonly used test items. The question is: *what sorts of internal representations are essential to the solution of typical intelligence test items, and what kinds of operations must be performed on those internal representations?* Possibly such an analysis will get us out of the circular, and nearly useless, claim of Arthur Jensen (1969) that "intelligence" is "what intelligence tests measure" (p. 8). Such a claim may help to fend off attacks on the tests by the truly timid or the feeble-minded, but it is ultimately an empty pretense.

First, some of the most commonly used "intelligence" test items of the non-verbal type are examined, and then some "intelligence" items of the verbal type are considered.

## Non-Verbal IQ Items

Among the commonly cited examples of exemplary non-verbal IQ items are the ones found in the *Cattell Culture Fair Intelligence Tests* and in *Raven's Progressive Matrices*. Jensen (1969, 1973, 1980) refers to these tests as nearly "pure" measures of "general intelligence". Since the *Cattell* tests incorporate items of the *Raven*-type, an examination of these should provide a fairly representative picture of some of the best non-verbal IQ tests in existence.

Figure 4.1 contains examples of the four item types that appear in the *Cattell* tests. (The third row in the figure, labeled "Matrices", represents the *Raven* type of item.) These samples come from a pamphlet prepared by the publishers of the *Cattell* tests to inform users about the test and its applications. Since the items shown are fairly simple ones by comparison to those that actually appear in the tests, whatever mental processes are required by these should be at least as important to the more complex items that actually appear in the tests.

For each type of item there is a separate set of instructions. For instance, in order to solve items of the "Series" type it is necessary to select the alternative on the right that best completes the sequential pattern that is displayed on the left. The examinee must note, among other things, that the rectangular bars on the left become longer as one progresses through the series from left to right. It is also the case that the increase in length is constant from one bar to the next.

What sorts of mental operations are necessary in order to solve items of the "Series" type? In addition to understanding the instructions themselves, which may present some difficulty to the lower range of examinees, there are other propositional operations that seem logically indispensable to the solution of such items. Setting aside the question of how the examinees distinguish between the lead-in material (the item stem) and the possible answers (the multiple-choice alternatives), may we not infer that they must internally represent the bars on the left in some manner or other? Perhaps the representations remain visual throughout the solution of the problem, but can it not be argued even if this is so that these representations must nonetheless serve as

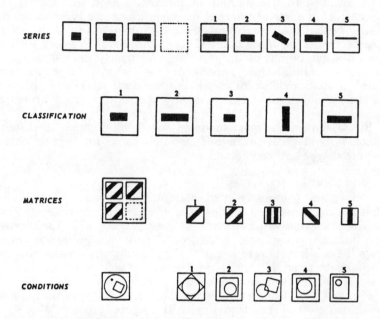

**FIGURE 4.1.** SAMPLE ITEMS FROM "AN INTRODUCTION TO IPAT (CATTELL'S) CULTURE FAIR INTELLIGENCE TESTING". COPYRIGHT © 1949, 1960, INSTITUTE FOR PERSONALITY AND ABILITY TESTING, INC. ALL RIGHTS RESERVED. REPRODUCED BY PERMISSION.

propositional subjects with which certain predicates must be associated?

For instance, necessary logical predicates of the second bar include (it would seem) the fact that it is the second one in the series (i.e., that it is positioned to the right of the first); that it is longer than the first bar; that it is oriented on the horizontal; and that it has the same width as the first. And no doubt other facts can be adduced. Each of these facts can be understood as a proposition for which the subject-predicate relation is an essential ingredient.

The question is whether these facts can be "known" in any sense at all by the test taker without some form of propositional logic in which to represent them. In addition, there is the implicit proposition (or fact) that the first and second bars are objects of the same type, and that they form a series of similar objects with the third bar. This requires that the "series" be treated as a logical subject which is distinct from its individual elements. Further, there is the proposition (or fact) that the increase in length from bar one to two to three is relatively constant. From this fact it may be inferred that the next item in the logical series must have the same properties as the preceding ones. In other words, it may be inferred that the same predicates will apply to the next logical subject in the series that have applied to preceding ones. (A necessary presupposition for all of this would seem to be the proposition that things will be orderly; i.e., that there is a logically discoverable answer to the test item.)

The item solver may rule out choice 2 because it is the same approximate length as the second bar in the series. He knows from the proposition that the bars in the series become progressively longer from left to right that the correct answer must be longer than the third bar in the series. Choice 3 may be ruled out because the bar in that alternative is not oriented on the horizontal. Here it seems that an implicit negation of the predicate "oriented on the horizontal" is required. (Again, it is acknowledged that the mental operations may in fact be performed on visual images, but does this eliminate the necessity of deep propositional structures? Frankly, it is difficult to imagine any way to eliminate the need for such structures.) Choice 4 can be eliminated because it does not satisfy the predicate of being longer than bar three in the series, and choice 5 is too narrow. It does not satisfy the predicate of being the same width as the other bars in the series.

While it might be correct to argue that not all of the propositions contained in the preceding remarks are necessary to the solution of the series problem, can it be argued that none of them is required? On the contrary, would it not make sense to suppose that many propositional forms are necessary which have not been highlighted in the previous analysis? Moreover, is it not also obvious that many if not all of the propositional structures illustrated will be required for the solution of any such problem?

The second type of item in Figure 4.1 seems to be somewhat simpler than the first. The directions tell the examinee to indicate which of the pictured elements does not go with the rest. Which one does not fit? Again, the bars, it would seem, are logical subjects with which certain crucial predicates must be associated. In this example, the predicate of horizontal orientation (being longer on the horizontal dimension than on the vertical) is crucial to the solution. The propositional operation of negation is equally essential. The problem is to find which element does not share the predicate(s) shared by all of the others. There may be some other way to represent the problem, but is there any method of representation which does not implicitly contain the propositional complexities just pointed out?

In the third type of problem, labeled "Matrices", Cattell was obviously influenced by the matrix format of the *Raven* non-verbal IQ test. The problem is to select the element from the several choices that best completes the matrix pattern. Simply put, the matrix type of item is merely a more complex version of the "Series" type of item. With a matrix there are more dimensions of pattern variation and hence a greater number of propositional structures are possible.

In the item at hand, on the third row of Figure 4.1, the test taker may note that there are various progressions in the matrix which may help to determine just what the missing element must be like. There is in fact a progression from left to right in each row, and from top to bottom in each column. There is even a progression across the diagonals that may be of some help. The question, it would seem, is what predicates must be associated with each of the elements of the pattern in order to uniquely determine the missing element of the whole pattern. The order in which the progressions are noticed may not be too important, but can it be denied that at least some of them must be noticed?

In the rather simple problem under consideration, it is sufficient to notice that the two patterns on the left side of the matrix are similar both in the direction of their cross-hatched lines, and in the number of those lines. From this it may be inferred that the ones on the right must also be similar, and that therefore the correct choice is the one which matches the pattern in the top right hand corner of the matrix. Thus, choice 1 is the correct answer. Other strategies would lead to the same result, but is there any conceivable strategy that does not depend on complex propositional operations? That is, is it possible to solve such problems without performing mental operations that set up subject-predicate relations which are true of the patterns in question? Or is it possible to avoid the negation of certain predicates? How about the conjoining of propositional meanings in complex ways?

In the fourth type of item, "Conditions", the task is considerably more complicated than in the previous items. The problem is to note the relation(s) between the dot and the various other elements enclosed in the square to the left and then find the square on the right where the dot can be placed in the same relation(s) to similar elements. In the example, the dot is inside the circle but outside the square. The only place where it can be placed in a similar relationship to a circle and square on the right is in Choice 3. In all of the other cases, the circle is completely contained within the square and it is not possible to place the dot inside the circle without also placing it inside the square at the same time.

As with previous examples, the question of how the examinee represents the fact that the larger square is not to be considered part of the immediate problem, and all of the other propositions that are contained implicitly or explicitly in the instructions to items of this type, are set aside at the outset. It is still necessary to recognize an implicit vocabulary (possibly a visual or merely geometric one) specifying such elements as DOT, CIRCLE, and SQUARE. It is possible that these elements need not necessarily be represented in the words of any particular natural language, but isn't a verbal representation highly likely? Roth's research (1978) seems to support the conclusion that all normals do in fact use verbal representations for such problems. But what if they did not? What if the representations were entirely visual (or in some other mental form, and not in words associated with a particular natural language)? Would this eliminate the necessity of propositional operations? Hardly. In fact is there any logical argument that would eliminate such operations? The problem is to conceive of a solution that would not in any way involve propositional complexities. This is a logical impossibility since the very representation of the problem itself must necessarily involve such complexities.

There must also, it seems, be an implicit (or explicit) vocabulary to distinguish the predicates INSIDE, NOT INSIDE (or OUTSIDE), and no doubt others as problems of the matrix type become increasingly complicated. Moreover, there are implicit superordinate operators such as NOT and AND. To solve the problem, the examinee, it would seem, must be able in some manner or other to represent internally propositions of the form, the DOT is INSIDE the CIRCLE, as well as the DOT is NOT INSIDE the SQUARE. Moreover, these propositions must be conjoined by some sort of AND operator to create a proposition that has the rough form, DOT INSIDE CIRCLE AND DOT NOT INSIDE SQUARE.

Such propositional forms have to be fitted to the visually presented facts. They must be pragmatically mapped onto those facts. Further, the actual pragmatic mappings are likely to be more complex than the ones sketched out here. This is inevitable as problems become more complex throughout tests of the matrix type.

If the foregoing argument concerning non-verbal IQ items is accepted, it can only enhance the plausibility of the hypothesis that deep semiotic abilities are the only logically possible basis for the solution of non-verbal IQ items of the type examined. Further, the most likely basis for the development of such semiotic abilities is the furtherance of the primary language. In case this hypothesis were correct, tests of the "non-verbal" type cannot in principle be entirely "language" free. They logically require propositional operations which presuppose grammar governed complexities. The question, then, if paradigm examples of "non-verbal" tests do not turn out to be entirely independent of linguistic (propositional) operations, what sorts of items can be expected to be "language" free?

### VERBAL IQ ITEMS
Some may argue that any analysis of "verbal" IQ items will be trivially relevant (and therefore *ir*relevant) to the hierarchical model under consideration. However, there are some good reasons for looking closely at "verbal" IQ items. For one, if the hierarchy is credible, it should be possible to demonstrate that in important ways "verbal" items have some common semiotic ground with "non-verbal" ones in the propositional operations that they require. For another, it should also be possible to examine the extent to which such items are distinct from so-called "language proficiency" items.

"Verbal" IQ items are, as Gunnarsson (1978) showed, sometimes excessively difficult to distinguish from items appearing in so-called "Reading" tests, and other categories of "Achievement" tests. Almost always, however, IQ items of the "verbal" type require the interpretation and/or production of words, or statements in a *particular language*. To this extent it is already difficult to follow the line that Jensen, Herrn-stein, and others do in claiming that such tests primarily measure innate ability rather than acquired language proficiency. It was the purpose of *Language in Education: Testing the Tests* (Oller and Perkins, 1978) to challenge the claims of the defenders of IQ testing in general. The principal objections raised there against certain claims of the IQ testers remain unanswered, in spite of certain valid criticisms of the statistical method of principal components analysis.[7]

At any rate, just what kinds of mental operations are required by IQ items of the "verbal" type? A typical item, one which appeared in the original Binet tests, requires the examinee to say what is wrong with a given statement such as the following:

> The judge told the prisoner: "You are to be hanged at dawn. Let this be a warning to you."

Most adults immediately laugh upon hearing the item. But it costs most of us a little thinking to explain why, and even more effort to see the vast propositional fabric on which our conclusion depends. The correct answer, is any statement to the effect that the prisoner can't be warned if he is dead.

The crux of the problem is a conflict between the necessary consequence that hanging will kill the prisoner and that warning implies an opportunity to repeat whatever offense the prisoner is accused of having committed. It takes almost no time for an adult to work out all of this. In fact, adults almost immediately find the judge's statement odd, even funny. However, what is not obvious is that many propositional meanings are taken into consideration in answering the item.

It is possible to differentiate the necessary network of related propositions into three categories: first, there are presuppositions which are necessary in order for us to associate any meaning at all with the asserted propositions; second, there are associated propositions which aid our comprehension but which are neither before nor after the stated assertions (we might term them "general semantic propositions"); and, third, there are implications which are in some sense subsequent to (or consequent upon) the asserted propositions.

For instance, because the judge hands down a death sentence, we may infer that the prisoner has been convicted of a capital crime. This inference is not a necessary one, in the strong logical sense, but it is a very likely one based on what we are apt to assume about the legal system in question, and it is both relevant and probably correct. A more obviously necessary presupposition is that the prisoner has been convicted of committing some serious crime. The fact that he is a prisoner, suggests the presupposition that he was captured at some time

---

[7]For the pertinent criticisms, see all of Part I in *Issues in Language Testing Research* (Oller, 1983b). Also see especially Chapter 22 of that volume where some of the criticisms are answered while others are accepted as valid.

in the past, just as the fact that the judge is a judge suggests the presupposition of an election or appointment to that office.

Associated propositional meanings would have to include the fact that a prisoner is someone who is detained against his will in a societal institution known as a prison; that a judge is someone empowered by the state with certain authorities within its legal system. In fact, the presupposed propositions also have associated propositional meanings. For instance, the presupposition that the trial of the prisoner has already occurred when the sentence is being handed down, has associated with it the semantic knowledge that trials occur in court-rooms; and that verdicts are usually reached by a juries, and so on.

There are also implications that follow from the assertions of the judge. Associated with the hanging is the semantically implied proposition (part of the meaning of the verb "hang" as applied to prison-ers) that it will involve placing a rope around the victim's neck, with the victim's hands restrained, and then, suspending the victim by the rope so that he will strangle or die of a broken neck. Implied proposi-tional meanings would also include that hanging kills the victim so this particular prisoner will die; that a warning implies an opportunity to repeat the presupposed offense, so this one will be of no effect. The warning will be cancelled in effect by the hanging, and so on.

No doubt the foregoing analysis leaves out more than it includes. However, it does suggest that an IQ item of the type analyzed involves a good deal of propositional reasoning of the very sort that goes on in the interpretation of ordinary discourse (for more on this topic, see Rumelhart, 1975; Schank, 1975, 1980; and Schank and Abelson, 1977). Is it not an open question whether there are any meanings at all which are not linked to the fabric of experience via the sort of propositional network illustrated with respect to the hanging example?

Here is another example from the Binet-type verbal IQ test. What is wrong with the statement:

> In a train wreck, the cars at the end are usually the ones most severely damaged.

Surprisingly, perhaps, most adults not only do not laugh at this item (in contrast to their reaction to the one about the hanging), but in fact, they meet it with a sort of blank stare. Many do not see anything wrong with it at all on first hearing. However, a bit of reflection proves that the statement is false.

To solve the puzzle it is necessary to consider what usually happens in a train wreck, and then to ask whether it is likely that the cars in the back will be the ones to receive most of the damage. In fact, trains travel on tracks. This is an associated proposition. That is, it is associated with the assertion about trains. Ordinarily, they travel in a forward linear direction. This too is an associated proposition which is a direct consequence of the linear nature of the tracks. From it, we can infer that the cars at the front are the ones which will logically receive the greater force of an impact if there is a collision.

This inference is an implication (by the definition given above) of the nature of trains and their usual linear motion in a forward direction. A further implication, is that the cars at the back are therefore the least likely to be damaged, since they are the ones which are the most protected due to the cushioning effect of the intervening cars as well as the fact that they are far less likely to be overtaken by something from behind than the cars in front are to run into something. It may be argued that the cars at the rear will receive the greatest damage if a stationary train is struck by another train from behind, but the one striking it will tend to receive the most damage in its lead cars. And, in any case, to reason that the statement about damage to trains is correct or incorrect on such a basis demonstrates the need to pragmatically map propositions onto the episodic facts of experience.

As in the hanging example, the problem solver requires access to much of the interpreted fabric of experience. There may be a multitude of strategies for working out these relationships but the fact that they are required seems unquestionable. Indeed, it seems that the ability to come up with the right propositional meanings, i.e., those which will lead to the solution of the problem, is crucially dependent on the pragmatic mapping of propositional meanings onto episodes of experience.

Here is one final example. In another typical item type, the examinee is presented with certain asserted information and then is asked to answer a question based on that information. For instance, the examinee might be told:

> Mary is taller than George but she is shorter than Sam or Harry. Who is the shortest?

Just what sort of mental acts are necessary to the solution of this problem? It seems simple enough on the surface, but there is more to it than immediately greets the analyst.

Consider first how a solution might be achieved through a visual strategy. Suppose we first imagine a female named Mary who is visibly taller than some male named George. (At this point, we have already made two propositional inferences about sex which go beyond the asserted information. We have also arrived at the proposition that both Mary and George are humans. It is difficult to imagine how we might derive at such inferential meanings from a strictly visual strategy, but let us continue.) Then, we may simply add two other male persons to our visual image, namely Sam and Harry. (Again, sex assignment is based on pragmatic propositional inferences based on the semantic values of the two names in question.) It is asserted that they are both taller than Mary. (However, a slight difficulty again arises for a strictly visual strategy since Sam and Harry are not compared with each other. How can we know for certain what height to assign to either of them? Though, it makes no difference to the problem at hand, height assignment to Harry and Sam would seem to be necessary to placing them in our visual image. Let's just assume this is accomplished, never mind how.) To answer the question, "Who is shortest?", we may now simply scan the image and pick out George.

Or, it would seem, a quicker non-visual (or only partially visual) strategy would be to reason that since George is shorter than Mary and Mary is shorter than Sam or Harry, George must be shorter than Sam or Harry, and therefore, the shortest of the four. This inference works because height is a transitive relationship.

No doubt, there are other strategies that will arrive at the same correct solution, but are there any that do not rely heavily on inferred propositional meanings? In fact, isn't it helpful (perhaps even necessary) to know what the question is in order to know what to do with the asserted propositional meanings? At least some problem solvers report that they need to have another pass at the asserted meanings after they know what it is they are looking for. For instance, consider how the problem would be changed if the question were, "Who is the next to the shortest person?", or "The third from the tallest?" Doesn't the need to know what the question is suggest that comprehension itself needs to be guided by some sort of propositionally formulated plan?

In addition to the reasoning already sketched out, there are some other propositional inferences that are lurking in the background just out of view. For instance, we assume that the measurement of the persons in the given assertions is done with all of them in a standing position, legs straight, head erect, etc. Further, we assume that hats don't count, that shoes are taken off, that it is unfair for anyone to stand on their tip-toes, that the ground must be level where the measuring takes place, etc. We do not expect the measurement to be done with some of the persons in kneeling or sitting position while others are standing, and so forth. Beyond these presupposed meanings there must be a great deal of additional propositional structure. But, perhaps this point is already established.

In the light of even this brief analysis, does it not seem clear that the solution of both "verbal" and "non-verbal" items is dependent on the utilization of propositional meanings of considerable complexity? Is it not also clear that presuppositions, associations, and implications must be supplied by the problem solver through abstract inferential reasoning? Further, doesn't all of this entail the utilization of some deep language system which has grammatical capabilities allowing such operations as predication, negation, conjunction, modification, and the like?

In his final chapter to the book, *The Human Brain*, Wittrock (1977) contends that "imagery" is crucial to the acquisition of "verbally presented" content. He cites the work of Allen Paivio and others showing that creating a meaningful image seems to have a direct and highly positive impact on retention and recall in many types of learning tasks. Could this be because of the fact that the creation of the appropriate sorts of images engages the main machinery of human intelligence? According to the semiotic model under consideration here, meaningfulness depends on the linking of propositional meanings in one form with similar meanings expressed in a different form. This hypothesis was proposed originally by Peirce (see Jakobson, 1980). It suggests that meaningfulness is dependent on translation--moving from one language system into another.

Paivio and others have demonstrated that the recall of a verbally presented form may be enhanced by causing the subject to link it up with a visual image that somehow expresses the same (or a similar) meaning. The translation hypothesis, suggests that the linking itself is the principal factor. Perhaps it facilitates retention and recall because it requires an active fitting of propositional meanings to each other-- a process that necessarily engages deep semiotic capacity.

In two dramatic demonstrations, Kieslar and McNeil (1962) and Wittrock (1963) showed that children who dealt with iconic presentations of various facts of molecular kinetics succeeded surprisingly well in recalling the principles a year later. In Wittrock's study, two-thirds of the children were able to remember the criterial concepts a year later. It was surprising that they were able to do this since they had only received two to four weeks of instruction and in spite of the fact that they were believed to be too young mentally to learn the concepts in the first place.

## CONCLUSION

The end result is only a slight amplification of the pragmatic mapping idea: namely, that the central function of intelligence is the linking of meanings expressed in different representational systems. It seems plausible at least to consider this possibility and to explore further some of its ramifications. In the chapters that follow the variance produced by educational and mental tests of various kinds is examined relative to various populations of subjects. In all of the discussion, it may be useful to keep in mind that correct answers to any of the test questions under consideration require the interpretation of certain semiotic forms in terms of certain other ones.

# Part II: Monolinguals and ESL Adults

# Chapter 5
# Competency and Monolinguals at the Secondary Level

In an effort to escape the criticism that many intelligence and achievement tests were of questionable relevance to everyday life, "competency" tests were developed in the late 1970s. They were supposed to assess ability to perform "real-life" tasks rather than the somewhat more "academic" tasks of most school tests. In this chapter what competency tests measure is in focus. To what extent can it be clearly demonstrated that such tests measure factors other than general proficiency in the primary language employed in the test items?

### SOME BACKGROUND ON COMPETENCY TESTING

The story really begins with the dissatisfaction of many educators with intelligence testing. At about the turn of the century, when Alfred Binet was developing what was to become the prototype of the modern IQ tests, he originally hoped to be able to predict success in school. Of course, it was supposed that success in school would be causally related to success in society at large, and therefore, the original intelligence testers were interested in this larger category of success as well. Other major factors which are generally believed to enter into "success" (whatever it is defined to be) are home background, effort, and native ability.

However, Arthur Jensen of Berkeley and Richard Herrnstein of Harvard have gone so far as to argue that native ability as measured by IQ tests is the basic determining factor in school performance as well as societal success. They argue that society works like a sorting mechanism. Persons of low ability, they contend, naturally precipitate to the bottom of the social hierarchy while persons of high ability rise to the top (Jensen, 1969, 1980; Herrnstein, 1973; and Herrnstein and Wagner, 1981).

Other theorists argued that educational achievement and the abilities that mental tests measure (whatever they may be) are resultant factors rather than causes. By this view, social stratification is itself the causal factor that determines educational achievement as well as scores on the tests (e.g., Gartner, Greer, and Reissman, 1974, and their collaborators). Yet another possibility is that there may be a dynamic interaction between native ability and other factors, including the social order itself (see Coles, 1978; Cummins, 1986; Spener, 1988). By this theory we might expect much alternation between the roles of cause and effect from one factor to another.

But what do the tests really measure? By the view of Jensen and Herrnstein, the IQ tests really measure native abilities to a very great extent. By the view of Gartner, et al, they really measure the effects of societal sorting to a very great extent (something which may not be very closely related to innate abilities). And, by a more moderate position between these two extremes, the IQ tests probably measure something less than true native ability and something more than mere societal discrimination (or sorting).

Interestingly, clear back at the turn of the century, Binet seemed to anticipate the crucial role of language in all of this. His tests revealed an overriding concern with language. Perhaps this concern helped to insure a tight link between "intelligence" tests and "achievement" tests. In fact, as we will see, this linguistic connection can be demonstrated in various ways.

Nearly two decades ago, Labov (1970) questioned the meaningfulness of scores attained on tests in majority English by children from various minority backgrounds. A short while later, seemingly unaware of the arguments advanced by Labov, David McClelland pointed out in an address at Educational Testing Service in 1971, that he had experienced difficulty in comprehending the English spoken in Jamaica. From this he inferred that perhaps the language of tests might be an important factor in test performance. Wolfram and Christian (1977) complained somewhat more explicitly that this is probably true with respect to children from white Appalachia.

Another problem which McClelland pointed out was that intelligence tests are almost universally validated against achievement tests, and vice versa, which results the tendency for them to gravitate toward each other. In fact, Gunnarsson (1978) showed that some intelligence, achievement, and even personality items are so similar as to be virtually indistinguishable. Further, he demonstrated that the rationales for the content of IQ and achievement tests often read like paraphrases of one another. In some cases the only significant difference between test items (or test rationales) aimed at different constructs would appear to be the labels on the test booklets.

In addition to the problem of content overlap in intelligence and achievement tests, as Roth (1978) has shown, the internal processing that enables children to solve abstract "non-verbal" problems such as Raven's Progressive Matrices may be tied directly to their use of language. He contends that "communication is instrumental for solving 'non-verbal' problems" (p. 2) and suggests metaphorically that "communicative efforts create a 'scaffolding'" which enables the problem-solver to reach what would otherwise be unattainable solutions (p. 4).

Because of all of the just mentioned problems in the traditional types of intelligence and achievement tests, McClelland, and others, have urged a shift in emphasis from innate capabilities and academic performances to life-skills which have more immediate importance to most persons. He and others, notably Robert Glazer, proposed sampling real life tasks:

Criterion sampling means that testers have got to get out of their offices where they play endless word and paper-and-pencil games and into the field where they actually analyze performance into its components (McClelland, 1971, pp. 179-180).

But, McClelland warned, the analysis could be carried too far:

> If we abandon general intelligence or aptitude tests, as proposed, and move toward criterion sampling based on job analysis, there is the danger that the tests will become extremely specific to the criterion involved (p. 184).

He cites the example of project ABLE where skills such as "measures angles", "sharpens tools and planes", and "identifies sizes and types of fasteners using gauges and charts" were singled out among fifty or so others. These categories, he regarded as too specific.

To counterbalance the possibility of items that are too specific, McClelland recommended attention to more general skills. Among the ones that he listed were, "reading, writing, calculating, and communication" (p. 185).

We might ask: have we not come full circle back to language abilities again? Can it be demonstrated that competency tests are not primarily measures of general language proficiency? Or putting the question somewhat differently, how important is knowledge of majority-variety English to performance on "competency" tests? The research reported below only scratches the surface of these questions, but it does offer some suggestive clues about the possible importance of language proficiency to competency tests.

### THE ADULT PERFORMANCE-LEVEL SURVEY

Perhaps the most widely used competency test battery in existence is the *Adult Performance-Level Survey (APL)*. According to the *Manual*, it was pretested on students in 36 states, 2,583 in all. The test *Manual* defines the main objective of the *APL* as a test of

> proficiency of both young and mature adults in skills necessary for minimal levels of educational and economic success in American society. . . . . Rather than emphasizing purely academic knowledge, the APL program focuses on functional skills that are highly relevant to everyday living (no date, Manual, p. 1).

The test purportedly aims at five skill areas and five content areas. The five skills include, "Identification of Facts and Terms", "Reading", "Writing", "Computation", and Problem Solving". The content areas are divided up into "Community Resources", "Occupational Knowledge", "Consumer Economics", Health", and "Government and Law". These categories can be arranged in such a way that their intersections define a matrix of possible test items as shown in Chart 5.1 on page 66 (from the *APL Manual*, p. 1).

Following this plan, the entire APL Survey, consisting of 40 items in all, can be divided into five parts, in two different ways. Each item serves double duty, both in a content area and in a skill area. Thus each part contains exactly 8 items (40 divided by 5).

To determine the extent to which each part score represents a different content or skill is a complex correlation problem. The question is, how much of the non-chance variance generated by each part score is unique to that part, and how much is common to the other parts? To the extent that each part produces specific variance (i.e., reliable variance which is unique to that part), it can be claimed that it contributes something distinctive to the total score on the test. On the other hand, to the extent that all of the parts produce overlapping variances, the possibility exists that they are measuring much the same complex of skills (whatever that those skills may turn out to be--a question returned to below).

### CHART 5.1
The "Content-by-Skills Matrix: Examples of Tasks" from the *Adult Performance Level Program* (*User's Guide*, n. d., p. 1)

| CONTENT/ SKILLS | Community Resources | Occupational Knowledge | Consumer Economics | Health | Government & Law |
|---|---|---|---|---|---|
| Identification of Facts and Terms | Knowing what a time zone is. | Knowing what skills are needed for clerical jobs. | Knowing what "bait & switch" is. | Knowing what a normal human temperature is. | Knowing what the Bill of Rights says. |
| Reading | Reading a bus schedule. | Reading a want-ad. | Reading a contract. | Reading a prescription label. | Reading a ballot. |
| Writing | Writing a letter to make hotel reservations. | Filling out a W-4 form. | Filing a consumer complaint. | Answering a medical questionnaire. | Writing a letter to a legislator. |
| Computation | Computing a plane fare. | Computing over-time earnings. | Finding the best buy. | Computing a daily dosage. | Computing a statute of limitations. |
| Problem Solving | Determining where to go for help with a problem. | Deciding what to say to a bother-some co-worker. | Deciding which of two decisions is better in economic terms. | Deciding which meal is best given a set of preconditions. | Determining if a given situation or action is legal. |

## A BRIEF REVIEW OF SOME STATISTICAL CONCEPTS
Readers who are already familiar with the statistical procedures of factor analysis and the computation of specificities may want to skip over this entire section (up to the next subhead). For others a brief review of certain statistical concepts may be helpful. (This review also provides an outline of the statistical approach applied in subsequent chapters of this book.)

First, it is necessary to define the concept "variance". The variance in a test is computed from the sum of squares of deviations from the mean (for the entire distribution of scores in question) divided by the number of cases minus one. Thus, the variance is the square of the standard deviation. (The standard deviation is often represented by the abbreviation $s$, and the variance by $s^2$.)

A second required statistical concept is the correlation between two distributions of scores drawn from the same sample of subjects. When high scorers on one test are also high scorers on the other test, and when low scorers on the one are low on the other, the two tests are positively correlated. The strongest possible positive correlation (referring to the linear Pearson product-moment $r$) is, of course, +1.00. A negative correlation arises when low scores on one test correspond to high scores on the other, and vice versa. The maximum negative correlation is -1.00. Regardless whether a correlation is positive or negative, it may vary in strength. To judge strength, in general we examine the correlation irrespective of its sign. That is, we look at the absolute value of the correlation. An absolute value of .00 would indicate no relationship at all between the tests in question. A value of .10 would indicate a weak relationship (in most cases, an insignificant one depending on the sample size); one of .30 would generally be taken to indicate a weak relationship; and one of, say, .90 would usually be taken to indicate a strong relationship.

The strength of a correlation is judged by its square. The square of the correlation is termed the "coefficient of determination" and is an index of the proportion of variance shared by the two tests in question. Thus, a correlation of .90, for example, would indicate a common variance of .81 (or 81%); while a correlation of .10, for instance, would indicate only a .01 overlap in variance (1 %).

Correlation is crucial to the definition of both reliability and validity. To the extent a test is correlated with itself (or with true measures of whatever the test measures), it may be said to be reliable. In this sense, all reliability estimates can be interpreted as estimates of self-correlation. Hence, the reliability of any test, call the test $i$, may be designated, $r_{ii}$. However, if we are thinking in terms of the test's correlation with true scores in the domain $i$, call the true scores in that domain $I$, then the reliability coefficient is sometimes designated $r_{iI}$. Whenever a correlation is interpreted as an index of reliability, it is assumed implicitly that the two measures in question are, in an important sense, the same.

But what if the two tests in question are not assumed to be the same, i.e., they are not taken to be two forms of the *same* test, but rather they are supposed to measure the same construct (i.e., the same underlying capacity or competence)? In this case, the identity of the two measures is not expected to be complete, and we may take their correlation not as an index of reliability but of *convergent* validity. For instance, if we have two tests, call them $i$ and $k$, which are aimed at the same construct, say, mathematical skill, then, the correlation $r_{ik}$ will be read as an index of convergent validity. The test writers, in such a case, will hope that the correlation is strong since the tests are supposed to measure the same construct. From a high convergent validity index, high reliability for both tests can be inferred. However, the reverse is not true. High reliability guarantees nothing about validity.

It follows, of course, that tests which are not reliable cannot have any convergent validity. If they do not correlate with themselves, so to speak, they must in fact be generating more or less random variance and therefore they cannot correlate with any other measures either. Thus, a test that is quite unreliable cannot have any convergent validity.

On the other hand, suppose that we have two tests which are supposed to measure distinct constructs which are not correlated with each other, e.g., mathematical ability and high-jumping ability. Call these tests $j$ and $m$ respectively. The correlation $r_{jm}$ will be an index of *divergent* validity. The test designers, in this case, hope that the correlation between them will be negligible because mathematical skill and high-jumping ability are believed to be distinct skills.

However, we cannot infer reliability from a low divergent validity index as we could from a high convergent index, because a low correlation may in fact be due to *un*reliability. On the other hand, a strong correlation between tests that are supposed to measure uncorrelated constructs would be undesirable: it would tend to show a lack of validity in one of the tests or in the theory concerning the constructs. As a result of these facts, divergent validity by itself is a relatively empty concept. It must also be possible to demonstrate convergent validity or divergence by itself remains relatively meaningless--it might mean mere unreliability of the tests and nothing more.

But suppose we want to judge the validity of multiple tests simultaneously. In order to do this it will be necessary to go beyond the technique of simple bivariate (two variable) correlation. Ordinarily, researchers work from correlation matrices that contain multiple bivariate correlations. By examining such matrices with appropriate statistical methods, usually some variety of factor analysis, it is possible to make meaningful inferences about many tests simultaneously.

The sort of reasoning that factor analysis begins with can be roughly illustrated by combining elements of the two previous examples. If we examine, for instance, the matrix of correlations between several measures aimed at math, call them $m$, $n$, and $o$, and several aimed at high-jumping, $j$, $k$, and $l$, we would expect to find that the correlations between tests aimed at the same construct should be higher than those between tests aimed at disparate constructs. When tests and constructs are combined in this way, inferences may be made about just which tests are measuring different constructs and which ones are measuring the same constructs. For instance, correlations $r_{mn}$, $r_{mo}$, $r_{no}$ (between the math tests) should be strong as should the correlations $r_{jk}$, $r_{jl}$, $r_{kl}$ (between the several jumping tests). However, the correlations across categories, those between math tests and jumping tests, $r_{mj}$, $r_{mk}$, $r_{ml}$, $r_{nj}$, $r_{nk}$, $r_{nl}$, $r_{oj}$, $r_{ok}$, and $r_{ol}$, should all be weak. Such comparisons would help to justify (or validate) the distinction between the math tests and the high-jumping tests. And, obviously, such designs can be made increasingly complex by adding more categorical distinctions--as in a hierarchical model along the lines of Chapter 2 above.

A fairly comprehensive conceptualization of classical factor problems in general can be achieved by appealing to the notion of the reliable variance in any test. According to the classical approach, reliable variance is the ratio of variance in true scores to variance in observed scores. By definition the observed scores have an error factor in them, while the true scores do not. Following the classical theory, a proper estimate of reliability is an estimate of the proportion of true score variance in the observed scores. Therefore, if we want to know how large the error term is in any given test, we may simply subtract the reliability from the total variance. If the total variance is standardized, it can always be expressed as a unit value (1.00). Hence, the error term (usually designated $e^2$) can be expressed in the following equation:

$$e^2 = 1 - r_{il} \text{ or } 1 = r_{il} + e^2 = s^2$$

where $s^2$ represents the total variance of the test in question. Extending the same reasoning, the reliable variance in a test may be split into two terms--(i) the variance shared with other tests, termed communality, designated as $h^2$; and (ii) the variance which is specific to the test in question, termed its specificity, designated as $b^2$. A little imagination will show that many ways of dividing up the communality can be conceived. Further, since the specificity of a given test is reliable by definition, it too (in principle at least) will be shared with all tests of the same type, and so, is really a different kind of common variance. However, for the purposes of this book we refer only to the terms of the classical model as shown in the following formula:

$$s^2 = 1 = h^2 + b^2 + e^2$$

## AN EMPIRICAL LOOK AT THE APL SURVEY

With the foregoing in mind we can now elaborate slightly on the central validity question: how much of the non-error variance (that is, the reliable variance) can be attributed to the specific constructs that the test (or part) is supposed to measure, and how much of the reliable variance can be attributed to a general factor (a common factor)? How large or small is the error term? Of the reliable factors (the communality and the specificity), which accounts for the greater amount of variance? Is either of them smaller than the error term, the unreliability factor? Finally, how can we best account for the reliable variance in the test and its parts? To what extent do the various parts of the *APL Survey* measure distinct capabilities (i.e., the posited constructs of interest)?

There can be no final answers to these questions because it is impossible in principle to obtain all of the evidence that would be required to achieve such answers. It is always possible to conceive of additional testing procedures or constructs that might be included in the analysis. Still, we can offer some relevant evidence on the basis of the data given in the test *Manual* by examining the variance in the various parts of the test to see how much is common to all of them ($h^2$), and how much is specific to each part ($b^2$). Also, we can make some reasonable inferences about the amount of variance attributable to ability in the primary language of the subjects and the only language of the tests, namely, English.

The analysis is primarily a question about correlations, but, for the sake of completeness, first the means and standard deviations are

presented as well as the reliabilities for each of the subtests and the
*APL* as a whole. These are given in Table 5.1. The means and standard
deviations are from the test *Manual* (n. d., p. 42). The estimated
reliabilities of the respective part scores are K-R 20 estimates also taken
from the *Manual* (p. 47) adjusted to full-length tests of 8 items each.
The adjustment was necessary since the K-R 20 estimates are equivalent
to split-half correlations (cf. Guilford and Fruchter, 1978, p. 426). Therefore, in order for the reliability estimates to be based on tests of the
same length as the intercorrelations between parts the length of each
part was adjusted from 4 to 8 items by the Spearman-Brown prophecy
formula. Otherwise, the reliability estimates would have been depressed
relative to the intercorrelations between parts.

**TABLE 5.1**

*APL Survey* Means, Totals Possible, Standard Deviations, and KR-20
Reliabilities Adjusted to Full-Length Tests, N = 2853

| SUBSCALES | Mean | Possible | s | KR-20 |
|---|---|---|---|---|
| CONTENT AREAS | | | | |
| Community Resources | 6.3 | 8 | .71 | .726 |
| Occupational Knowledge | 5.6 | 8 | .94 | .780 |
| Consumer Economics | 5.2 | 8 | .76 | .718 |
| Health | 5.7 | 8 | .87 | .788 |
| Government and Law | 5.1 | 8 | .73 | .701 |
| SKILLS AREAS | | | | |
| Identification of | | | | |
| Facts and Terms | 4.1 | 8 | .74 | .758 |
| Reading | 6.3 | 8 | .89 | .765 |
| Writing | 5.7 | 8 | .69 | .710 |
| Computation | 5.6 | 8 | .94 | .773 |
| Problem Solving | 6.2 | 8 | .78 | .758 |
| *APL Survey* Total | 27.91 | 40 | 3.78 | .925 |

The various subtests were all of roughly similar difficulty though
the Identification of Facts and Terms was clearly the most challenging
(note the mean of 4.1 which is a full point lower than any of the
others). On the whole test items were answered correctly 69.78% of
the time. More importantly, all subtests proved to be reliable at the
.7 level or above in spite of their brevity. This is noteworthy in view
of the fact that each subtest is only 8 items in length. The overall
reliability of the entire battery was .925 (adjusted to the full length
of 40 items) for this sample.

The next step was to obtain the correlations between parts.
Tables 5.2 and 5.3 give the initial correlation matrices for the APL

part scores broken down into Content and Skill Areas, respectively. Next the classical method of principal factoring was applied to extract the common variance from each set of part scores. It was already clear in fact from the raw correlations that there existed a good deal of communality underlying each of the part scores.

In applying the classical factoring method, an iterative approach was used to obtain estimates of communalities[8] which were then placed on the diagonal of each of the correlation matrices before factoring. The results of these analyses are reported in Table 5.4. They show a substantial communality underlying both sets of part scores. The common factors which have been extracted can be regarded as much the same in each case since they are based on different methods of partitioning the same test variances (once by Content Areas and once by Skill Areas; see the matrix given above as Chart 5.1). This general factor accounted for 64.7% of the total variance in all of the parts divided by Content Areas, and 64.7% by Skill Areas.

TABLE 5.2

*APL Survey* Intercorrelations among Content Area Subscales (Form AS1), N = 2853

| Subscales | 1 | 2 | 3 | 4 | 5 |
|---|---|---|---|---|---|
| 1 Community Resources | 1.00 | .59 | .52 | .56 | .52 |
| 2 Occupational Knowledge | | 1.00 | .59 | .60 | .55 |
| 3 Consumer Economics | | | 1.00 | .59 | .54 |
| 4 Health | | | | 1.00 | .52 |
| 5 Government and Law | | | | | 1.00 |

The next step was to compute specificity estimates for each of the parts of the *APL* both under Content Areas and Skill Areas). This was done by subtracting the respective communality from the reliability estimate for the part score in question. The results of this analysis are given in Table 5.5, column three. It can be seen that the specificity estimates are generally less than the error terms which are reported in column four of Table 5.5, but are never as much as half the estimated communality shared with the other parts. The bulk of the

---

[8]After determining how many factors could be extracted with eigenvalues greater than unity (i.e. greater than the total variance in any single test), as a starting point the square of the multiple correlation between the part score (or test) in question and the other parts was placed on the diagonal. It is known that the square of the multiple correlation gives the lowest possible limit of communality, while the reliability of the test in question gives the highest possible limit. The matrix was then factor analyzed and the squares of multiple correlations were replaced with new estimates of communalities based on the inferred factors. If the new estimates of communalities were not negligibly different from the former ones, the matrix was factored again, new estimates were obtained, and so forth, until the new estimates reached a point of negligible difference from the preceding ones.

reliable variance is accounted for by the general factor that is common
to the various part scores.

TABLE 5.3
*APL Survey* Intercorrelations among Skill Area Subscales (Form AS1),
N = 2853

| Subscales | 1 | 2 | 3 | 4 | 5 |
|---|---|---|---|---|---|
| 1 Facts and Terms | 1.00 | .58 | .53 | .55 | .62 |
| 2 Reading | | 1.00 | .58 | .59 | .57 |
| 3 Writing | | | 1.00 | .51 | .52 |
| 4 Computation | | | | 1.00 | .53 |
| 5 Problem Solving | | | | | 1.00 |

TABLE 5.4
Principal Factor Solutions (with iterations) for Content and Skill Areas
on the *APL Survey* (Form AS1), N = 2853

| Subscales for Content Areas | Loading on general factor | Communality |
|---|---|---|
| 1 Community Resources | .728 | .530 |
| 2 Occupational Knowledge | .791 | .626 |
| 3 Consumer Economics | .750 | .563 |
| 4 Health | .764 | .584 |
| 5 Government and Law | .702 | .493 |
| Subscales for Skill Areas | Loading on general factor | Communality |
| 1 Facts and Terms | .768 | .590 |
| 2 Reading | .785 | .617 |
| 3 Writing | .707 | .500 |
| 4 Computation | .724 | .525 |
| 5 Problem Solving | .751 | .564 |

But just what is this general factor? It receives its highest loadings from the Occupational Knowledge and Reading subscores, but
receives loadings nearly as high from all of the other subscales as well.
In spite of the differences in content across subscales, which are substantial, all of the subscales require processing of verbal sequences in
English. While it cannot be said definitively that proficiency in English
language skills, especially reading, is the only possible common variable

across all of the tests in question, it is certainly a plausible contender for a substantial share in the observed general factor.

Some might argue that the observed general factor is simply because of the heterogeneity of the subjects tested and the common skills required by the various parts of the examination. However, this argument seems to circumvent the real issue leaving the basic question unresolved. What we need to find out is the extent to which the "common skills" underlying the various tasks (and the "heterogeneity of the subjects" on these skills) can be distinguished from or identified with the ability to use language for communicative purposes. Also, the subjects tested were in fact a relatively homogeneous group at least in respect to grade level--all of them were eleventh graders.

TABLE 5.5
Specificities and Error Terms for the Subscales of the *APL Survey* (Form AS1), N = 2853

| Subscales CONTENT | KR-20 | $h^2$ | $b^2$ | $e^2$ |
|---|---|---|---|---|
| 1 Community Resources | .726 | .530 | .196 | .274 |
| 2 Occupational Knowledge | .780 | .626 | .154 | .220 |
| 3 Consumer Economics | .718 | .563 | .155 | .282 |
| 4 Health | .788 | .584 | .204 | .212 |
| 5 Government and Law | .701 | .493 | .208 | .299 |
| SKILLS | | | | |
| 1 Facts and Terms | .758 | .590 | .168 | .242 |
| 2 Reading | .765 | .617 | .148 | .235 |
| 3 Writing | .710 | .500 | .210 | .290 |
| 4 Computation | .773 | .525 | .248 | .227 |
| 5 Problem Solving | .758 | .564 | .194 | .242 |

## CONCLUSION

In subsequent chapters, with different tests and different subject populations, additional evidence is sought on the role of both primary and non-primary language skills in relation to other test constructs. The general factor identified in this chapter is probably due in substantial measure to proficiency in the primary language of the subjects tested. Upon reflection, it seems obvious enough that language proficiency *must* be a large part of what goes to make up "competency" in the broad sense of the latter term. However, to the extent that *English language* skills are a primary factor measured by such competency tests, the *APL* and other tests like it may present a somewhat different challenge to the vast and growing (cf. Tucker and Gray, 1980; Ortiz and Yates, 1983; Cummins, 1986) *non-English minorities* than its label implies. Where disproportionately large and increasing numbers of such minority students are being identified incorrectly as mentally retarded, learning disabled, or language disordered in American schools (cf. Coles, 1978; Cummins, 1984; Oller and Damico, in press; Hamayan and Damico, in press), the probable role of the language factor in such tests cannot be lightly dismissed. Nor is there any refuge for the test users in the attempt to trivialize the role of language by saying, "Oh, but of course, everyone always knew that." On the contrary, if language should turn out to play the central role that some theoreticians admit it does, and which the evidence here shows that it probably does, it will be necessary to offer alternatives to students of limited English proficiency--alternatives that do not depend so heavily on proficiency in English, or, what amounts to the same thing, that provide an equal opportunity for all of our students to achieve it.

# Chapter 6
## Competency Scores and English
## Proficiency of Adult ESL Students[9]

The design of the study reported in this chapter is much the same as in Chapter 5, except here, the subject population is a group of adults from diverse cultural backgrounds for whom English is a non-primary language. Again attention is focussed on "competency" tests. The main instruments used here are three different forms of the *Tests of Adult Basic Education*. They are intended to measure life skills in such areas as reading, vocabulary, math computation, and math concepts. What is focussed on is the extent to which the separate instruments actually contain specific variance, and the extent to which their variance is attributable to a general factor (in this case a possible second language factor for the group studied). Of secondary interest is the in-house English proficiency test used at the Defense Language Institute for the placement of its students (the *English Comprehension Level*). The variance in the latter test, assuming that it has some validity, is useful in relation to the final question, namely, how much of the common variance underlying all of the tests investigated (the various forms of the *TABE* as well as the *ECL*) can be attributed to an English factor.

### RATIONALE OF THE *TABE* BATTERY
The *Tests of Adult Basic Education* (1975) were explicitly patterned after the *California Achievement Tests*. In constructing the battery, designers used test items from the *California Achievement Tests*. It may be noted at the outset that it is a little surprising that a competency battery should be built out of items drawn from an achievement battery. The fact that competency tests are supposed to assess "life skills" and to that extent to be different in purpose from achievement tests seems to suggest that the competency tests should also be different in content and approach. Be that as it may, the designers of the *TABE* battery did claim to make adjustments in the items they took from the *California Achievement Tests* in order to make them appropriate for examinees from culturally diverse backgrounds. In particular, they tried to reduce ethnic and sex biases in the battery (*TABE Technical Report*, 1976) and to eliminate abstract language requirements. For the easiest version of the *TABE* battery the designers

---

[9]This chapter benefitted from the assistance of both Virginia Streiff and Virginia Berk, both of whom at the time the data were collected were at the University of Texas at San Antonio.

75

cut the subsections aimed at prescriptive grammar and usage. They also attempted to adapt the items in such a way as to reflect adult usage, experience, and interests (*TABE Publisher's Manual*, 1976), though Hieronymus (1972) has found the *TABE* battery inadequate on just these criteria.

Another problem is that in spite of the fact that the battery is supposed to measure "life skills" and therefore to be aimed at more or less specific criteria (apropos of the remarks by McClelland quoted in Chapter 5), nonetheless, according to its own authors, the *TABE* battery is supposed to measure fairly general skills. These include reading comprehension, vocabulary, mathematical computation, and mathematical concepts.

Taking all of the foregoing into account, some of the people who would likely be included in the target population for the test battery would be adult students in the United States who have learned English as a second language. But, is the *TABE* appropriate for such a group? Or is it, in addition to whatever other problems it may have, heavily influenced by a general factor of proficiency in English?

PROCEDURE

To address the foregoing issues, and to seek at least partial answers to the questions raised, scores attained by adult foreign students on three versions of the *TABE* battery were examined. The subjects tested were all enrolled at the English Language Center of the Defense Language Institute (San Antonio, Texas at Lackland Air Force Base).[10] Scores on the *English Comprehension Level* (the in-house proficiency instrument used at DLI) were also used.

In response to the possibility that a large though spurious general factor due to mere heterogeneity in the subject pool might arise, two design features are worth mentioning: first the subject pool was divided by ability into three groups. In fact, this was done at the time of the original testing, on the basis of overall competence in English. The least advanced group (n = 172) took the easy version (E) of the *TABE* battery, the intermediate group (n = 187) took the medium difficulty version (M), and the most advanced group (n = 486) took the difficult form (D). (From here on the groups and/or the test forms in question will be referred to as E, M, and D.) These three forms of the *TABE* battery were based on items drawn from the 1970 version of the *California Achievement Tests* at reading levels 2-4, 4-6, and 7-9, respectively. (While a chief complaint against IQ tests was that they were related too closely to achievement tests and vice versa, it would seem that the circle may have remained essentially unbroken even as com-

---

[10]The original testing was done by staff at the Defense Language Institute for the purpose of determining grade equivalent reading levels for their *English Comprehension Level* test. The latter test is used as a basis for placement at the DLI English Language Center. The author and his erstwhile collaborators are grateful for the assistance of DLI staff in making the data for this study available to us. However, it must be added that any errors contained here and the ideas expressed pertain to the author alone.

petency tests were added to the picture.) The division of the subject pool could be expected to reduce the strength of any general factor that might be obtained. This is due to the fact that such a procedure in effect partitions the total heterogeneity into the three subsamples of subjects. Any such reduction will automatically help to eliminate any spurious tendency for a large general factor to emerge simply as a result of large differences that are likely to exist between low scorers and high scorers on the tests. The second precaution taken to prevent any spurious heterogeneity from generating an equally spurious general factor was built into the design in the manner in which subjects were selected for the study, as described in the following section.

### SUBJECTS

No subject falling below the mid-point on the *English Comprehension Level* was included in the study. The purpose of this screening was to eliminate any subjects whose lack of ability in English would effectively render their scores on the *TABE* battery meaningless (and which would also spuriously contribute to a greater heterogeneity in the data sets). In all, 845 subjects were tested. They ranged from approximately 18 to 30 years of age. The majority were of Iranian or Arab extraction, though some Spanish speakers, and some subjects from oriental backgrounds were also represented.

### TESTS

The three forms of the *TABE* battery (E, M, and D) correspond closely to Levels 2, 3, and 4 of the *California Achievement Tests*. All three forms contain the same four sections as the *CAT*: Reading Comprehension, Vocabulary, Math Computation, and Math Concepts. Forms M and D also include sections labeled Language Mechanics and Spelling. Presumably, it was believed by the designers that the latter pair of tests do not tap the sorts of "abstract" language abilities which they took pains to try to eliminate from other portions. In addition to the *TABE* scores, the total score on the *English Comprehension Level* was also used.

The *TABE* Reading Comprehension subtest requires examinees to locate topics in a table of contents and an index and to answer multiple choice questions about several short passages. The Vocabulary subtest consists of items where an underlined word presented in a brief context is to be matched with the best of four possible synonyms, e.g., "*beyond* the barn" where the choices are (1) at, (2) in, (3) near, (4) past. The Math Computation test requires the selection of correct answers to problems in addition, subtraction, multiplication, and division from a field of four alternatives in each case. In the Math Concepts subtest subjects respond to word problems and to items about mathematical symbols and geometric figures. The Language Mechanics subtest focusses on punctuation, capitalization, and grammatical usage (in the prescriptive sense of "grammar"). The Spelling subtest requires subjects to select incorrectly spelled items from lists of words. The format and the items in all of the subtests of the *TABE* battery are very similar to the ones that actually appeared in the *California Achievement Tests*, Levels 2, 3, and 4 (1970).

The *English Comprehension Level* routinely administered at DLI is also a multiple choice instrument. It consists of two subtests, Reading Comprehension and Aural Comprehension. Items are presented in single sentence contexts with responses reflecting points of vocabulary, grammar, and phonology. The Reading Comprehension portion consists of multiple choice items requiring the identification of synonyms, paraphrases, or grammatically appropriate choices in a written format. The Aural Comprehension test is similar except the lead-in portion of each item is presented auditorily. Here is an example showing what *ECL* phonology items are like:

He likes to ride. What does he like to do?
    (a) read
    (b) red
    (c) ride
    (d) write.

The lead-in is presented on an audio tape and the problem is to determine which of several words appeared in the utterance. The difficulty is supposed to be focussed on phoneme discrimination.

An example of the paraphrase type which could be presented either in an aural or written format is the following:

Are you ready to order now?
    (a) Would you like to leave the restaurant now?
    (b) How about paying the bill at this time?
    (c) Should you enter the building now?
    (d) Have you already decided what to eat?

(Since only the total score is used in the analyses which follow, the differences between the two subtests on the *ECL* are mentioned only to give a better picture of the meaning of the total score on that test. If it were argued that the *ECL*, in the form described, is a somewhat narrow test of English language skills, such a claim could not be disputed. However, it does focus almost exclusively on English language abilities.)

## AN EMPIRICAL LOOK AT THE *TABE* BATTERY

The main goal was to find out how much of the variance underlying the subtests could be attributed to a common general factor and how much would be specific to each subtest. More importantly, it was asked how much of the common variance underlying all of the tests might be attributable to language skills.

To begin with the usual descriptive statistics for groups E, M, and D are presented in Tables 6.1, 6.2, and 6.3. In the first column of each table, the means are given, followed by the total possible points in column two, the standard deviations in three, and finally the KR-21 reliability estimates (for full length tests) in column four.

**TABLE 6.1**

Means, Standard Deviations, and KR-21 Reliabilities for the *English Comprehension Level* and Subscores on the *Tests of Adult Basic Education*, Form E, N = 172

| Tests | Mean | Possible | *s* | KR-21 |
|---|---|---|---|---|
| *English Comprehension Level* | 50.28 | (100) | 13.28 | .925 |
| *Tests of Adult Basic Education* | | | | |
|   Vocabulary | 29.65 | (40) | 4.26 | .734 |
|   Reading Comprehension | 22.82 | (45) | 8.07 | .907 |
|   Math Computation | 69.57 | (72) | 2.47 | .765 |
|   Math Concepts | 28.87 | (45) | 7.36 | .895 |

**TABLE 6.2**

Means, Standard Deviations, and KR-21 Reliabilities for the *English Comprehension Level* and Subscores on the *Tests of Adult Basic Education*, Form M, N = 187

| Tests | Mean | Possible | *s* | KR-21 |
|---|---|---|---|---|
| *English Comprehension Level* | 65.15 | (100) | 12.64 | .925 |
| *Tests of Adult Basic Education* | | | | |
|   Vocabulary | 18.16 | (40) | 4.80 | .726 |
|   Reading Comprehension | 20.59 | (42) | 5.95 | .824 |
|   Math Computation | 54.52 | (68) | 7.75 | .901 |
|   Math Concepts | 25.95 | (40) | 6.06 | .857 |
|   Language Mechanics | 4.19 | (109) | 1.32 | ---- |
|   Spelling | .66 | (32) | .61 | ---- |

It can be seen that the Language Mechanics and Spelling tests on forms M and D of the TABE battery were too difficult for these subjects. As a result, no reliabilities are reported because there is essentially no reliable variance in these subtests for the subject population examined. Therefore, these subtests are eliminated from subsequent analyses.

As might be expected, subjects at all levels had the least difficulty with Math Computation. This is, presumably, because they are able to fall back on their primary language, and perhaps deeper semiotic skills, for those computations. (Also see Chapter 7 below and Flahive, 1980.) Those who took version E of the *TABE* battery in fact obtained a mean near the ceiling on the scale. As a result, the correlations obtained for this subtest will be relatively uninformative because there is practically no variance in the sample. Therefore, this test was excluded from subsequent analyses.

TABLE 6.3
Means, Standard Deviations, and KR-21 Reliabilities for the *English
Comprehension Level* and Subscores on the *Tests of Adult Basic
Education*, Form D, N = 486

| Tests | Mean | Possible | s | KR21 |
|---|---|---|---|---|
| *English Comprehension Level* | 78.23 | (100) | 7.83 | .837 |
| *Tests of Adult Basic Education* | | | | |
| Vocabulary | 20.55 | (40) | 5.42 | .795 |
| Reading Comprehension | 20.42 | (45) | 6.27 | .837 |
| Math Computation | 31.73 | (48) | 8.00 | .907 |
| Math Concepts | 29.05 | (50) | 6.74 | .844 |
| Language Mechanics | 4.19 | (109) | 1.32 | ---- |
| Spelling | .66 | (32) | .61 | ---- |

The next step, then, was to examine the intercorrelations of the
various measures. With the exclusion of the Language Mechanics and
Spelling sections of the *TABE* M and D versions, and the Math Computation section on the E version, all of the intercorrelations are reported in Tables 6.4, 6.5, and 6.6. To extract the common variance underlying all of the tests, principal factoring with iterations was used as in
Chapter 5.

TABLE 6.4
Correlations between the Total Score on the *English Comprehension
Level* and the Subscores on the *Tests of Adult Basic Education*,
Form E, N = 172

| Tests | 1 | 2 | 3 | 4 | 5 |
|---|---|---|---|---|---|
| 1   *ECL* | 1.000 | .490 | .377 | --- | .300 |
| *Tests of Adult Basic Education* | | | | | |
| 2   Vocabulary | | 1.000 | .341 | --- | .280 |
| 3   Reading Comprehension | | | 1.000 | --- | .606 |
| 4   Math Computation | | | | 1.000 | --- |
| 5   Math Concepts | | | | | 1.000 |

In Table 6.7 the results for *TABE* Form E are presented. As
expected a general factor emerged accounting for 55% of the common
variance. The heaviest loaders on this general factor were the Reading
Comprehension and Math Concepts subscales. Since the latter test
requires solution of word-problems (e.g., "If George starts out with five
dollars and spends fifty cents for chewing gum, a dollar fifty for *Time
Magazine*, . . . "), it is not surprising that it should relate strongly to

the same general factor as the Reading Comprehension test which accounted for 57.2% of the variance in this factor.

**TABLE 6.5**
Correlations between the Total Score on the *English Comprehension Level* and the Subscores on the *Tests of Adult Basic Education*, Form M, N = 187

| Tests | 1 | 2 | 3 | 4 | 5 |
|---|---|---|---|---|---|
| 1   *ECL* | 1.000 | .578 | .409 | .370 | .573 |
| *Tests of Adult Basic Education* | | | | | |
| 2   Vocabulary | | 1.000 | .502 | .375 | .575 |
| 3   Reading Comprehension | | | 1.000 | .545 | .600 |
| 4   Math Computation | | | | 1.000 | .706 |
| 5   Math Concepts | | | | | 1.000 |

**TABLE 6.6**
Correlations between the Total Score on the *English Comprehension Level* and the Subscores on the *Tests of Adult Basic Education*, Form D, N = 486

| Tests | 1 | 2 | 3 | 4 | 5 |
|---|---|---|---|---|---|
| 1   *ECL* | 1.000 | .477 | .519 | .287 | .396 |
| *Tests of Adult Basic Education* | | | | | |
| 2   Vocabulary | | 1.000 | .547 | .150 | .315 |
| 3   Reading Comprehension | | | 1.000 | .433 | .586 |
| 4   Math Computation | | | | 1.000 | .680 |
| 5   Math Concepts | | | | | 1.000 |

In Table 6.8 the results for *TABE* Form M are presented. Again a single general factor emerged (explaining 62.1% of the total variance) and again the heaviest loadings came from Reading Comprehension and Math Concepts. However, in this case Math Concepts accounted for the greatest amount of variance, 81.2%, while Reading Comprehension accounted for 49.2%. Then, in Table 6.9 results are presented for *TABE* Form D. Here a somewhat different picture emerges. Two distinct factors can be discerned. The first seems to be predominantly defined by the math scores, while the second is primarily an English language factor. However, there are significant loadings on both factors from Math Concepts and Reading Comprehension which tends to obscure the distinction between the two factors somewhat, though deep semiotic skills and English language proficiency as well, are clearly involved in both factors.

*TABLE 6.7*

Principal Factor Solution with Iterations for the *English Comprehension Level* and the Subscores on the *Tests of Adult Basic Education*, Form E, N = 172

| Tests | Loading on the General Factor | Communality with the General Factor |
|---|---|---|
| *English Comprehension Level* | .578 | .334 |
| *Tests of Adult Basic Education* | | |
|     Vocabulary | .544 | .296 |
|     Reading Comprehension | .756 | .572 |
|     Math Computation | --- | --- |
|     Math Concepts | .652 | .426 |

*TABLE 6.8*

Principal Factor Solution with Iterations for the *English Comprehension Level* and the Subscores on the *Tests of Adult Basic Education*, Form M, N = 187

| Tests | Loading on the General Factor | Communality with the General Factor |
|---|---|---|
| *English Comprehension Level* | .646 | .418 |
| *Tests of Adult Basic Education* | | |
|     Vocabulary | .683 | .467 |
|     Reading Comprehension | .701 | .492 |
|     Math Computation | .692 | .478 |
|     Math Concepts | .901 | .812 |

The final step in the analysis of the three *TABE* forms is to examine the amount of common variance in each test in relation to the amount of specific variance. In Table 6.10, all three subsamples are included. In column one the reliability estimates are given again for ease of reference; in column two, the estimated communalities ($h^2$) are given; in column three the difference between columns one and two, or the estimated specificity of each test ($b^2$) is given; and the error term ($e^2$) appears in column four.

The results shown in Table 6.10 reveal substantial specificities on all of the tests for group E. In fact, there, the specificities are greater in all cases than are the error estimates. However, there are also substantial communalities with a single general factor in all of the tests. Since the largest of these communalities falls to Reading Comprehension, and the next largest to Math Concepts, is it not reasonable to conclude that English language skills must play a large part in that general factor?

**TABLE 6.9**
Principal Factor Solution with Iterations (Varimax Rotation) for the *English Comprehension Level* and the Subscores on the *Tests of Adult Basic Education*, Form D, N = 486

| Tests | Factor One | Factor Two | Communality |
|---|---|---|---|
| *English Comprehension Level* .253 | | .599 | .423 |
| *Tests of Adult Basic Education* | | | |
| Vocabulary | .068 | .764 | .588 |
| Reading Comprehension | .440 | .679 | .655 |
| Math Computation | .795 | .128 | .649 |
| Math Concepts | .800 | .336 | .755 |

**TABLE 6.10**
Estimates of Specificity and Error for the *English Comprehension Level* and the Subscores on the *Tests of Adult Basic Education*, Forms E (N =172), M (N =187), and D (N = 486)

| Tests (E, M, and N, respectively) | KR-21 | $h^2$ | $b^2$ | $e^2$ |
|---|---|---|---|---|
| *English Comprehension Level* | .925 | .334 | .591 | .075 |
| *Tests of Adult Basic Education* | | | | |
| Vocabulary (E) | .734 | .296 | .438 | .266 |
| Reading Comprehension (E) | .907 | .572 | .335 | .093 |
| Math Computation (E) | --- | --- | --- | --- |
| Math Concepts (E) | .895 | .426 | .469 | .105 |
| | | | | |
| *English Comprehension Level* | .925 | .418 | .507 | .075 |
| *Tests of Adult Basic Education* | | | | |
| Vocabulary (M) | .726 | .467 | .259 | .274 |
| Reading Comprehension (M) | .901 | .492 | .409 | .099 |
| Math Computation (M) | .824 | .478 | .346 | .176 |
| Math Concepts (M) | .857 | .812 | .045 | .143 |
| | | | | |
| *English Comprehension Level* | .837 | .423 | .414 | .163 |
| *Tests of Adult Basic Education* | | | | |
| Vocabulary (D) | .795 | .588 | .207 | .205 |
| Reading Comprehension (D) | .837 | .655 | .182 | .163 |
| Math Computation (D) | .907 | .649 | .258 | .093 |
| Math Concepts (D) | .844 | .755 | .089 | .156 |

For M the results also seem to sustain the hypothesis that there must be a large language component in the general factor extracted. Here the specificity for Math Concepts is only 4.5% as against an error term of 14.3% and a communality with the general factor of 81.2%. Reading Comprehension has the next largest share in the general factor (49.2%) but still has a substantial specificity (40.9%) which is considerably larger than its estimated error (9.9%).

The results are less clear with respect to D. Although the Math Concepts test still shows the largest communality with other tests, and the smallest specificity, perhaps this should not surprise anyone since it contains both arithmetic and reading aspects. Also, if we look back to the varimax rotated factor solution presented in Table 6.9, we see that Reading Comprehension, Math Concepts, and the *English Comprehension Level* all loaded significantly on both of the two principal factors. However, it was apparent that the first factor could best be defined in relation to arithmetic skills, while the second was more clearly a language factor (especially involving variance from the Vocabulary subscale).

## CONCLUSIONS

As in Chapter 5, where the *Adult Performance Level Survey* (a competency test intended for native speakers of English) was examined, the results here seem to support the conclusion that whatever is measured by the *TABE* battery (in this case as applied to adult non-native speakers of English) may be due in considerable measure to general ability to manipulate language--in this case, the English of the tests. Another point that may bear additional attention in the future is the apparent fact that the difference between "competency" and "achievement" tests, in some cases, may turn out to be as much a matter of labeling as of content. At least, this seems to be the case for the three forms of the *TABE* battery examined here.

# Chapter 7
# Non-Verbal Intelligence and English Proficiency of Adult ESL Students[11]

The research reported in this chapter also used a sample of adult ESL students at the Defense Language Institute (DLI) at Lackland. They were given tests of English proficiency and also of non-verbal intelligence. The instructions for the non-verbal tests were given both in English and in the native languages of the students tested. Earlier, working with a group of advanced ESL learners, Flahive (1980) had reported substantial correlations between scores on the *Raven Progressive Matrices* (a test aimed at non-verbal intelligence; discussed in Chapter 4 above), and scores on such language oriented tests as the *McGraw Hill Reading* test, and the *Test of English as a Foreign Language*. In this study the primary aim was to find out how much of the variance in the non-verbal scores in the data sample from DLI was specific and how much was common to the ESL tests. The question was whether it would be possible to identify a deep language or semiotic factor in the variance common to the ESL and non-verbal IQ scores.

## WHAT IS NON-VERBAL IQ?

If we followed the approach of Jensen (1969), we might say that "non-verbal IQ" is what non-verbal intelligence tests measure. However, as Roth (1978) has shown in interviews with children who have taken the *Raven Progressive Matrices* test, there is a lot of propositional reasoning in the solution of non-verbal IQ test items. In fact, if the argument in Chapter 4 is on the right track, it is more than just difficult to solve non-verbal IQ items without propositionally complex reasoning. As was argued there, such reasoning, it would seem, is a kind of deep language or semiotic skill which can probably only be developed to a high level of proficiency through the acquisition and use of some particular language.

But suppose we assume that non-verbal IQ really is something more than deep language or semiosis without speech. Suppose we assume that it is some kind of intelligence that is intrinsically unassociated with any sort of propositional logic at all. What sort of subject

---

[11]The research reported in this chapter was completed with the kind assistance of V. Streiff, Anne Krueger, Virginia Berk, and Sandra Di Quinzio, John Ball and Joyce Osborn who were then at the University of Texas at San Antonio. As throughout, the conclusions and ideas expressed are the sole responsibility of the author.

population and what sort of tests would tend to optimally reveal the divergent validity of non-verbal IQ scores?

For several reasons subjects learning a second language would seem to be an ideal population to study. With such a population, there would be less reason to expect to find a spuriously high correlation between verbal and non-verbal scores than there would be in cases where the native language is used as the divergent criterion. In the case of a second language as a divergent validity criterion, the time at which study of the second language is begun (or the length of exposure to it) would appear to be only randomly related to the non-verbal intelligence of the subjects. Why would smarter (non-verbally intelligent) subjects tend to start learning the second language earlier, or why would less intelligent subjects tend to start later?

On the other hand, if the native language were used, some correlation between non-verbal scores and proficiency in the primary language would be expected due simply to the fact that the development of these factors would necessarily have occurred hand in hand. In using the native language as a criterion, therefore, it could be argued that a lack of radical divergence is no great surprise. But what if we failed to find divergence between non-verbal scores and second language proficiency? Wouldn't this be a bit more interesting?

Suppose we found that a sizable chunk of the variance in non-verbal intelligence were predictable on the basis of *second* language proficiency. Wouldn't this tend to increase the suspicion that non-verbal test items actually require some sort of propositional ability?

PROCEDURE

Three ESL proficiency tests and a non-verbal IQ measure were administered to a group of 72 foreign students at DLI.[12] The ESL tests were regarded as divergent validity criteria for the non-verbal intelligence test. According to the hypothesis that non-verbal intelligence is quite distinct from verbal ability, low to nil correlations between the various measures should be expected. However, the semiotic model discussed above in Chapter 2 would suggest significant and even substantial correlations.

SUBJECTS

The examinees were randomly selected from all three levels at DLI--beginning, intermediate, and advanced. The selection was deliberately spread over the whole spectrum of scores on the *English Comprehension Level* (the DLI ESL proficiency test; for a description see Chapter 6 above). This was done in order to maximize the available variance in the divergent validity criteria. Since there is little or no

[12]The author is grateful to the staff at the Defense Language Institute for making this study possible. Of course, they are not at all responsible for what is said here though this study could not have been completed without their assistance.

reason to expect that beginning learners of ESL should be less intelligent than intermediate to advanced learners, this feature of the design should have biased the outcome in favor of the divergent validity of the non-verbal IQ test, and thus, against the semiotic model of Chapter 2. All of the examinees were involved in an intensive ESL program requiring four hours of classroom work and two hours of lab daily. They came from a great diversity of backgrounds, and educational levels ranging from sixth grade to college. The majority were speakers of Arabic, or Persian. Spanish but several Asian languages were also represented.[13]

### TESTS

The second language proficiency tests included the *English Comprehension Level* (described above in Chapter 6, pp. 78-78), a standard cloze test (approximately 500 words long) based on an every tenth word deletion ratio (for a total of 50 items), and a multiple choice cloze test. In addition, the *Test of Non-Verbal Reasoning* (Richardson, Bellows, and Henry, 1963) was used as a measure of non-verbal intelligence. Each of these tests is described (with the exception of the *ECL* which was already discussed in Chapter 6 above).

Both of the cloze passages came from a text on flying (a topic of interest to the trainees at the Lackland Air Force Base). According to the Dale-Chall formula (1948), both texts fell at approximately the fourth grade level in difficulty. Alternative answers for the multiple choice cloze always included the exact word as the correct answer. The inappropriate responses, however, also had some semantic or syntactic appropriateness to increase their attractiveness. For instance, here is an example of one of the multiple choice items that was used:

> The two _____ began building their own toy flying machine.
>
> (a) immediate
> (b) brothers
> (c) person
> (d) did

The *Test of Nonverbal Reasoning* consists of 24 items which require the examinee to select the two figures from six alternatives which share some geometric feature(s) with a given set of figures. Its authors claim that it has been used "successfully with a variety of business and industrial applicants and employees" (Richardson, Bellows, and Henry, 1963, unnumbered page; see list of tests below). The test is brief and easy to administer. It takes only ten minutes to complete.

---

[13]Of course, it is true that persons who come from higher socioeconomic backgrounds (and who tend to thus get higher scores on non-verbal and other sorts of IQ tests) also tend to be persons who have had the opportunity to study English as a foreign language abroad. Therefore, some of the more advanced students could be expected to fall into this category. To the extent that this is so, the correlation between non-verbal IQ and ESL attainment would tend to be spuriously inflated. In subsequent research, this potential contaminating factor should be examined more closely.

The instructions are not very complicated and are supplemented by easy to understand examples:

> Each problem in the test is made up of ten figures. The first four figures are all alike in some way, and two of the last six figures are like the first four. Your task is to select those two and write their numbers in the space at the right of the item.

> Look at the sample below. The first four figures are all squares. Of the last six figures, only the first and sixth are squares. The numbers 1 and 6 have been written in the spaces under ANSWERS.

> Here are three more sample problems for you to work on. Do them now.

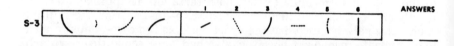

All tests were administered during the same week. They were given in the order, *ECL*, multiple-choice cloze, non-verbal IQ, and standard cloze. It was expected that practice on the multiple choice cloze test would provide an easier transition to standard cloze to which the subjects had little or no previous experience. The cloze tests were both scored by the exact-word criterion. This method yields only slightly lower reliability and validity than the method of counting any contextually appropriate response as correct, and it is less time consuming. (On the validity of the exact word scoring of cloze tests, see Oller, 1972; Hanzeli, 1976; Streiff, 1978, and Oller, 1979).

## DATA ANALYSIS

Although the main concern was the divergent validity of the non-verbal IQ test, in Table 7.1, the means, possible totals, standard deviations, and the KR-21 reliability estimates for each test are presented. The reliabilities are adjusted by the Spearman-Brown prophecy formula in order to obtain estimates appropriate to full-length tests in each case. To facilitate comparisons across tests, a percentage score is given in parentheses next to the raw score mean in each case.

It can be seen that the Standard Cloze Test was the most difficult for these subjects, and next most difficult was the *Test of Non-Verbal Reasoning*. The Multiple Choice Cloze, by contrast, was the easiest of all and the *English Comprehension Level* was next easiest. As has been observed by other researchers (Hinofotis and Snow, 1980; Hale, et al., 1988) multiple choice cloze tests are bound to be easier because they do not require either the creation anew or the retrieval from memory of the missing items. In fact, they only require selection from a field of distractors, which is a considerably easier task. It is interesting that this subject population found the *Test of Non-Verbal Reasoning* somewhat more challenging than at least two of the ESL tests.

*TABLE 7.1*

Means, Standard Deviations, and KR-21 Reliabilities for the *English Comprehension Level*, a Multiple Choice Cloze Test, a Standard Cloze Test, and the *Test of Non-Verbal Reasoning*, N = 72

| Tests | Mean | (%) | Total Possible | Standard Deviation | KR-21 |
|---|---|---|---|---|---|
| ECL | 63.35 | (63.35%) | 100 | 22.98 | .870 |
| Multiple Choice Cloze | 34.88 | (69.76%) | 50 | 13.58 | .870 |
| Standard Cloze | 11.79 | (23.58%) | 50 | 9.51 | .795 |
| *Non-Verbal Reasoning* | 7.43 | (30.96%) | 24 | 5.09 | .582 |

*TABLE 7.2*

Correlations between the *English Comprehension Level*, a Multiple Choice Cloze Test, a Standard Cloze Test, and the *Test of Non-Verbal Reasoning*, N = 72

| Tests | 1 | 2 | 3 | 4 |
|---|---|---|---|---|
| *English Comprehension Level* | 1.000 | .546 | .576 | .397 |
| Multiple Choice Cloze | | 1.000 | .727 | .436 |
| Standard Cloze | | | 1.000 | .488 |
| Non-Verbal Reasoning | | | | 1.000 |

Table 7.2 reports the correlations between the tests. Because the *Test of Non-Verbal Reasoning* had lower reliability than the other tests, as well as less variance (note its standard deviation in Table 7.1), the correlations between it and the other measures are no doubt depressed. However, there is some indication of divergent validity inasmuch as the correlations between the non-verbal measure and the ESL tests are always lower than the correlations between the various ESL measures. Still, they are not as much lower as might be expected

90     *Language and Bilingualism: More Tests of Tests*

according to the claim of the test's own authors that it "is truly non-verbal and non-language" (Richardson, et al., 1963, no page number).

Table 7.3 reports the results of a principal factor analysis over the four tests in question. As is usually expected when only four tests are input to the analysis, only one factor with an eigenvalue greater than unity emerged. This factor accounted for 65% of the total variance and 31.1% of the variance in the *Test of Non-Verbal Reasoning*. The significance of these findings is clearer in light of Table 7.4 (on page 91, below) which gives reliabilities, communalities (with the single general factor), specificities, and error estimates for each of the four tests. From this table, it is apparent that the *Test of Non-Verbal Reasoning* has more common variance with the general factor than it has specific variance. Also, the specificity for this test, the *Test of Non-Verbal Reasoning*, is less than 70% of its error term. According to Kaufman (1979), in such a case, the estimated specificity should not be interpreted. This is because of the considerable likelihood that such an estimate may be unreliable.

**TABLE 7.3**

Principal Factor Solution with Iterations for the *English Comprehension Level*, a Multiple Choice Cloze Test, a Standard Cloze Test, and the *Test of Non-Verbal Reasoning*, N = 72

| Tests | Loading on the General Factor | Communality with the General Factor |
|---|---|---|
| *English Comprehension Level* | .672 | .451 |
| Multiple Choice Cloze | .815 | .664 |
| Standard Cloze | .877 | .769 |
| Non-Verbal Reasoning | .558 | .311 |

**CONCLUSION**

While it would probably not be correct to say that a second language factor plays a role in the *Test of Non-Verbal Reasoning*, it seems clear that the general factor extracted in this study (see Table 7.3) *is* best defined as a factor of ESL proficiency. It received its strongest loadings from the Standard Cloze and the Multiple Choice Cloze. Nevertheless, it cannot be said that second language proficiency mediates performance on the *Test of Non-Verbal Reasoning*. What would seem more likely is that perhaps a deep language factor (or a composite of semiotic factors) mediates performance on both the ESL tests and on the *Test of Non-Verbal Reasoning*. (Also see Chapter 8, which follows immediately, on this same issue.)

*TABLE 7.4*

Reliabilities, Communalities, Specificities, and Error Estimates for Scores on the *English Comprehension Level*, a Multiple Choice Cloze Test, a Standard Cloze Test, and the *Test of Non-Verbal Reasoning*, N = 72

| Tests | KR-21 | Communality | Specificity | Error |
|---|---|---|---|---|
| *English Comprehension Level* | .870 | .451 | .419 | .130 |
| Multiple Choice Cloze | .870 | .664 | .206 | .130 |
| Standard Cloze | .795 | .769 | .026 | .205 |
| Non-Verbal Reasoning | .582 | .311 | .271 | .418 |

# Part III: English Proficiency and Achievement of Bilingual Children

# Chapter 8
# Language, Achievement, and Non-Verbal Intelligence Tests of Bilingual Children

## with Steve Chesarek
## Montana State University at Bozeman

Studies of minority groups in America have often focussed on the contrast between the minority in question and the majority. The focus here is different. In this chapter we are concerned with the factors that are measured by various tests aimed at specific areas under the general headings of achievement, intelligence, and language proficiency. The data samples come from the elementary school at Crow Agency, Montana. The tests used in this study included the *Peabody Individual Achievement Tests* (with sections on Mathematics, Reading Comprehension, Reading Recognition, Spelling, and General Information), five of the twelve subtests of the *Revised Illinois Test of Psycholinguistic Abilities* (including Auditory Reception, Auditory-Vocal Association, Visual-Motor Association, Verbal Expression, and Grammatic Closure), the *Peabody Picture Vocabulary Test*, the *Bellugi Syntax Measure*, *Raven's Progressive Matrices*, and *Cattell's Culture Fair Intelligence Tests*, Scale 2, Forms A and B. As in previous chapters, the purpose was to find out how much of the variance underlying the several tests would be attributable to a common factor, and how much would be specific to each test. As before, it was also asked to what extent it might be reasonable to interpret the variance in the common factor as a general factor of semiotic capacity.

## PROCEDURE

### SUBJECTS

According to G. H. Matthews (1976), about 85% of the children at the school, even a couple of years after the time of testing, still used Crow as their primary language. English ability varied from near nothing to practically native. The total enrollment at the elementary school was approximately 275 children at the time of the testing. The data sample of first and second graders in 1971-72 consisted of between 73 and 78 children. The sample from 1972-73 was actually divided into two segments consisting of 69 to 73 first and second graders, and 22 to 24 third graders (most of whom were included in the sample of second graders taken in 1971-72). All of the children were more or less bilingual in Crow and English, but were generally dominant in Crow.

All of the tests were administered individually. This was done because experience at Crow Agency had shown that the children performed better on individually administered tests. This procedure seemed consistent with the objective of finding out what the children *could* actually do rather than trying to demonstrate what they could *not* do. All of the testing was done over a period of about four to six weeks in each case. The data were collected in academic years 1971-72 and 1972-73. Some of the children were tested in both academic years, but due to population mobility and attrition at the school the overlap in the data samples across grade levels was far from complete.

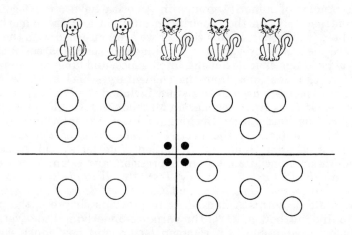

ILLUSTRATION 8.1. ITEM 9 FROM THE *PIAT* MATHEMATICS TEST.

## TESTS

Since the tests used in this study were more varied than those discussed in previous chapters, somewhat more space is given to their description. As in Chapter 4 above, here too, content analysis of tests is used as a basis for assessing possible interpretations of the common variance underlying the various tests. See also the discussion in the DATA ANALYSIS section. The content analysis follows the approach used by Gunnarsson (1978).

### THE PEABODY INDIVIDUAL ACHIEVEMENT TESTS

Each of the five tests in this battery is administered in a one-on-one interview setting. Four of the five sections are supplemented with pictures which are exemplified below. All five require substantial interaction between the examiner and examinee. For these tests, the interaction took place predominantly in English, occasionally supplemented with explanations in Crow. Only the fifth subtest requires that examinees formulate responses in English. In the other cases the examiner does nearly all of the talking. Each subtest terminates when the examinee misses three items in a row.

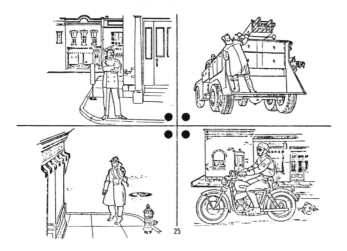

**ILLUSTRATION 8.2.** ITEM 25 FROM THE *PIAT*
READING COMPREHENSION TEST.

### MATHEMATICS
Each item begins with a series of pictures followed by a verbal prompt. Illustration 8.1 below gives an idea of the layout of each item. Beneath the stem, the rest of the page is divided into four sections. The child is asked to indicate the quadrant that corresponds to some numerical aspect of the items pictured in the stem. For instance, Illustration 8.1, which corresponds to Plate 9 (the ninth item) shows two dogs and three cats in the lead-in. The child is asked to count them and indicate the quadrant which contains the same number of circles as there are dogs and cats combined. Problems become progressively more difficult. Plate 74 (not pictured here), for example, requires the examinee to know the sum of the internal angles of a triangle. (The object pictured in that plate is an obtuse triangle.)

### READING COMPREHENSION
In this subtest, the child is asked to read a sentence that is printed on one page and then on the next page to pick the one of four pictures that best represents the meaning of the previously read sentence. For example, the child reads,
The policeman was standing at the village corner.
and then sees Plate 25 (given above as Illustration 8.2). He must select quadrant 1. As in all of the subtests, the items become progressively more difficult. For instance, the following sentence goes with Plate 84 (not shown here):
The pundit who was exorbitantly pedantic and obviously erudite in his didactic activities, was the subject of unan-

imous adulation, from those who had matriculated, as a
result of his elucidating discourse.
The alternative choices show a lecturer in front of a class with an
abstruse looking formula written neatly on the board; another lecturer
in front of a class with the students talking to each other and throwing
paper airplanes (his formula is scrawled on the board); a man receiving
an award at a banquet; and a man at a banquet being gestured at by
the speaker at the podium. Perhaps the last picture is the correct
choice (?) because the pundit is said to be the "subject of unanimous
adulation".

READING RECOGNITION
    This test requires the examinee to match a pictured object,
letter, or word with one of four other items; then, to name letters of
the alphabet; then, to read aloud various lists of words. For example,
the words "run", "play", and "jump" appear as items 19, 20, and 21,
and "nihilism", "pharyngeal", and "pterodactyl" appear as items 78, 79,
and 80.

SPELLING
    This part begins with a task which requires telling the difference
between letters and pictures of objects. For instance, in one of the early
plates, a puppy is displayed in three of the quadrants and the letter
"a" is displayed in the fourth. The child must say which one is different.
Also included in this portion are the printed symbols for addition,
subtraction, and division. The test continues with a task where the child
must pick the correct spelling of a given word as shown in Illustration 8.3.

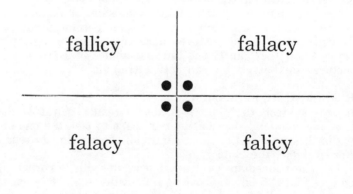

ILLUSTRATION 8.3. ITEM 74 FROM THE *PIAT* SPELLING TEST.

GENERAL INFORMATION
Here questions are put which require short answers. For instance, in item 17 the child is asked,
What season comes next after winter?
In item 62, the question is
What international prizes are awarded to persons making the greatest contribution to mankind?

*ILLINOIS TEST OF PSYCHOLINGUISTIC ABILITIES*
The experimental edition of this test was published in 1961. It consisted of 9 subtests aimed at various aspects of mental ability based on the theorizing of Charles Osgood (1957a, 1957b). A revised edition was then published in 1968. Here we will concentrate on the five subtests from the revised edition which were used in testing the Crow children of this study.

AUDITORY RECEPTION
This test was formerly called Auditory Decoding. The child is asked to affirm or negate questions such as,
Do airplanes fly?
Do dogs bark?
Do chairs yawn?
and so forth. Supposedly, this test assesses the child's "ability to derive meaning from verbally presented material" (Kirk, McCarthy and Kirk, 1968, p. 9). In brief, the test requires the rejection of implied anomalous assertions. It may be objected that the test allows a 50% chance of guessing the correct answer since the responses are "yes" or "no".

AUDITORY-VOCAL ASSOCIATION
This subtest is a closure task. It consists of 42 analogies presented orally. For example, the examinee hears,
I cut with a saw; I pound with a _____ ,
and must complete the analogy. This subtest is similar in format to the Grammatic Closure subtest described below. The main difference, it would seem, is that there the focus is on surface syntax or morphology, and here it is on the functions of things in experience (an aspect of pragmatics).

VISUAL-MOTOR ASSOCIATION
A pictured object is indicated at the extreme right hand side of a page. To the left, four other objects are displayed. The child must pick the one of the four on the left that goes with the one on the right. For example, in one item, an infant in diapers is pictured on the right and a nail, a straight pen, a paper clip, and a safety pin appear on the left. The child must select the safety pin because it is the only one that has an obvious association with the baby in diapers. Associations tested here include the relations between a hammer and nails, a horse and cow, bread and butter, as well as abstract relations of the sort

typical of the items found in the *Raven Progressive Matrices* and in the *Cattell* tests which are described in greater detail below (Also, see Chapter 4 above.)

### VERBAL EXPRESSION

This test was formerly called Vocal Encoding. In administering it, the examiner hands the child a familiar object and asks him to tell all about it. While explaining the examples, the examiner may prompt the child by asking questions such as, "What it is?" " What's it made of?" "What color is it?" "What do you use it for?" but in the test proper no prompts are allowed except, "Tell me more about it," or "What else can you tell me about it?"

### GRAMMATIC CLOSURE

Each item is similar in form to the ones that appear in the Auditory-Vocal Association test described above. For example, the child hears,

Here is a bed; here are two _____.

At the same time pictures are presented showing just one bed on one side of the page and more than one on the other. The examiner points to the appropriate pictures in sequence while the lead-in portion is presented aloud. According to the authors, the use of pictures is supposed to "avoid contaminating the test with difficulty in the receptive process" (Kirk, McCarthy, and Kirk, 1968, p. 12). Presumably, the authors also hoped to differentiate this test from the Auditory-Vocal Association Test where the receptive process is supposed to be in focus.

ILLUSTRATION 8.4. ITEM 93 FROM THE *PEABODY PICTURE VOCABULARY TEST.*

### THE PEABODY PICTURE VOCABULARY TEST

This test is intended to be a measure of verbal intelligence. Each item consists of a page divided up into four quadrants with different objects or activities depicted in each quadrant. For example, Illustration 8.4 (page 100, above) is Plate 93 from the test. The examinee is told to show where the sheep are in the pictures. The examiner is warned against giving inadvertent clues. For instance, articles such as "the" and "a" are to be avoided in phrasing the prompts,

Show me _____ .

or,

Point to _____ .

This creates some syntactic oddities in the manner in which items are presented, but has not deterred educators from using the test very widely.

### THE BELLUGI SYNTAX MEASURE

This is the only test used in the present study which is not published and widely available. It was designed originally to measure understanding of syntactic relations--e.g., between agent and object, possessor and possessed, relative clause and main clause. The original version was lengthened.

Each item consisted of a pair of pictures where the two elements displayed were in some way syntactically complementary to each other. For instance, on half of the page a boy might be pictured washing a girl and on the other half,

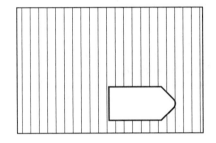
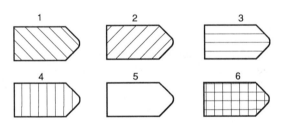

ILLUSTRATION 8.5. A PATTERN LIKE SIMPLER ONES IN *RAVEN'S PROGRESSIVE MATRICES.*

the girl would be washing the boy. The instruction given the examinee would be,

One of these pictures shows a girl washing a boy. The other one shows a boy washing a girl. Show me, "The boy washes the girl".

It is to be expected that the reliability of this test would be depressed by the binary nature of the choices, and also by the pragmatic (and syntactic) strangeness of some of the questions. (The obtained reliability was only .37; see below.)

### RAVEN'S PROGRESSIVE MATRICES

It is generally assumed that this test is a measure of "non-verbal IQ". Jensen (1969, 1973, and 1980) argues that this test,along with *Cattell's Culture Fair Intelligence Tests* (discussed below) is a relatively pure measure of the general factor of intelligence proposed by Spearman (1904). He sees *Raven's Progressive Matrices* and the *Cattell* tests as being relatively free of any "verbal" contamination.

However, Raven himself, the famous British creator of the *Matrices*, claimed that in order for his test to serve as a suitable measure of Spearman's general factor of intelligence, the *Matrices*

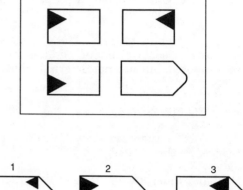

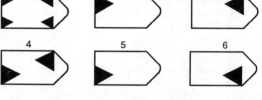

**ILLUSTRATION 8.6.** A BIDIMENSIONAL MATRIX OF THE *RAVEN TYPE*.

would need to be supplemented by a verbal IQ test. Therefore, it would seem that there is room for discussion about whether the *Matrices* constitute a "pure" or biased measure of general intelligence. Apparently, Raven thought of Spearman's "g" as a composite of verbal and non-verbal skills.

At any rate, each item in *Raven's Progressive Matrices* requires the subject to examine a pattern presented pictorially (or on a form board) and to select from six alternatives the patch that completes a missing portion of the pattern. There are basically two types of matrices. Illustration 8.5 (above) shows an example of the first type. In it, there is a relatively singular pattern. Illustration 8.6 shows an example of the second type with a multidimensional progression of patterns. The answer to 8.5 is choice 1 and to 8.6 it is 6.

### CATTELL'S CULTURE FAIR IQ TESTS, SCALE 2, A AND B

These tests are intended for the age range from 8 to 14 years, so they could be used only with the third graders in this study. Both Forms A and B consist of four subtests each. The first of these contains 12 items where the child must select a pattern that forms the best continuation of three given forms. This is the Series type of item illustrated above in Chapter 4 and analyzed in some depth there (pp. 59-62). The second type of item, Classification, requires that the child reject the element in a series which does not fit (again, for an illustration and discussion, see pp. 62-65 above). There are 14 items of the Classification type. The third set of items is very much like the examples from the *Raven Progressive Matrices* given as Illustrations 8.3 and 8.4. There are 12 items of this type. Finally, the last set of items, Conditions, requires the examinee to look at a pattern of geometric figures where a dot has been placed inside or outside, beneath, or above one or more other figures. The problem is to select from five choices the one where the dot can be placed in the same relation to similar geometric figures (not identical ones necessarily) that it had in the lead-in portion. There are 8 items of this type. The entire test requires less than 30 minutes to administer (3 minutes for Series, 4 for Classification, 3 for Matrices, and 2 and 1/2 for Conditions).

### WHAT DO THE FOREGOING TESTS MEASURE?

The question of validity can be addressed in part by examining the content of the several tests. We begin by examining the tests that are the least obviously "verbal" in nature. Of course, all of them require some use of language (though not necessarily English) to make the tasks understandable to the examinees. But what about the items proper? Let's first look more closely at the "non-verbal" IQ tests.

Do the non-verbal tests require language? If the argument in Chapter 4 above is roughly correct, it would seem that indeed they must. Whether they require overt or even covert *speech* on the other hand, is another matter. Perhaps they do. Perhaps they don't. But either way it seems that they must depend on deep propositional operations.

For instance, consider the Conditions type of item that appears in *Cattell's Culture Fair Intelligence Tests*, Scale 2, Forms A and B. Is it conceivable that the relations between the dot and the other geometric figures could be represented in any form that is not propositionally complex? We do not believe so for reasons given above in Chapter 4. It seems possible that the representation might be largely visual, or in any case a non-speech image of some sort, but it does not seem possible to us that it could lack the normal complexities which distinguish diverse forms of propositions (i.e., deep language forms), e.g., predication, negation, and conjunction. With the population studied here, it is quite possible that any covert speech forms might be in Crow rather than in English, but this is not a counter-argument. On the contrary, it agrees with the semiotic model above in Chapter 2.

There are some interesting similarities between items appearing in the various tests and subtests. For instance, the subtest labeled Mathematics in the *Peabody Individual Achievement Tests* contains some items that are quite similar both to those appearing in *Raven's Progressive Matrices* and to the ones in the matrices portion of the *Cattell* tests. On the basis of previous research, it is generally acknowledged that math tests require verbal skills to a rather large extent (see Kaufman, 1979). Moreover, for independent reasons, mathematicians such a C. S. Peirce and other logicians (John Lotz and Alonzo Church to name two) have long insisted that math and logic are derivative from natural language propositions. This seems doubly true in the case of the *Peabody* Mathematics test where all of the problems are posed in a verbal form. Consider the difficulty of discovering the sum of the three internal angles of a triangle without a fairly sophisticated level of language proficiency. Is it possible to obtain or internally express such a concept without a propositional system of some complexity? Or, of equal importance, could the question be imagined in a non-propositional form?

The only other test in the various batteries discussed above which seems to be oriented toward a non-verbal aspect of cognition is the Visual-Motor Association subtest which appears in the *Illinois Test of Psycholinguistic Abilities*. But here too, propositional reasoning involving such operations as predication, negation, and conjunction seems necessary. For instance, how will the examinee represent internally the fact that you drive nails with a hammer, or that diapers may be (or at least used to be) pinned on with safety pins, or that cows and horses are both domestic animals? Can any form even be conceived of that lacks propositional complexities? Of course we can conceive of complex visual images that are not obviously propositions, but this is not what is required. What is necessary, logically speaking, is to show that a visual image can be construed in such a way as not to involve propositional complexities in any form whatever. This is solidly impossible.

With respect to the other tests mentioned, is there any need to discuss the centrality of a general factor of language proficiency? In all of those cases, since the tests rather obviously require the use of speech forms with propositional complexities, it follows that they also depend, at least to that extent, on language proficiency. However, the more interesting aspect of the argument we are considering is that even the tests which minimize the utilization of overt speech forms may nevertheless still require use of deep language or semiotic capacities. In all of this discussion, of course (as emphasized above in Chapter 3), it remains crucial to make a fundamental distinction between speech, which may be the most common outward manifestation of language, and language itself. Similarly, it is important to keep in mind that language in its most abstract semiotic form cannot be identified with any particular grammatical system. This is a subtle but crucial point.

Examining test content seems to sustain the hunch that a general factor of language proficiency will probably be important to all of the tests in question. It remains to examine the variance generated by the tests in our data sample.

## DATA ANALYSIS

As in the preceding chapters, we begin by reporting the standard descriptive statistics. Since we wanted to use the maximum number of cases for each computation, pair-wise deletion of missing cases was used. Table 8.1 gives the results for the first and second graders who were tested in 1971-72; Table 8.2 reports on the sample of first and second graders from 1972-73; and Table 8.3 presents the findings from the third graders tested in 1972-73. Comparison of the means, reported in the first column of each table, seems to reveal an across-the-board improvement from 1971-72 to 1972-73 for the first and second graders at Crow Agency. Since some of the children tested in 1972-73 were also tested in 1971-72, it may be that the gain partly reflects the previous year's practice. The second column of each table indicates the number of valid cases on which the computations were based in each instance. Column three gives the standard deviation, and column four the estimated reliability for each test.

*TABLE 8.1*

Means, Number of Cases, Standard Deviations, and Estimated Reliabilities for the *Peabody Individual Achievement Tests*, the *Raven's Progressive Matrices*, the *Peabody Picture Vocabulary Test*, and Portions of the *Revised Illinois Test of Psycholinguistic Abilities*: First and Second Graders at Crow Agency in 1971-72, N > 72 < 79

| Tests | Mean | N | s | $r_{ii}$ |
|---|---|---|---|---|
| *Peabody Individual Achievement Tests* | | | | |
| Mathematics | 19.962 | 78 | 7.178 | .83 |
| Reading Recognition | 19.090 | 78 | 8.253 | .89 |
| Reading Comprehension | 18.244 | 78 | 7.602 | .78 |
| Spelling | 19.488 | 78 | 8.379 | .55 |
| General Information | 13.141 | 78 | 5.890 | .70 |
| *Raven's Progressive Matrices* | 19.027 | 73 | 5.686 | .60 |
| *Peabody Picture Vocabulary* | 50.178 | 73 | 7.185 | .67 |
| *Illinois Test of Psycholinguistic Abilities* | | | | |
| Auditory Reception | 19.227 | 75 | 7.120 | .63 |
| Auditory-Vocal Association | 16.373 | 75 | 6.796 | .86 |
| Visual-Motor Association | 23.147 | 75 | 4.112 | .45 |
| Verbal Expression | 19.253 | 75 | 7.460 | .63 |
| Grammatic Closure | 8.413 | 75 | 4.877 | .78 |

All of the reliability estimates, except for some in Table 8.3 below, were taken from published sources. For instance, the ones reported for the various parts of the *Peabody Individual Achievement Tests* came from Dunn and Markwardt (1970, p. 11). Those in Tables 8.1 and 8.2 (which happen to be the same incidentally) are based on norms for first graders, while those in Table 8.3 were generally based on norms for third graders.

For the tests in Table 8.3, published estimates were used for children in the third grade or the next closest grade for which an estimate was given in the appropriate test manual. Where no published estimate could be obtained, we computed a KR-21 estimate based on our data sample (adjusted for full length tests). This was necessary only in the case of the *Cattell* tests and the *Bellugi Syntax Measure*. For the *Illinois Test of Psycholinguistic Abilities*, the estimates come from Paraskevopoulos and Kirk (1969, p. 108). The ones reported in Tables 8.1 and 8.2 are stability estimates reported for six year olds corrected for restricted range. Those given in Table 8.3 are similar estimates for eight year olds. The reliability estimates for the *Peabody Picture Vocabulary Test* come from Dunn (1965). For the first and second graders we used his reliability estimate for six year olds, and for the third grade sample we used his estimate for eight year olds.

*TABLE 8.2*

Means, Number of Cases, Standard Deviations, and Estimated Reliabilities for the *Peabody Individual Achievement Tests*, the *Raven's Progressive Matrices*, the *Peabody Picture Vocabulary Test*, and Portions of the *Revised Illinois Test of Psycholinguistic Abilities*: First and Second Graders at Crow Agency in 1972-73, N > 68 < 74

| Tests | Mean | N | $s$ | $r_{ii}$ |
|---|---|---|---|---|
| *Peabody Individual Achievement Tests* | | | | |
| Mathematics | 22.959 | 73 | 8.329 | .83 |
| Reading Recognition | 20.575 | 73 | 5.951 | .89 |
| Reading Comprehension | 19.726 | 73 | 5.173 | .78 |
| Spelling | 20.164 | 73 | 5.974 | .55 |
| General Information | 16.027 | 73 | 5.757 | .70 |
| *Raven's Progressive Matrices* | 20.609 | 69 | 5.188 | .60 |
| *Peabody Picture Vocabulary* | 53.261 | 69 | 7.703 | .67 |
| *Illinois Test of Psycholinguistic Abilities* | | | | |
| Auditory-Vocal Association | 18.884 | 69 | 8.197 | .86 |
| Grammatic Closure | 9.725 | 69 | 5.538 | .78 |

Both of the estimates for *Raven's Progressive Matrices* come from the *Manual* (Raven, 1965, p. 18) for the age range between 5 1/2 and 7 1/2 years. For the *Cattell* and *Bellugi* tests no reliability figures could be found, though an estimate of .80 is reported by Cattell for high school freshmen. For this reason, we used KR-21 estimates (corrected to full length) based on the third grade data just for these two tests.

The next stage of the analysis was to examine the correlation matrices for each data sample. These are given in Tables 8.4, 8.5, and 8.6. An examination of these tables revealed substantial relationships among some of the tests. However, because of the sheer numbers of correlations involved, it would have been difficult to arrive at sound conclusions just by examining the multitude of correlations in question. For this reason principal factor solutions were computed. These analyses are given in Tables 8.7, 8.8, and 8.9, and are easier to interpret.

**TABLE 8.3**

Means, Number of Cases, Standard Deviations, and Estimated Reliabilities for the *Peabody Individual Achievement Tests*, *Cattell's Culture Fair Intelligence Tests*, Scale 2, Forms A and B, the *Peabody Picture Vocabulary Test*, the Auditory Vocal Association Test from the *Revised ITPA*, and the *Bellugi Syntax Measure*: Third Graders at Crow Agency in 1972-73, N > 21 < 25

| Tests | Mean | N | $s$ | $r_{ii}$ |
|---|---|---|---|---|
| *Peabody Individual Achievement Tests* | | | | |
| Mathematics | 32.083 | 24 | 7.835 | .68 |
| Reading Recognition | 34.250 | 24 | 8.764 | .94 |
| Reading Comprehension | 30.708 | 24 | 5.505 | .73 |
| Spelling | 33.333 | 24 | 7.631 | .78 |
| General Information | 24.792 | 24 | 10.990 | .77 |
| *Cattell's IQ Test* Form A | 22.5909 | 22 | 6.254 | .84 |
| *Cattell's IQ Test* Form B | 25.727 | 22 | 5.717 | .80 |
| *Peabody Picture Vocabulary* | 60.348 | 23 | 8.499 | .79 |
| *Illinois Test of Psycholinguistic Abilities* | | | | |
| Auditory-Vocal Assoc. | 25.565 | 23 | 5.845 | .83 |
| *Bellugi Syntax Measure* | 27.826 | 23 | 3.284 | .37 |

**TABLE 8.4**

Intercorrelations for the *Peabody Individual Achievement Tests*, the Raven Progressive Matrices, the *Peabody Picture Vocabulary Test*, and Portions of the *Revised Illinois Test of Psycholinguistic Abilities*: First and Second Graders at Crow Agency in 1971-72, N > 72 < 79

| Tests | 1 | 2 | 3 | 4 | 5 | 6 | 7 | 8 | 9 | 10 | 11 | 12 |
|---|---|---|---|---|---|---|---|---|---|---|---|---|
| 1 *PIAT* Math | 1.000 | .578 | .613 | .566 | .712 | .596 | .354 | .486 | .583 | .216 | .384 | .518 |
| 2 *PIAT* Read Rec | | 1.000 | .961 | .871 | .674 | .575 | .329 | .502 | .659 | .408 | .520 | .635 |
| 3 *PIAT* Reading Comp | | | 1.000 | .846 | .723 | .599 | .362 | .510 | .645 | .449 | .503 | .673 |
| 4 *PIAT* Spelling | | | | 1.000 | .665 | .520 | .261 | .476 | .636 | .403 | .489 | .637 |
| 5 *PIAT* General Info | | | | | 1.000 | .592 | .549 | .559 | .744 | .484 | .544 | .691 |
| 6 *Raven's Progressive Matrices* | | | | | | 1.000 | .420 | .563 | .526 | .289 | .445 | .446 |
| 7 *Peabody Picture Vocabulary Test* | | | | | | | 1.000 | .590 | .596 | .253 | .501 | .620 |
| 8 *ITPA* Auditory Reception | | | | | | | | 1.000 | .669 | .258 | .355 | .591 |
| 9 *ITPA* Auditory-Vocal Association | | | | | | | | | 1.000 | .399 | .527 | .681 |
| 10 *ITPA* Visual-Motor Association | | | | | | | | | | 1.000 | .338 | .316 |
| 11 *ITPA* Verbal Expression | | | | | | | | | | | 1.000 | .477 |
| 12 *ITPA* Grammatic Closure | | | | | | | | | | | | 1.000 |

In Table 8.7, two factors appear. The first receives its heaviest loadings from the *PIAT* Reading Recognition and Reading Comprehension subscales (.919, and .910). It also receives significant loadings from everything but the *Peabody Picture Vocabulary Test* (.080). This is surprising since the Peabody is supposed to be a "verbal" IQ test, and would normally be expected to correlate strongly with such a highly verbal factor. The second factor receives its heaviest loading from the *Peabody Picture Vocabulary Test* (.850), but also gets significant loadings from *all* of the other tests as well. Apparently we have two factors in this case which are very nearly general to all of the tests. The only tests which do not have fairly substantial communalities with the others are the two *ITPA* subtests. In particular, the Visual-Motor Association subscale does not correlate very strongly with either of the two common factors (.384 with one, and .259 with two). Interestingly, however, the *Raven* test (the non-verbal intelligence measure) correlates about equally with both common factors (.491 with one, and .473 with two).

**TABLE 8.5**

Intercorrelations for the *Peabody Individual Achievement Tests*, the Raven Progressive Matrices, the *Peabody Picture Vocabulary Test*, and Portions of the *Revised Illinois Test of Psycholinguistic Abilities*: First and Second Graders at Crow Agency in 1972-73, N > 68 < 74

| Tests | 1 | 2 | 3 | 4 | 5 | 6 | 7 | 8 | 9 |
|---|---|---|---|---|---|---|---|---|---|
| 1 *PIAT* Math | 1.000 | .620 | .580 | .602 | .499 | .520 | .335 | .644 | .363 |
| 2 *PIAT* Reading Rec. | | 1.000 | .921 | .852 | .638 | .507 | .277 | .625 | .503 |
| 3 *PIAT* Reading Comp. | | | 1.000 | .832 | .650 | .510 | .315 | .586 | .533 |
| 4 *PIAT* Spelling | | | | 1.000 | .636 | .609 | .279 | .543 | .528 |
| 5 *PIAT* General Information | | | | | 1.000 | .462 | .443 | .646 | .669 |
| 6 *Raven's Progressive Matrices* | | | | | | 1.000 | .233 | .485 | .368 |
| 7 *Peabody Picture Vocabulary Test* | | | | | | | 1.000 | .482 | .437 |
| 8 *ITPA* Auditory-Vocal Association Test | | | | | | | | 1.000 | .588 |
| 9 *ITPA* Grammatic Closure Test | | | | | | | | | 1.000 |

**TABLE 8.6**

Intercorrelations for the *Peabody Individual Achievement Tests*, Cattell's *Culture Fair Intelligence Tests*, Scale 2, Forms A and B, the *Peabody Picture Vocabulary Test*, the Auditory Vocal Association Test (from the *ITPA*), and the *Bellugi Syntax Measure*: Third Graders at Crow Agency in 1972-73, N > 22 < 25

| Tests | 1 | 2 | 3 | 4 | 5 | 6 | 7 | 8 | 9 | 10 |
|---|---|---|---|---|---|---|---|---|---|---|
| 1 *PIAT* Math | 1.000 | .266 | .358 | .351 | .733 | .620 | .820 | .582 | .402 | .511 |
| 2 *PIAT* Read. Rec. | | 1.000 | .848 | .894 | .260 | .076 | .150 | .097 | .072 | .475 |
| 3 *PIAT* Reading Comp. | | | 1.000 | .823 | .320 | .156 | .246 | .035 | .053 | .446 |
| 4 *PIAT* Spelling | | | | 1.000 | .373 | .193 | .228 | .155 | .138 | .587 |
| 5 *PIAT* General Information | | | | | 1.000 | .350 | .481 | .714 | .663 | .517 |
| 6 *Cattell's IQ Test*, Form A | | | | | | 1.000 | .665 | .288 | .368 | .535 |
| 7 *Cattell's IQ Test*, Form B | | | | | | | 1.000 | .337 | .292 | .382 |
| 8 *Peabody Picture Vocabulary Test* | | | | | | | | 1.000 | .705 | .579 |
| 9 *ITPA* Auditory-Vocal Association | | | | | | | | | 1.000 | .462 |
| 10 *Bellugi Syntax Measure* | | | | | | | | | | 1.000 |

TABLE 8.7

Principal Factor Analysis with Iterations (Varimax Rotation) for the *Peabody Individual Achievement Tests*, the *Raven Progressive Matrices*, the *Peabody Picture Vocabulary Test*, and Portions of the *Revised Illinois Test of Psycholinguistic Abilities*: First and Second Graders at Crow Agency in 1971-72, N > 72 < 79

| Tests | Factor One | Factor Two | $h^2$ |
|---|---|---|---|
| 1 *PIAT* Mathematics | .537 | .443 | .486 |
| 2 *PIAT* Reading Recognition | .919 | .274 | .919 |
| 3 *PIAT* Reading Comprehension | .910 | .311 | .925 |
| 4 *PIAT* Spelling | .862 | .260 | .811 |
| 5 *PIAT* General Information | .606 | .621 | .752 |
| 6 *Raven's Progressive Matrices* | .491 | .473 | .465 |
| 7 *Peabody Picture Vocabulary Test* | .080 | .850 | .729 |
| 8 *ITPA* Auditory Reception | .342 | .657 | .548 |
| 9 *ITPA* Auditory-Vocal Association | .511 | .681 | .725 |
| 10 *ITPA* Visual-Motor Association | .384 | .259 | .214 |
| 11 *ITPA* Verbal Expression | .404 | .473 | .387 |
| 12 *ITPA* Grammatic Closure | .497 | .625 | .637 |

In Table 8.8 we see a pattern quite similar to the one in 8.7. Again there are two factors. Again, the strongest correlates of the first factor are three of the subtests in the *Peabody Individual Achievement Tests* which are clearly aimed at reading skills. Again, however, the *Peabody Picture Vocabulary Test* does not correlate much at all (.117) with the first factor (a reading factor?) but correlates substantially with the second factor (.604). Again, both factors seem to be fairly general ones receiving significant loadings from nearly all of the tests. In this case, the non-verbal intelligence measure (the *Raven* test) loads most strongly on the first factor (.521) along with several tests that are heavy on verbal requirements. However, the second factor also has substantial language requirements and also receives a significant, though modest, loading from the *Raven* test (.329). It may be that in 8.7 and in 8.8, the difference between the two factors can be partly attributed to extraneous variables such as the time of testing, methods and instructions given, and the like. This possibility is supported by the fact that the *Peabody Individual Achievement Tests* load most heavily on the first factor in each case while the subscales of the Illinois Test of Psycholinguistic Abilities load most heavily on the second factor in each case.

When we come to Table 8.9, the pattern is somewhat different. Three factors can be identified, and the distinctions between them are somewhat sharper than they were for the preceding groups. Perhaps this is due in part to the reduction of the heterogeneity of the sample.

In Table 8.9 only third graders are included in the data sample while in both of the preceding tables, first *and* second graders were included.

**TABLE 8.8**

Principal Factor Analysis with Iterations (Varimax Rotation) for the *Peabody Individual Achievement Tests*, the *Raven Progressive Matrices*, the *Peabody Picture Vocabulary Test*, and Portions of the *Revised Illinois Test of Psycholinguistic Abilities*: First and Second Graders at Crow Agency in 1972-73, N > 68 < 74

| Tests | Factor One | Factor Two | $h^2$ |
|---|---|---|---|
| 1 *PIAT* Mathematics | .553 | .422 | .484 |
| 2 *PIAT* Reading Recognition | .906 | .292 | .906 |
| 3 *PIAT* Reading Comprehension | .859 | .327 | .845 |
| 4 *PIAT* Spelling | .863 | .303 | .836 |
| 5 *PIAT* General Information | .491 | .658 | .673 |
| 6 *Raven's Progressive Matrices* | .521 | .329 | .380 |
| 7 *Peabody Picture Vocabulary Test* | .117 | .604 | .378 |
| 8 *ITPA* Auditory-Vocal Assoc. Test | .440 | .706 | .692 |
| 9 *ITPA* Grammatic Closure Test | .349 | .647 | .540 |

The first factor again receives its heaviest loadings from the three subtests of the *Peabody Individual Achievement Tests* which require reading performances (namely, Reading Recognition, .950; Spelling, .931; and Reading Comprehension, .874). It also gets a moderate loading from the *Bellugi Syntax Measure* (.456). The second factor receives its heaviest loadings from the *Peabody Picture Vocabulary Test* (.903); the *ITPA* Auditory-Vocal Association subtest (.764); the *PIAT* General Information subtest (.719); the *Bellugi Syntax Measure* (.514); and from the *PIAT* Mathematics subtest (.430). The strongest correlates of the third factor are the *Cattell* Form B (.921), the *PIAT* Mathematics subtest (.782), and the *Cattell* Form A (.669). This third factor also receives modest loadings from the *PIAT* General Information subtest (.370) and the *Bellugi Syntax Measure* (.325).

Is it possible that the first two factors are primarily dependent on knowledge of English? This does not seem implausible in view of the variables that contribute the most to these factors. But what about the third factor? Could it be more closely related to skill in the primary language which is Crow for most of these children? Since the nonverbal item types were explained in Crow, it does not seem unlikely that many of the children may be relying on reasoning in their primary language to solve the problems in the *PIAT* Mathematics subtest and in the two *Cattell* tests. The weak but significant loadings from the *Bellugi Syntax Measure* and from the *PIAT* General Information subtest on this factor, however, remain a bit mysterious.

TABLE 8.9
Principal Factor Analysis with Iterations (Varimax Rotation) for Intercorrelations for the *Peabody Individual Achievement Tests, Cattell's Culture Fair Intelligence Tests*, Scale 2, Forms A and B, the *Peabody Picture Vocabulary Test*, the Auditory-Vocal Association Test (from the *ITPA*), and the *Bellugi Syntax Measure*: Third Graders at Crow Agency in 1972-73, N > 22 < 25

| Tests | Factor One | Factor Two | Factor Three | $h^2$ |
|---|---|---|---|---|
| 1 *PIAT* Mathematics | .220 | .430 | .782 | .846 |
| 2 *PIAT* Reading Recognition | .950 | .070 | .027 | .909 |
| 3 *PIAT* Reading Comprehension | .874 | .017 | .173 | .795 |
| 4 *PIAT* Spelling | .931 | .150 | .124 | .905 |
| 5 *PIAT* General Information | .231 | .719 | .370 | .707 |
| 6 *Cattell's IQ Test*, Form A | .074 | .240 | .669 | .510 |
| 7 *Cattell's IQ Test*, Form B | .098 | .158 | .921 | .882 |
| 8 *Peabody Picture Vocabulary* | .013 | .903 | .196 | .854 |
| 9 *ITPA Auditory-Vocal Assoc.* | .009 | .764 | .183 | .617 |
| 10 *Bellugi Syntax Measure* | .456 | .514 | .325 | .577 |

Table 8.10 gives specificity and error estimates for all three data samples. To condense all of the figures into one table, the traditional factor analytic abbreviations are used for reliability ($r_{ii}$), communality ($h^2$), specificity ($b^2$), and error ($e^2$). In cases where the specificity would have been negative, zeroes are entered on the assumption that the reliability estimates must have been spuriously low in those cases. There were 14 cases where this happened out of a total of 31 specificity estimates. Since this is nearly 50% of the instances, it may arouse suspicion that the specificities of the tests in question may be low to nil. This unnerving possibility (one that challenges the divergent validity of nearly all the tests examined) seems disturbingly probable when we examine the mean specificity as against the mean error estimate for all of the tests, .104 versus .289. Since the error term is, on the average, 2.77 times larger than the estimated specificity, it is difficult to argue that the tests in question generally have divergent validity.

If we examine the tests which seem to be the most obvious measures of constructs other than a language factor, we find little convincing evidence of interpretable specificities. For instance, although *Raven's* test shows specificities of .135 (for first and second graders in 1971-72), and .220 (for first and second graders in 1972-73), the respective error estimates are both .40. This fact, if we follow Kaufman (1979) and others, renders the specificities uninterpretable. However, the communalities of the *Raven* test are substantial, .465 and .380, respectively.

TABLE 8.10

Estimates of Specificity and Error for the *Peabody Individual Achievement Tests, Cattell's Culture Fair Intelligence Tests*, Scale 2, Forms A and B, *Raven's Progressive Matrices*, the *Peabody Picture Vocabulary Test*, the *Illinois Test of Psycholinguistic Abilities, Cattell's Culture Fair Intelligence Tests*, Scale 2, Forms A and B, and the *Bellugi Syntax Measure*

| Tests | Grades 1 & 2, 1971-72 | | | | Grades 1 & 2, 1972-73 | | | | Grade 3, 1972-73 | | | |
|---|---|---|---|---|---|---|---|---|---|---|---|---|
| | $r_{ii}$ | $h^2$ | $b^2$ | $e^2$ | $r_{ii}$ | $h^2$ | $b^2$ | $e^2$ | $r_{ii}$ | $h^2$ | $b^2$ | $e^2$ |
| *PIAT* Mathematics | .83 | .486 | .344 | .17 | .83 | .484 | .346 | .17 | .68 | .846 | .000 | .32 |
| *PIAT* Reading Recog | .89 | .919 | .000 | .11 | .89 | .906 | .000 | .11 | .94 | .909 | .031 | .06 |
| *PIAT* Reading Comp | .78 | .925 | .000 | .22 | .78 | .845 | .000 | .22 | .73 | .795 | .000 | .27 |
| *PIAT* Spelling | .55 | .811 | .000 | .45 | .55 | .836 | .000 | .45 | .78 | .905 | .000 | .22 |
| *PIAT* General Inform | .70 | .752 | .000 | .30 | .70 | .673 | .027 | .30 | .77 | .707 | .063 | .23 |
| *Raven's Prog Matrices* | .60 | .465 | .135 | .40 | .60 | .380 | .220 | .40 | -- | --- | --- | -- |
| *Peabody Picture Vocab* | .67 | .729 | .000 | .33 | .67 | .378 | .292 | .33 | .79 | .854 | .000 | .21 |
| *ITPA* Auditory Reception | .63 | .548 | .082 | .37 | -- | --- | --- | -- | -- | --- | --- | -- |
| *ITPA* Aud-Vocal Assoc | .86 | .725 | .135 | .14 | .86 | .692 | .168 | .14 | .83 | .617 | .213 | .17 |
| *ITPA* Visual-Motor Assoc. | .45 | .214 | .236 | .55 | -- | --- | --- | -- | -- | --- | --- | -- |
| *ITPA* Verbal Expression | .63 | .387 | .243 | .37 | -- | --- | --- | -- | -- | --- | --- | -- |
| *ITPA* Grammatic Closure | .78 | .637 | .143 | .22 | .78 | .540 | .240 | .22 | -- | --- | --- | -- |
| *Cattell's IQ Test* Form A | -- | --- | --- | -- | -- | --- | --- | -- | .83 | .510 | .320 | .16 |
| *Cattell's IQ Test* Form B | -- | --- | --- | -- | -- | --- | --- | -- | .74 | .882 | .000 | .26 |
| *Bellugi Syntax Measure* | -- | --- | --- | -- | -- | --- | --- | -- | .37 | .577 | .000 | .63 |
| Column Means for $b^2$ and $e^2$ | | .115 | .302 | | | .108 | .260 | | | .063 | .253 | |
| Grand Means for $b^2$ and $e^2$ | | | | | | | | | | .104 | .274 | |

The other "non-verbal" measures are, of course, the *Cattell* tests. If we average the estimated specificities we obtain a mean of .160, versus a mean error for the two tests of .210. Again, the specificities are uninterpretable if we follow the conservative procedure recommended by Kaufman.

The only other test which would appear to be at least partly non-verbal (disregarding instructions for the items, which are usually verbal) is the *ITPA* Visual-Motor Association test. It shows a specificity of .236 in the first data sample, but an error term of .55. Again, we cannot interpret the specificity as indicative of divergent validity.

## CONCLUSION

It seems that the non-verbal intelligence measures, for the Crow-English bilinguals in this study, may be weak in divergent validity. For another, it would appear that language skills probably do play a substantial role in all of the tests examined. Also, the hypothesis that abstract reasoning as required by math problems and by "non-verbal" IQ items probably causes bilinguals to fall back on skills in their primary language is sustained.

# Chapter 9
# Language and Achievement of Hopi-English Bilinguals, Grades 2-6[14]

In this chapter, language and achievement tests were investigated with a new sample of the population of subjects studied by Streiff in 1978. In that study, Hopi-English bilingual children took the *California Achievement Tests* along with written and oral cloze tests. Here only written cloze tests were used, but measures of fluency in English and Hopi were added. As in previous chapters, the focus was on the tests rather than the persons tested. The purpose was to find out more about the role of language proficiency in achievement tests.

## PROCEDURE

### SUBJECTS
Fifty-nine Hopi children from grades three to six were tested on the reservation in Northern Arizona. This number represented all of the Hopi children in these grades who were present on the days of testing. (It was originally intended to include the second grade as well, but the written cloze procedure proved to be too difficult for them.) The teachers, assisted by their aides, judged children at the second grade level (not tabled) to be somewhat stronger in Hopi than in English, and this pattern generally held up throughout the grades. However, only one child in the entire sample was judged to be monolingual in Hopi while four were judged to be monolingual in English.

## TESTS

### CLOZE
An every-fifth-word deletion rate was used. An attempt was made to match the material to the expected reading levels of the children. In fact, the selected passages proved to be challenging for all four grades. Nevertheless, sufficient variance was generated to enable us to draw the desired comparisons with variances in the achievement battery. To maximize the meaningful variance in the cloze scores at each level, any contextually appropriate response was counted as correct. This method has been shown in previous research to yield somewhat higher reliabilities and stronger concurrent validity coefficients than the exact-word method of scoring though the two methods are strongly correlated (see Oller, 1972, 1979; also Brown, 1983, 1988a and

---

[14]The author thanks V. Streiff who collaborated in this research. Though she is not responsible for the views expressed in this chapter, without her help the work could not have been done.

1988b). In fact, in the present study, correlations between scores based on the exact-word criterion and scores based on the criterion of contextual appropriateness ranged from .895 to .960. (These correlations are not tabled in this chapter, but were routinely computed along with a number of other statistics not discussed.) Therefore, to simplify the analysis the contextually appropriate criterion was used for all of the analyses reported below.

## DOMINANCE AND FLUENCY SCALES

Five-point Likert-type scales were used. The Dominance scale was based on the research of Spolsky, Holm, and Murphy (1974), which also served as the basis for the Lau-scale (cf. Oller, 1979, pp. 98-100). It required the rater to indicate whether the child was (1) monolingual in Hopi, (2) dominant in English, (3) equally skilled in Hopi and English, (4) dominant in English, or (5) monolingual in English. Thus, a high score on this scale represents a perceived tendency for the child to prefer Hopi over English while a low score indicates the reverse. In addition, there were two fluency scales: one for Hopi, and one for English. Each of these was also a five-point scale with high ability at one end and low ability at the other. The scales were both coded so that a high score on either scale corresponded to high ability (native) in the respective language while the lowest score meant the child could barely communicate in the language.

It is well known by now that there are significant problems with subjective ratings of this type. For instance, previous research (cf. Teitelbaum, 1976) has shown that they are not always as reliable as might be hoped. Also, it is known that ratings assigned on more than one scale at the same time tend to be influenced by a significant halo effect (Yorozuya and Oller, 1980). Nevertheless, it seemed desirable to attempt to obtain some indication of how the teachers perceived the language abilities of the children. Further, it was hoped that the teachers' knowledge of the fact that the children were also being tested for proficiency in English might enhance the accuracy of their evaluations. In order to keep things as simple as possible, raters were only asked to assess preference for one language or the other and "fluency" in the two languages. It would have been possible to seek finer discriminations, but in the setting where the testing was to be done, it seemed wise to use an uncomplicated rating form.

## THE CALIFORNIA ACHIEVEMENT TESTS

This battery of tests was administered early in the fall semester at Hopi while the cloze tests were given from three to five weeks later. Scores from the subscales of the *California Achievement Tests* used in the present study included Reading Vocabulary, Reading Comprehension, Language Mechanics, Language Expression, Spelling, Math Computation, and Math Concepts and Applications. All of these tests are in a multiple choice format.

READING VOCABULARY

There are three types of items in this subtest. The first involves the most common sort of synonym matching. A word is given in a stem and the examinee must select from a field of alternatives the choice that is nearest in meaning to the given word. The second item type requires the identification of the opposite of the given word. And a third type deals with lexical items which have multiple meanings.

READING COMPREHENSION

In this subtest attention is focussed on asserted facts, inferences, analysis of characters, figurative uses of language, and distinctions between real and imagined elements. Questions in multiple choice format follow brief texts in each case.

LANGUAGE MECHANICS

This portion assesses knowledge of writing conventions including the capitalization of such elements as "I", proper nouns, the beginning letter of each sentence, and content words in titles. Also, marks of punctuation are tested in this section.

LANGUAGE EXPRESSION

Surface morphology and grammatical usage are the target domains of this subscale. Attention is focussed on the use of pronouns, verbs, and adjectives, subject/verb agreement, and various modifiers.

SPELLING

This test tries to assess knowledge of phonemic/graphemic cor-respondences as well as idiosyncratic spellings of certain syllabic or morphemic units (e.g., "-ies" as in "city/cities", "-ence" versus "-ance" as in "occurrence" versus "insurance", etc.).

MATH COMPUTATION

This is an arithmetic test where the examinee is required to select the answers from fields of distractors to problems in addition, subtraction, multiplication, and division.

MATH CONCEPTS AND APPLICATIONS

This subtest assesses knowledge of counting, theory of numbers, and ability to interpret propositions containing negative elements such as "no" and "none". Judgments are also required concerning scalar quantities (e.g., temperature and linear measurements). Knowledge of geometric figures and relationships is also assessed along with ability to read graphs and to solve "story" problems in arithmetic.

RESULTS AND DISCUSSION

The distribution of perceived abilities on a Spolsky-type dominance scale are displayed in Table 9.1. Judgments of relative fluency in Hopi and English are shown in Table 9.2. In grades 3 and 6 children are judged to be stronger in Hopi, but somewhat stronger in English in grades 4 and 5. On the average, there is a slight preference for Hopi and the children are rated somewhat below the mid-point on the fluency scale in both languages.

Means, standard deviations, and reliabilities for each test are given by grade level in Table 9.3. The reliabilities for the Cloze scores are KR 21 estimates adjusted for full length tests, and those for the *California Achievement Tests* are KR 20 estimates similarly adjusted. The latter were taken from the *California Achievement Tests Technical Bulletin 1* (1979). No reliabilities are given for the subjective rating scales, but the other tests show uniformly high reliabilities.

**TABLE 9.1**
Dominance Ratings by Grade Level for Hopi-English Bilinguals in Northern Arizona

| Grade | Only Hopi (1) | Mainly Hopi (2) | Equal (3) | Mainly English (4) | Only English (5) | Mean |
|---|---|---|---|---|---|---|
| 3 N = 15 | 0 | 9 | 1 | 2 | 3 | 2.933 |
| 4 N = 19 | 1 | 1 | 10 | 7 | 0 | 3.211 |
| 5 N = 10 | 0 | 1 | 5 | 3 | 1 | 3.400 |
| 6 N = 15 | 0 | 7 | 7 | 1 | 0 | 2.600 |
| Column Totals | 1 | 18 | 25 | 12 | 4 | |
| Grand Mean Rating | | | | | | 3.286 |

Table 9.3 shows consistent upward progress in the Cloze scores (7.27, 15.42, 20.00, 27.00), but the pattern of change in the dominance ratings and fluency ratings is notably less consistent. From grades 3 to 5 dominance appears to be shifting from Hopi to English (2.93, 3.21, 3.40), but at grade 6, this pattern reverses itself. The mean rating drops back to 2.60. Also, from grades 3 to 5 gains in English seem to be occurring (3.13, 3.44, 3.60), but again at grade 6, this pattern is reversed. The mean rating drops back to 3.13. The Hopi fluency ratings seem to show no particular pattern of change, and the English ratings are not consistent with the steady upward trend of cloze scores.

In the achievement tests fairly consistent gains appear. Exceptions are Spelling and the two math tests. On the Spelling test the third graders attain a higher mean (14.40) than any of the subsequent grades, and, consistent with the English Fluency Ratings, the sixth graders get the lowest mark (12.13). Also in mathematics, the children at grade 6 attain lower scores (16.67 and 19.40) than those at grade 5 (20.90 and 25.20), dropping back about the level of grade 4 (15.21, and 22.57).

TABLE 9.2
Fluency Ratings in English and Hopi

| Grade/Language | 1 Low | 2 | 3 Mid | 4 | 5 High | Mean |
|---|---|---|---|---|---|---|
| 3 English | 0 | 7 | 3 | 1 | 4 | 3.133 |
| Hopi | 3 | 2 | 2 | 0 | 8 | 3.533 |
| 4 English | 0 | 2 | 6 | 11 | 0 | 3.438 |
| Hopi | 1 | 4 | 5 | 9 | 0 | 3.158 |
| 5 English | 0 | 1 | 4 | 3 | 2 | 3.600 |
| Hopi | 1 | 1 | 2 | 4 | 2 | 3.500 |
| 6 English | 0 | 5 | 5 | 3 | 2 | 3.133 |
| Hopi | 0 | 1 | 4 | 6 | 4 | 3.867 |
| **Column Totals** | | | | | | |
| English | 0 | 15 | 18 | 18 | 8 | |
| Hopi | 5 | 8 | 13 | 19 | 14 | |
| **Grand Means** | | | | | | |
| English | | | | | | 3.326 |
| Hopi | | | | | | 3.514 |

TABLE 9.3
Means, Standard Deviations, and Reliabilities for Cloze, Subjective Ratings, and the *California Achievement Tests*

| Tests | Grade 3 N = 15 | | | Grade 4 N = 19 | | | Grade 5 N = 10 | | | Grade 6 N = 15 | | |
|---|---|---|---|---|---|---|---|---|---|---|---|---|
| | $m$ | $s$ | $r_{ii}$ | $m$ | $s$ | $r_{ii}$ | $m$ | $s$ | $r_{ii}$ | $m$ | $s$ | $r_{ii}$ |
| Cloze | 7.27 | 6.91 | .940 | 15.42 | 10.75 | .962 | 20.00 | 9.66 | .941 | 27.00 | 7.40 | .882 |
| Dominance | 2.93 | 1.28 | ---- | 3.21 | .79 | ---- | 3.40 | .84 | ---- | 2.60 | .63 | ---- |
| English Fluency | 3.13 | 1.30 | ---- | 3.44 | .70 | ---- | 3.60 | .97 | ---- | 3.13 | 1.06 | ---- |
| Hopi Fluency | 3.53 | 1.73 | ---- | 3.16 | .96 | ---- | 3.50 | 1.27 | ---- | 3.87 | .92 | ---- |
| Reading Vocab | 7.00 | 2.83 | .919 | 7.89 | 4.56 | .953 | 14.20 | 4.47 | .947 | 14.93 | 5.06 | .942 |
| Reading Comp | 12.93 | 4.60 | .953 | 14.00 | 6.07 | .958 | 19.20 | 6.27 | .958 | 20.87 | 6.02 | .953 |
| Language Mech | 10.20 | 4.16 | .947 | 9.95 | 3.42 | .936 | 13.80 | 4.13 | .942 | 15.40 | 2.97 | .936 |
| Language Expr | 13.00 | 3.40 | .958 | 15.47 | 5.35 | .953 | 20.60 | 6.45 | .958 | 24.53 | 4.93 | .942 |
| Spelling | 14.40 | 3.20 | .907 | 13.63 | 3.17 | .907 | 14.20 | 4.47 | .925 | 12.13 | 2.92 | .925 |
| Math Comput | 10.53 | 5.17 | .925 | 15.21 | 4.25 | .942 | 20.90 | 6.82 | .930 | 16.67 | 4.15 | .919 |
| Math Concepts | 19.87 | 7.40 | .823 | 22.57 | 3.92 | .851 | 25.20 | 9.02 | .870 | 19.40 | 3.66 | .837 |

The next step in the analysis was to compute the correlation matrices for each grade level. These are presented in Tables 9.4 through 9.7. These tables are not interpreted fully, but it may be useful to comment briefly on the relationship between the Cloze scores and the subjective assessments of language proficiency. From the correlations in Table 9.4 (for the third graders, there seems to be a strong halo effect in the three subjective scales. The correlations between them would seem to be spuriously high. This effect is weaker in Table 9.5 (for grade 4), but reappears in Table 9.6 (grade 5). It is absent again from Table 9.7 (grade 6). This fluctuation could be due as much to differences in the raters as in the subjects rated. It is interesting that the correlation between Cloze and the English Fluency Rating is always positive (though not always statistically significant), while the correlation between Cloze and the Hopi Fluency Rating is always negative. This suggests that perceptions of skill in English and in Hopi may in fact be only weakly related to actual proficiency. With adjustments for sample size, the mean correlation between Cloze with the English Fluency Rating was .507, and with Hopi it was -.346.

### TABLE 9.4
Correlations between Cloze, Subjective Ratings, and the California Achievement Tests for Grade 3 at Hopi, N = 15

| Tests | 1 | 2 | 3 | 4 | 5 | 6 | 7 | 8 | 9 | 10 | 11 |
|---|---|---|---|---|---|---|---|---|---|---|---|
| 1 Cloze | 1.000 | .204 | .162 | -.156 | .490 | .133 | .189 | .507 | .337 | .052 | .379 |
| 2 Dominance Rating | | 1.000 | .949 | -.952 | .276 | .508 | -.413 | -.049 | -.027 | .254 | -.039 |
| 3 English Fluency Rating | | | 1.000 | -.892 | .175 | .526 | -.348 | -.032 | -.116 | .180 | .002 |
| 4 Hopi Fluency Rating | | | | 1.000 | -.395 | -.534 | .233 | -.085 | -.054 | -.282 | -.044 |
| 5 Reading Vocabulary | | | | | 1.000 | -.450 | .382 | .475 | .378 | .445 | .587 |
| 6 Reading Comprehension | | | | | | 1.000 | .019 | .278 | -.080 | .407 | .218 |
| 7 Language Mechanics | | | | | | | 1.000 | .621 | -.146 | .038 | .484 |
| 8 Language Expression | | | | | | | | 1.000 | .262 | .264 | .656 |
| 9 Spelling | | | | | | | | | 1.000 | .245 | .349 |
| 10 Math Computation | | | | | | | | | | 1.000 | .492 |
| 11 Math Concepts and Applications | | | | | | | | | | | 1.000 |

### TABLE 9.5
Correlations between Cloze, Subjective Ratings, and the *California Achievement Tests* for Grade 4 at Hopi, N = 19

| Tests | 1 | 2 | 3 | 4 | 5 | 6 | 7 | 8 | 9 | 10 | 11 |
|---|---|---|---|---|---|---|---|---|---|---|---|
| 1 Cloze | 1.000 | .304 | .476 | -.244 | .534 | .712 | .152 | .644 | .147 | .048 | .039 |
| 2 Dominance Rating | | 1.000 | .416 | -.120 | .270 | .279 | .396 | .424 | .033 | .135 | .282 |
| 3 English Fluency Rating | | | 1.000 | -.701 | .332 | .354 | .384 | .309 | .411 | .340 | .260 |
| 4 Hopi Fluency Rating | | | | 1.000 | -.034 | -.162 | -.116 | -.156 | -.383 | -.009 | -.196 |
| 5 Reading Vocabulary | | | | | 1.000 | .566 | .402 | .683 | .494 | .107 | .392 |
| 6 Reading Comprehension | | | | | | 1.000 | .366 | .691 | .404 | .123 | .306 |
| 7 Language Mechanics | | | | | | | 1.000 | .490 | .418 | .188 | .561 |
| 8 Language Expression | | | | | | | | 1.000 | .319 | .171 | .193 |
| 9 Spelling | | | | | | | | | 1.000 | .349 | .363 |
| 10 Math Computation | | | | | | | | | | 1.000 | .482 |
| 11 Math Concepts and Applications | | | | | | | | | | | 1.000 |

Also, the correlation between the English Fluency Rating and the Hopi Fluency Rating was always negative (adjusted mean $r$ = -.679). This relationship is probably inflated by the halo effect, but it shows that when the raters judged proficiency in English to be high, they judged Hopi proficiency to be weak, and vice versa. This judgment is probably incorrect, however, since careful research generally reveals a substantial positive relationship between first and second language skills. (See the discussion in Chapters 2-4 above. Also see Chapter 11 below for evidence of a positive relationship between first and second language skills in the Spanish-English bilinguals discussed there.)

*TABLE 9.6*
Correlations between Cloze, Subjective Ratings, and the *California Achievement Tests* for Grade 5 at Hopi, N = 10

| Tests | 1 | 2 | 3 | 4 | 5 | 6 | 7 | 8 | 9 | 10 | 11 |
|---|---|---|---|---|---|---|---|---|---|---|---|
| 1 Cloze | 1.000 | .559 | .750 | -.299 | .795 | .492 | .554 | .829 | .064 | -.595 | -.262 |
| 2 Dominance Rating | | 1.000 | .900 | -.934 | .183 | .256 | .281 | .441 | .271 | -.147 | .319 |
| 3 English Fluency Rating | | | 1.000 | -.815 | .484 | .437 | .507 | .685 | .381 | -.192 | -.130 |
| 4 Hopi Fluency Rating | | | | 1.000 | .059 | -.070 | -.169 | -.244 | -.372 | -.071 | .214 |
| 5 Reading Vocabulary | | | | | 1.000 | .713 | .412 | .690 | -.024 | -.429 | -.145 |
| 6 Reading Comprehension | | | | | | 1.000 | .628 | .621 | .109 | .047 | .194 |
| 7 Language Mechanics | | | | | | | 1.000 | .814 | .165 | .106 | .505 |
| 8 Language Expression | | | | | | | | 1.000 | .115 | -.195 | .124 |
| 9 Spelling | | | | | | | | | 1.000 | -.145 | .170 |
| 10 Math Computation | | | | | | | | | | 1.000 | .649 |
| 11 Math Concepts and Applications | | | | | | | | | | | 1.000 |

*TABLE 9.7*
Correlations between Cloze, Subjective Ratings, and the *California Achievement Tests* for Grade 6 at Hopi, N = 15

| Tests | 1 | 2 | 3 | 4 | 5 | 6 | 7 | 8 | 9 | 10 | 11 |
|---|---|---|---|---|---|---|---|---|---|---|---|
| 1 Cloze | 1.000 | .504 | .729 | -.696 | .767 | .572 | .676 | .527 | .380 | .516 | .113 |
| 2 Dominance Rating | | 1.000 | .298 | -.592 | .192 | .172 | .547 | .073 | -.046 | .462 | -.512 |
| 3 English Fluency Rating | | | 1.000 | -.348 | .694 | .741 | .458 | .532 | .201 | -.335 | -.169 |
| 4 Hopi Fluency Rating | | | | 1.000 | -.326 | -.133 | -.714 | -.427 | -.260 | -.445 | .188 |
| 5 Reading Vocabulary | | | | | 1.000 | .824 | .401 | .732 | .300 | .400 | .240 |
| 6 Reading Comprehension | | | | | | 1.000 | .430 | .576 | .208 | .409 | .421 |
| 7 Language Mechanics | | | | | | | 1.000 | .506 | .265 | .278 | .076 |
| 8 Language Expression | | | | | | | | 1.000 | .376 | .166 | .284 |
| 9 Spelling | | | | | | | | | 1.000 | .092 | .328 |
| 10 Math Computation | | | | | | | | | | 1.000 | .179 |
| 11 Math Concepts and Applications | | | | | | | | | | | 1.000 |

Another noteworthy fact about the subjective ratings is that the correlations between subjectively judged dominance and fluency were not always as strong as they should have been. Since dominance is presumably determined entirely by the relationship of proficiencies in the two languages, insofar as the fluency ratings indicate proficiency, they should be correspondingly (i.e., strongly) correlated with the Dominance Ratings. In fact, the adjusted mean correlation between the English Fluency Ratings and the Dominance Ratings was .603 (positive as expected), and between the Hopi Fluency Ratings and the Dominance Ratings, the adjusted mean correlation was -.589 (negative as expected).

120    *Language and Bilingualism: More Tests of Tests*

In view of the occasional correlations above .9 which are obtained between the fluency scales, these correlations are low.

The next phase of the analysis was to factor each of the correlation matrices using the principal factoring method with iterative estimates of communalities on the diagonal of each correlation matrix (see Chapter 5 above for an explanation of the method). The varimax rotation for each of these solutions is given in Tables 9.8-9.11.

**TABLE 9.8**
Principal Factor Analysis with Iterations (Varimax Rotation) for Cloze, Subjective Ratings, and the *California Achievement Tests*: Third Graders at Hopi 1978-79, N = 15

| Tests | Factor One | Factor Two | Factor Three | Factor Four | $h^2$ |
|---|---|---|---|---|---|
| Cloze | .238 | .635 | .458 | -.290 | .754 |
| Dominance Rating | .987 | -.081 | .076 | .062 | .991 |
| English Fluency Rating | .957 | -.053 | -.043 | .023 | .921 |
| Hopi Fluency Rating | -.941 | -.036 | .054 | -.166 | .918 |
| Reading Vocabulary | .284 | .619 | .276 | .397 | .698 |
| Reading Comprehension | .555 | .230 | -.141 | .395 | .537 |
| Language Mechanics | -.332 | .803 | -.361 | .078 | .892 |
| Language Expression | .004 | .808 | .108 | .167 | .693 |
| Spelling | -.086 | .122 | .859 | .213 | .806 |
| Math Computation | .197 | .167 | .149 | .688 | .563 |
| Math Con and Appl | -.034 | .654 | .218 | .454 | .683 |

In Table 9.8 the bulk of the variance in the first factor is attributable to the three subjective rating scales. All of them load on it at .941 or above. That factor also receives a moderate loading from Reading Comprehension (.555). The second factor probably represents some sort of general proficiency in English since it receives its heaviest loadings from Language Expression (.808), Language Mechanics (.803), Math Concepts and Applications (.654), Cloze (.635), and Reading Vocabulary (.619). Factor three was defined primarily by the Spelling test (.859), though it also received a modest loading from Cloze (.458). The fourth factor received its primary loadings from Math Computation (.688) and Math Concepts and Applications (.454) though it also was weakly related to Reading Vocabulary (.397) and Reading Comprehension (.395). The measures with the largest communalities were the three subjective ratings, Dominance, .991, English, .921, and Hopi, .911, closely followed by Language Mechanics (.892), and Cloze (.754). However, all of the tests showed substantial communalities.

TABLE 9.9

Principal Factor Analysis with Iterations (Varimax Rotation) for Cloze, Subjective Ratings, and the *California Achievement Tests*: 4th Graders at Hopi 1978-79, N = 19

| Tests | Factor One | Factor Two | Factor Three | Factor Four | $h^2$ |
|---|---|---|---|---|---|
| Cloze | .845 | -.066 | .255 | -.101 | .794 |
| Dominance Rating | .338 | .364 | .215 | -.287 | .375 |
| English Fluency Rating | .269 | .387 | .851 | -.030 | .948 |
| Hopi Fluency Rating | -.079 | .112 | -.859 | -.193 | .794 |
| Reading Vocabulary | .682 | .301 | -.001 | .227 | .607 |
| Reading Comprehension | .816 | .163 | .101 | .127 | .719 |
| Language Mechanics | .321 | .576 | .118 | .086 | .456 |
| Language Expression | .817 | .208 | .085 | .167 | .719 |
| Spelling | .240 | .376 | .275 | .849 | .995 |
| Math Computation | .022 | .475 | .108 | .119 | .252 |
| Math Con. and Appl. | .128 | .901 | -.140 | .071 | .852 |

In the fourth grade data sample, four factors emerged. The first was defined best by Cloze (.845), Language Expression (.817), Reading Comprehension (.816), and Reading Vocabulary (.682). The second received its heaviest loadings from Math Concepts and Applications (.901), Language Mechanics (.576), and Math Computation (.475). It also received weak positive loadings from the English Fluency Rating (.387), Spelling (.376), the Dominance Rating (.364), and Reading Vocabulary (.301). The third factor appeared to be largely a function of the two fluency ratings (Hopi -.859 and English .851), and the fourth was defined chiefly by Spelling (.849) which also loaded weakly on all three of the other factors. In this case, the factors with the highest communalities were Spelling (.995), the English Fluency Rating (.949), Math Concepts and Applications (.852), the Hopi Fluency Rating (.794), and Cloze (.794). Math Computation, and the Dominance Rating had low communalities (.252, and .375, respectively).

For the fifth grade sample, three factors appeared. The first received its heaviest loadings from Language Expression (.879), Reading Vocabulary (.826), Language Mechanics (.790), Cloze (.778), Reading Comprehension (.767), and the English Fluency Rating (.523). The second factor was defined principally by the three subjective ratings scales (Hopi Fluency, -.988, Dominance, .921, and English, .809). The third got its main loadings from the two mathematics tests, Math Concepts and Applications (.823), and Math Computation (.791). It also received modest (and unexplained) negative loadings from Cloze (-.473) and from Reading Vocabulary (-.362) as well as a small positive loading from

Language Mechanics (.392). The variables with the largest communalities were the subjective scales (Hopi, .978, English .956, and Dominance, .947) followed by Cloze (.918), Language Expression (.847), Language Mechanics (.826), and Reading Vocabulary (.816).

**TABLE 9.10**
Principal Factor Analysis with Iterations (Varimax Rotation) for Cloze, Subjective Ratings, and the *California Achievement Tests*:
Fifth Graders at Hopi 1978-79, N = 10

| Tests | Factor One | Factor Two | Factor Three | $h^2$ |
|---|---|---|---|---|
| Cloze | .778 | .298 | -.473 | .918 |
| Dominance Rating | .212 | .921 | -.230 | .947 |
| English Fluency Rating | .523 | .809 | -.166 | .956 |
| Hopi Fluency Rating | .026 | -.988 | .042 | .978 |
| Reading Vocabulary | .826 | -.059 | -.362 | .816 |
| Reading Comprehension | .767 | .089 | .136 | .615 |
| Language Mechanics | .790 | .218 | .392 | .826 |
| Language Expression | .879 | .272 | -.023 | .847 |
| Spelling | .064 | .386 | .093 | .161 |
| Math Computation | -.202 | .035 | .791 | .668 |
| Math Con and Appl | .191 | -.130 | .823 | .731 |

In the sixth grade sample, again there were three factors. Both the first and the second received substantial loadings from Cloze (.632, and .670, respectively). However, the first was defined most clearly by Reading Comprehension (.949), Reading Vocabulary (.822), and the English Fluency Rating (.743), while the second received its main loadings from the Hopi Fluency Rating (-.936), and Language Mechanics (.689). It also got modest loadings from the Dominance Rating (.502) and from Language Expression (.432). Both factors one and two also received weak loadings from Math Computation (.415, and .304). The third factor received a substantial negative loading from the Dominance Rating (-.809) and a significant positive loading from Math Concepts and Applications (.643). It also received weak loadings from Spelling (.399) and Language Expression (.368). The variables with the largest communalities were the Dominance Rating (.996), Reading Comprehension (.942), the Hopi Fluency Rating (.921), Cloze (.849), and Reading Vocabulary (.808).

The final step in the analysis was to examine the specificities of the measures. Except for the subjective ratings scales, these are given for all of the tests in Table 9.12 along with communalities, reliabilities, and error terms for each grade level. The column means are averages for each grade while the row means are averages for each measure.

*TABLE 9.11*

Principal Factor Analysis with Iterations (Varimax Rotation) for Cloze, Subjective Ratings, and the *California Achievement Tests*: Sixth Graders at Hopi 1978-79, ( N = 15)

| Tests | Factor One | Factor Two | Factor Three | $h^2$ |
|---|---|---|---|---|
| Cloze | .632 | .670 | .005 | .849 |
| Dominance Rating | .300 | .502 | -.809 | .996 |
| English Fluency Rating | .743 | -.290 | -.051 | .638 |
| Hopi Fluency Rating | .123 | -.936 | .173 | .921 |
| Reading Vocabulary | .822 | -.292 | -.217 | .808 |
| Reading Comprehension | .949 | .056 | .195 | .942 |
| Language Mechanics | .356 | .689 | -.041 | .603 |
| Language Expression | .506 | .432 | .368 | .579 |
| Spelling | .138 | .363 | .399 | .310 |
| Math Computation | .415 | .304 | -.143 | .668 |
| Math Con. and Appl. | .264 | -.073 | .643 | .731 |

The grand mean of all communalities was .671, for specificities, .268, and error terms, .074. The Cloze scores showed the greatest average communality (.829) and the least specificity (.102). All of the tests except for Cloze, and Math Concepts and Applications had average specificities that were considerably more than twice their respective error terms. Math Computation had the least communality (.442) and the greatest specificity (.487). Next in line, was Language Expression with a specificity of .370 and a communality of .568. Perhaps the fact that this test concentrates on surface elements of English is the best explanation for the relatively low communality and high specificity for this population of subjects.

CONCLUSION

It is interesting that in the aggregate the two tests which seem to contribute the most in terms of explaining variance in all the other tests, and also to contribute least in the sense of adding specific (unique and reliable) variance of their own were Cloze and Math Concepts and Applications. Both of these tests rely heavily on ability to process text--to understand propositional meanings, including assertions, presuppositions, associations, and implications in temporally progressive and causally linked sequences. The expectation that deep language or semiotic capacities would figure largely in all of the tests examined here is generally sustained.

**TABLE 9.12**

Estimates of Specificity and Error for Cloze, Subjective Ratings, and the *California Achievement Tests*

| Tests | $r_{ii}$ | Grade 3 N = 15 $h^2$ | $b^2$ | $e^2$ | $r_{ii}$ | Grade 4 N = 19 $h^2$ | $b^2$ | $e^2$ |
|---|---|---|---|---|---|---|---|---|
| 1 Cloze | .940 | .754 | .186 | .060 | .962 | .794 | .168 | .038 |
| 2 Reading Vocabulary | .919 | .698 | .221 | .081 | .953 | .607 | .346 | .047 |
| 3 Reading Comp. | .953 | .537 | .416 | .047 | .958 | .719 | .239 | .042 |
| 4 Language Mech. | .947 | .892 | .055 | .053 | .936 | .456 | .480 | .064 |
| 5 Language Expr. | .958 | .693 | .265 | .042 | .953 | .719 | .234 | .047 |
| 6 Spelling | .907 | .806 | .101 | .093 | .907 | .995 | .000 | .093 |
| 7 Math Comput. | .925 | .563 | .362 | .075 | .942 | .252 | .690 | .058 |
| 8 Math Con. | .823 | .683 | .140 | .177 | .851 | .852 | .000 | .149 |

| | | | | | | | | |
|---|---|---|---|---|---|---|---|---|
| Col. Means for $h^2$, $b^2$, and $e^2$ | | .703 | .218 | .072 | | .674 | .270 | .067 |

Grand Means for $h^2$, $b^2$, and $e^2$

**TABLE 9.12**
(continued)

| | $r_{ii}$ | Grade 5 N = 10 $h^2$ | $b^2$ | $e^2$ | $r_{ii}$ | Grade 6 N = 15 $h^2$ | $b^2$ | $e^2$ | Row Means $h^2$ | $b^2$ | $e^2$ |
|---|---|---|---|---|---|---|---|---|---|---|---|
| 1 | .941 | .919 | .022 | .059 | .882 | .849 | .033 | .118 | .829 | .102 | .069 |
| 2 | .947 | .816 | .131 | .053 | .942 | .808 | .134 | .058 | .732 | .208 | .060 |
| 3 | .958 | .615 | .343 | .042 | .953 | .942 | .011 | .047 | .703 | .252 | .044 |
| 4 | .942 | .826 | .116 | .058 | .936 | .603 | .333 | .064 | .694 | .246 | .060 |
| 5 | .958 | .847 | .111 | .042 | .942 | .579 | .363 | .058 | .710 | .243 | .047 |
| 6 | .925 | .161 | .764 | .075 | .925 | .310 | .615 | .075 | .568 | .370 | .084 |
| 7 | .930 | .668 | .262 | .070 | .919 | .286 | .633 | .081 | .442 | .487 | .071 |
| 8 | .870 | .731 | .139 | .130 | .837 | .489 | .348 | .163 | .689 | .157 | .155 |

| | | | | | | | | | | | |
|---|---|---|---|---|---|---|---|---|---|---|---|
| Col. Means | | .698 | .236 | .066 | | .608 | .309 | .083 | | | |

Grand Means (Columns and Rows) $h^2$, $b^2$, and $e^2$       .671  .258  .074

# Chapter 10
# Language and Achievement of Navajo-English Bilinguals at Grades 3-9[15]

Like Chapter 9 above, this chapter too is a follow-up to V. Streiff (1978) with differences in the method and in the population studied. Here, scores attained by Navajo-English bilinguals on the *Comprehensive Tests of Basic Skills* and on a written cloze test are examined. As in previous chapters, the objective was to find out how much of the variance in each of the subtests examined could be attributed to a common factor underlying all of the tests and how much of it would be specific to the respective subtests. Again, a central question was to see how much of the common variance might be attributed to a deep and general factor of semiotic capacities.

## THE BILINGUAL SETTING
The present study was conducted in a school where, from pre-kindergarten through the second grade, instruction takes place in the primary language of the children (Navajo). In subsequent grades, the primary language continues to be a medium of instruction in culture, although increasing amounts of material are presented in the secondary language (English). Throughout the first four years, the children receive instruction in oral English. Reading in English is introduced in second grade, but reading in Navajo, and instruction in Navajo culture, continue in the primary language through the ninth grade. Here, all of the tests were administered in English, so no comparison can be drawn with performance in the primary language (but see Chapters 11 and 12 below). However, rough measures of language dominance were obtained from the Lau-type scale also used in Chapter 9 above.

## SUBJECTS
Fully 85% of the 181 Navajo children in the data sample were judged by their teachers to have been monolingual in Navajo when they first entered school. (This percentage, which does not appear in the table, is identical to the estimate of monolingual Crow speaking children entering school at Crow Agency in Montana. Refer to Chapter 8 above.) Perhaps these judgments can be regarded with somewhat more confidence than those of studies where the raters do not speak the primary

---

[15]This chapter was completed only because of the help of Paul Streiff formerly of the Bureau of Indian Affairs and more recently associated with Edgewood Independent School District in San Antonio, Texas. His help is gratefully acknowledged, but he is exonerated from any responsibility for the conclusions expressed.

126    *Language and Bilingualism: More Tests of Tests*

language of the children and therefore have less opportunity to observe their skills (cf. Teitelbaum, 1976).

The subjects of this study were distributed over the grades from 3 through 9 as shown in column 1 of Table 10.1. All of the children attended school near their homes on the Navajo Reservation in Northern Arizona. Few were judged by their teachers to be monolingual in English. In columns two through six, Table 10.1 shows the number judged to fall at each of the five points on the Lau dominance scale. Since the rating procedure was probably not completely reliable (also see Chapter 9 above), perhaps the details of the picture presented in Table 10.1 should be relied on less than the overall pattern. It would appear that gains in English were being made throughout the seven year spread from grade 3 to 9. The overall trend seems to be toward a balanced form of bilingualism. This entails movement from Navajo dominance toward greater skill in English. None of the children were judged to be monolingual in Navajo beyond grade 6, though several in grades 6 through 8 were judged to be monolingual in English. However, the grand mean still shows a slight preference for Navajo over English. It may be inferred that children were making gains in both languages as they progressed through the grades. In grade 9, 82% were judged to be balanced bilinguals.

TABLE 10.1
Dominance in Navajo and English Judged by Teachers, N = 181

| Grade | N | Only Navajo (1) | Mainly Navajo (2) | Equal (3) | Mainly Engl. (4) | Only English (5) | Mean |
|---|---|---|---|---|---|---|---|
| 3 | 30 | 10 | 16 | 3 | 1 | 0 | 1.833 |
| 4 | 27 | 3 | 17 | 6 | 1 | 0 | 2.185 |
| 5 | 23 | 1 | 15 | 6 | 1 | 0 | 2.304 |
| 6 | 40 | 1 | 24 | 13 | 1 | 1 | 2.425 |
| 7 | 22 | 0 | 10 | 9 | 1 | 2 | 2.318 |
| 8 | 22 | 0 | 4 | 12 | 3 | 3 | 3.227 |
| 9 | 17 | 0 | 2 | 14 | 1 | 0 | 2.941 |
| Column Totals | | 15 | 88 | 63 | 9 | 6 | |
| Grand Mean | | | | | | | 2.462 |

TESTS
Written cloze tests were adapted from the passages used by V. Streiff (1978). An every eighth word deletion ratio was used to obtain 50 blanks. By the Dale and Chall readability formula, the texts ranged in difficulty from lower 3rd grade to upper 6th. The children at grades

3, 4, and 5 received 3rd, 4th, and 5th grade material respectively. Children in grades 6 and 7 received material at the lower 6th level and children at grades 8 and 9, received material at the upper 6th level. Judging by the average reading levels of the children in the data samples, these readability levels were expected to be challenging for the children in grades 3 through 6, but more nearly within reach of the children at grades 7 through 9. The cloze tests were all administered during the month of February 1979.

In addition to the cloze tests, scores from the *Comprehensive Tests of Basic Skills*, administered in September 1978, were also obtained. (Hence, there was a lag of approximately five months between the achievement testing and the language proficiency testing.) The *Comprehensive Tests of Basic Skills* consist of eight subtests. These are labeled Reading Comprehension, Reading Vocabulary, Language Mechanics, Language Expression, Spelling, Math Computation, Math Concepts, and Math Applications. The Reading Vocabulary subtest is a multiple choice test requiring the identification of synonyms. The subtest labeled Reading Comprehension consists of short passages followed by multiple choice questions. The Spelling portion requires examinees to differentiate correct and incorrect spellings. The Language Mechanics subtest focusses on punctuation and capitalization. Language Expression involves sentence completion tasks aimed at certain parts of speech, and word choice, as well as some items dealing with paragraph organization. Math Computation presents arithmetic problems requiring addition, subtraction, multiplication, and division. The Math Concepts portion includes verbally formulated problems concerning measurements of time, denominations of money, and linear quantities. There are also some items dealing with geometric relationships, e.g., the fact that a square is formed from two equilateral triangles. Finally, the Math Applications subtest requires mathematical skills for verbally presented problems.

Levels 1, 2, and 3, of the *Comprehensive Tests of Basic Skills* were administered. Grades 3 and 4 took Level 1; 4 and 5 took Level 2; and 7, 8, and 9, Level 3. One of the reported virtues of the *Comprehensive Tests of Basic Skills* is that care was taken to try to eliminate cultural bias. In order to accomplish this, reviewers representing minority groups were employed to screen items. Comparisons of the performance of majority and minority groups item by item were also examined to detect items unduly difficult for certain minorities. The tests were also specifically designed to tap the broad range of skills drawn from Bloom's taxonomy (1956). One review commends the test for "generally sound quality and great adaptability" (Findley, 1978).

## RESULTS AND DISCUSSION

Because the children at the various grade levels did not all take the same tests, it was necessary to examine performance at each grade level separately. In order to maximize the meaningful variance in the cloze scores, any contextually appropriate word was counted as correct. Previous research has shown that this scoring method generates somewhat higher reliabilities and concurrent validity coefficients (cf. Oller, 1979). As in previous chapters, the usual descriptive statistics are routinely examined. These are given in Table 10.2 for Grades 3 through 9. The reliabilities reported for the Cloze tests are KR-21 estimates adjusted for full length tests. Those reported for the *Comprehensive Tests of Basic Skills*, however, are those given in the *Manual* for the respective grade levels. In fact, all of the tests were quite reliable.

**TABLE 10.2**

Means and Standard Deviations for Grades 3 to 9 at Rock Point on the *Comprehensive Tests of Basic Skills* and Written Cloze Tests

| Tests | Grade 3 N = 30 | | | Grade 4 N > 22 < 28 | | | Grade 5 N >21 < 24 | | |
|---|---|---|---|---|---|---|---|---|---|
| | *m* | *s* | $r_{ii}$ | *m* | *s* | $r_{ii}$ | *m* | *s* | $r_{ii}$ |
| Cloze | 13.23 | 11.57 | .95 | 13.37 | 8.03 | .95 | 16.52 | 7.45 | .92 |
| *Comprehensive Tests of Basic Skills* | | | | | | | | | |
| Reading Voc | 2.85 | .37 | .92 | 3.00 | .26 | .93 | 3.40 | .41 | .92 |
| Read Comp | 2.97 | .40 | .94 | 3.34 | .37 | .94 | 3.62 | .48 | .92 |
| Lang Mech | 3.34 | .59 | .85 | 3.73 | .52 | .86 | 3.89 | .47 | .82 |
| Lang Expr | 3.44 | .32 | .90 | 3.59 | .40 | .91 | 4.06 | .37 | .88 |
| Spelling | 3.30 | .42 | .89 | 3.76 | .36 | .91 | 3.76 | .49 | .89 |
| Math Comp | 2.88 | .21 | .95 | 3.06 | .31 | .95 | 3.56 | .26 | .92 |
| Math Con | 2.87 | .27 | .89 | 3.22 | .29 | .89 | 3.48 | .48 | .82 |
| Math Appl | 3.01 | .26 | .91 | 3.12 | .35 | .92 | 3.46 | .49 | .89 |

**TABLE 10.2**
(continued)

| | Grade 6 N > 35 < 40 | | | Grade 7 N > 18 < 23 | | | Grade 8 N > 20 < 23 | | | Grade 9 N > 14 < 18 | | |
|---|---|---|---|---|---|---|---|---|---|---|---|---|
| | *m* | *s* | $r_{ii}$ | *m* | *s* | $r_{ii}$ | *m* | *s* | $r_{ii}$ | *m* | *s* | $r_{ii}$ |
| C | 20.03 | 8.29 | .91 | 28.36 | 9.71 | .93 | 32.68 | 10.04 | .93 | 36.24 | 5.67 | .93 |
| *CTBS* | | | | | | | | | | | | |
| RV | 3.42 | .35 | .94 | 4.19 | .53 | .93 | 4.48 | .74 | .94 | 4.65 | .62 | .91 |
| RC | 3.95 | .60 | .93 | 4.59 | .84 | .92 | 4.95 | .62 | .93 | 5.17 | .56 | .91 |
| LM | 4.52 | .51 | .82 | 5.05 | .41 | .77 | 5.28 | .49 | .80 | 5.26 | .45 | .78 |
| LE | 4.39 | .35 | .89 | 4.68 | .69 | .89 | 4.89 | .61 | .90 | 4.99 | .57 | .85 |
| Sp | 4.37 | .55 | .90 | 4.73 | .43 | .88 | 5.30 | .49 | .89 | 5.57 | .58 | .88 |
| MC | 3.89 | .26 | .94 | 4.23 | .31 | .94 | 4.70 | .35 | .95 | 5.27 | .32 | .94 |
| Mn | 3.82 | .49 | .85 | 4.38 | .36 | .85 | 4.65 | .59 | .89 | 5.15 | .58 | .86 |
| MA | 3.87 | .45 | .90 | 4.47 | .44 | .89 | 4.99 | .59 | .91 | 5.34 | .58 | .87 |

It appears from Table 10.2 that children at grade 3 did almost as well as those at grade 4 on the Cloze task, but it must be remembered that they actually took different tests. Substantial gains are indicated beyond grade 4 because of the fact that the texts used at the more advanced levels became increasingly difficult. Gains across the grade levels on the *Comprehensive Tests of Basic Skills* are modest but fairly steady on all the tests with the exception of Language Mechanics between grades 8 and 9.

The next step was to compute correlations between the nine test scores for each grade. These are given in Tables 10.3 through 10.9. In order to use the maximum number of cases for each calculation, a pair-wise procedure for deleting missing cases was employed. For this reason, the number of cases varied within each data set, except for the third grade sample where scores existed for all subjects on all nine tests. The correlations were generally positive, and in the predicted direction. In the few cases where negative correlations appeared, they were weak and failed to reach significance at the .05 level. It is interesting to note that in spite of the time lapse between the administration of the *Comprehensive Tests of Basic Skills* and the Cloze tests there were generally positive and significant correlations between the Cloze scores and the subtests on the achievement battery.

**TABLE 10.3**

Correlations between a Cloze Test, and the Various Parts of the *Comprehensive Tests of Basic Skills* for Grade 3 at Rock Point, N = 30

| Tests | 1 | 2 | 3 | 4 | 5 | 6 | 7 | 8 | 9 |
|---|---|---|---|---|---|---|---|---|---|
| 1 Cloze | 1.000 | .200 | .203 | .696 | .137 | .516 | .254 | .553 | .076 |
| *Comprehensive Tests of Basic Skills* | | | | | | | | | |
| 2 Read Voc | | 1.000 | .340 | .364 | -.141 | .532 | .313 | .182 | -.117 |
| 3 Read Comp | | | 1.000 | .437 | -.167 | .324 | .002 | .153 | .479 |
| 4 Language Mechanics | | | | 1.000 | .056 | .447 | .284 | .622 | .124 |
| 5 Language Expression | | | | | 1.000 | -.079 | -.182 | .203 | .079 |
| 6 Language Spelling | | | | | | 1.000 | .344 | .278 | .109 |
| 7 Math Computation | | | | | | | 1.000 | .291 | -.148 |
| 8 Math Concepts | | | | | | | | 1.000 | -.041 |
| 9 Math Applications | | | | | | | | | 1.000 |

The next step was to examine the common factors underlying the correlation matrices through principal factoring. (Again, a pair-wise method of deleting missing data was employed in order to maximize the number of valid cases entering into each correlation.) The results of these analyses are given in Tables 10.10 through 10.16. In Table 10.10, three distinct factors appeared. The first received its heaviest loadings from Cloze (.802), Language Mechanics (.801), and Math Concepts (.738). The second factor received its strongest loadings from

Reading Vocabulary (.691), Spelling (.531), and Math Computation (.432). The third factor received substantial loadings only from Reading Comprehension (.837) and Math Applications (.626).

***TABLE 10.4***

Correlations between a Cloze Test, and the Various Parts of the *Comprehensive Tests of Basic Skills* for Grade 4 at Rock Point, N > 22 < 28

| Tests | 1 | 2 | 3 | 4 | 5 | 6 | 7 | 8 | 9 |
|---|---|---|---|---|---|---|---|---|---|
| 1 Cloze | 1.000 | .475 | .302 | .343 | .317 | .417 | .268 | .527 | .401 |
| *Comprehensive Tests of Basic Skills* | | | | | | | | | |
| 2 Read Voc | | 1.000 | .230 | .261 | .248 | .557 | .345 | .125 | .496 |
| 3 Reading Comp | | | 1.000 | .451 | .486 | .352 | .399 | .271 | .210 |
| 4 Language Mechanics | | | | 1.000 | .396 | .500 | .411 | .410 | .540 |
| 5 Language Expression | | | | | 1.000 | .559 | .209 | .638 | .417 |
| 6 Spelling | | | | | | 1.000 | .158 | .286 | .412 |
| 7 Math Computation | | | | | | | 1.000 | .295 | .262 |
| 8 Math Concepts | | | | | | | | 1.000 | .326 |
| 9 Math Applications | | | | | | | | | 1.000 |

***TABLE 10.5***

Correlations between a Cloze Test, and the Various Parts of the *Comprehensive Tests of Basic Skills* for Grade 5 at Rock Point, N > 21 < 24

| Tests | 1 | 2 | 3 | 4 | 5 | 6 | 7 | 8 | 9 |
|---|---|---|---|---|---|---|---|---|---|
| 1 Cloze | 1.000 | .614 | .514 | .572 | .788 | .240 | .075 | .424 | .532 |
| *Comprehensive Tests of Basic Skills* | | | | | | | | | |
| 2 Read Voc | | 1.000 | .493 | .088 | .453 | -.045 | -.032 | .440 | .437 |
| 3 Reading Comp | | | 1.000 | .389 | .622 | .118 | -.044 | .444 | .443 |
| 4 Language Mechanics | | | | 1.000 | .576 | .298 | -.144 | .449 | .384 |
| 5 Language Expression | | | | | 1.000 | .361 | -.002 | .452 | .509 |
| 6 Spelling | | | | | | 1.000 | .002 | -.003 | .165 |
| 7 Math Computation | | | | | | | 1.000 | .313 | .081 |
| 8 Math Concepts | | | | | | | | 1.000 | .304 |
| 9 Math Applications | | | | | | | | | 1.000 |

The tests with the largest communalities were Reading Comprehension (.842), Language Mechanics (.755), and Cloze (.661). Also it is interesting that all three of the identified factors received their strongest loadings from tests that required the exercise of substantial proficiency in English (namely, Cloze, Reading Vocabulary, and Reading

Comprehension). The Language Expression subtest showed the weakest communality (.200) with the three factors extracted and Math Computation had the next lowest communality (.316).

TABLE 10.6

Correlations between a Cloze Test, and the Various Parts of the *Comprehensive Tests of Basic Skills* for Grade 6 at Rock Point,
N > 36 < 40

| Tests | 1 | 2 | 3 | 4 | 5 | 6 | 7 | 8 | 9 |
|---|---|---|---|---|---|---|---|---|---|
| 1 Cloze | 1.000 | .314 | .458 | .384 | .406 | .327 | .436 | .571 | .376 |
| *Comprehensive Tests of Basic Skills* | | | | | | | | | |
| 2 Read Voc | | 1.000 | .321 | .293 | .325 | .309 | .099 | .039 | .069 |
| 3 Reading Comp | | | 1.000 | .396 | .518 | .381 | .185 | .140 | .259 |
| 4 Language Mechanics | | | | 1.000 | .465 | .357 | .414 | .421 | .223 |
| 5 Language Expression | | | | | 1.000 | .156 | .213 | .105 | .049 |
| 6 Spelling | | | | | | 1.000 | -.046 | .297 | .256 |
| 7 Math Computation | | | | | | | 1.000 | .469 | .183 |
| 8 Math Concepts | | | | | | | | 1.000 | .525 |
| 9 Math Applications | | | | | | | | | 1.000 |

TABLE 10.7

Correlations between a Cloze Test, and the Various Parts of the *Comprehensive Tests of Basic Skills* for Grade 7 at Rock Point,
N > 18 < 23

| Tests | 1 | 2 | 3 | 4 | 5 | 6 | 7 | 8 | 9 |
|---|---|---|---|---|---|---|---|---|---|
| 1 Cloze | 1.000 | .429 | .667 | -.136 | .542 | .248 | -.249 | .474 | .171 |
| *Comprehensive Tests of Basic Skills* | | | | | | | | | |
| 2 Read Voc | | 1.000 | .388 | .051 | .378 | .313 | -.023 | .337 | .328 |
| 3 Reading Comp | | | 1.000 | .443 | .619 | .280 | .094 | .393 | .411 |
| 4 Language Mechanics | | | | 1.000 | .153 | .213 | .371 | .097 | .218 |
| 5 Language Expression | | | | | 1.000 | .427 | -.101 | .672 | .351 |
| 6 Spelling | | | | | | 1.000 | -.026 | .312 | .223 |
| 7 Math Computation | | | | | | | 1.000 | -.113 | .608 |
| 8 Math Concepts | | | | | | | | 1.000 | .251 |
| 9 Math Applications | | | | | | | | | 1.000 |

The picture for the fourth graders was somewhat different. For one thing, there were only two significant factors. Cloze loaded almost equally on these two factors (.449 and .422). The first factor received its heaviest loadings from Language Expression (.748), Math Concepts

---

(.724), Language Mechanics (.604), and Reading Comprehension (.518). The second was defined primarily by Reading Vocabulary (.996) and Spelling (.512). It also received a significant loading from Math Applications (.477). The latter also loaded at .424 on the first factor as well.

**TABLE 10.8**

Correlations between a Cloze Test, and the Various Parts of the *Comprehensive Tests of Basic Skills* for Grade 8 at Rock Point, N > 20 < 23

| Tests | 1 | 2 | 3 | 4 | 5 | 6 | 7 | 8 | 9 |
|---|---|---|---|---|---|---|---|---|---|
| 1 Cloze | 1.000 | .422 | .726 | .578 | .836 | .651 | .509 | .428 | .705 |
| *Comprehensive Tests of Basic Skills* | | | | | | | | | |
| 2 Read Voc | | 1.000 | .702 | .172 | .529 | .176 | .160 | .547 | .362 |
| 3 Reading Comp | | | 1.000 | .471 | .826 | .404 | .491 | .384 | .683 |
| 4 Language Mechanics | | | | 1.000 | .571 | .446 | .370 | .382 | .489 |
| 5 Language Expression | | | | | 1.000 | .550 | .426 | .543 | .678 |
| 6 Spelling | | | | | | 1.000 | .656 | .115 | .615 |
| 7 Math Computation | | | | | | | 1.000 | .309 | .676 |
| 8 Math Concepts | | | | | | | | 1.000 | .543 |
| 9 Math Applications | | | | | | | | | 1.000 |

**TABLE 10.9**

Correlations between a Cloze Test, and the Various Parts of the *Comprehensive Tests of Basic Skills* for Grade 9 at Rock Point, N > 14 < 18

| Tests | 1 | 2 | 3 | 4 | 5 | 6 | 7 | 8 | 9 |
|---|---|---|---|---|---|---|---|---|---|
| 1 Cloze | 1.000 | .559 | .541 | .150 | .296 | .463 | .304 | .462 | .198 |
| *Comprehensive Tests of Basic Skills* | | | | | | | | | |
| 2 Read Voc | | 1.000 | .840 | .608 | .590 | .662 | .450 | .422 | .093 |
| 3 Reading Comp | | | 1.000 | .507 | .690 | .580 | .543 | .542 | .266 |
| 4 Language Mechanics | | | | 1.000 | .379 | .309 | .486 | .305 | .115 |
| 5 Language Expression | | | | | 1.000 | .044 | .607 | .443 | .461 |
| 6 Spelling | | | | | | 1.000 | .138 | .107 | -.106 |
| 7 Math Computation | | | | | | | 1.000 | .925 | .667 |
| 8 Math Concepts | | | | | | | | 1.000 | .726 |
| 9 Math Applications | | | | | | | | | 1.000 |

Again it would seem that language skills figure largely in both factors. It may also be noteworthy that no separate math factor appears, though the Math Computation test did show the lowest communality with the two factors which were extracted (.204).

**TABLE 10.10**
Principal Factor Analysis with Iterations (Varimax Rotation) for a Cloze
Test and the *Comprehensive Tests of Basic Skills*: Third
Graders at Rock Point in 1978-79, N = 30

| Tests | Factor One | Factor Two | Factor Three | $h^2$ |
|---|---|---|---|---|
| Cloze | .802 | .102 | .084 | .661 |
| *Comprehensive Tests of Basic Skills* | | | | |
| Reading Vocabulary | .223 | .690 | .052 | .529 |
| Reading Comp | .158 | .342 | .837 | .842 |
| Language Mechanics | .801 | .230 | .246 | .755 |
| Language Expression | .228 | -.383 | -.032 | .200 |
| Spelling | .441 | .531 | .149 | .498 |
| Math Computation | .297 | .432 | .202 | .316 |
| Math Concepts | .738 | .030 | -.030 | .546 |
| Math Applications | .034 | -.149 | .626 | .415 |

**TABLE 10.11**
Principal Factor Analysis with Iterations (Varimax Rotation) for a
Cloze Test and the *Comprehensive Tests of Basic Skills*: Fourth
Graders at Rock Point in 1978-79, N > 22 < 28

| Tests | Factor One | Factor Two | $h^2$ |
|---|---|---|---|
| Cloze | .449 | .422 | .380 |
| *Comprehensive Tests of Basic Skills* | | | |
| Reading Vocabulary | .054 | .996 | .994 |
| Reading Comprehension | .517 | .213 | .312 |
| Language Mechanics | .604 | .318 | .466 |
| Language Expression | .748 | .186 | .594 |
| Spelling | .459 | .512 | .473 |
| Math Computation | .350 | .285 | .204 |
| Math Concepts | .724 | .081 | -.531 |
| Math Applications | .424 | .477 | .408 |

At the fifth grade level, again three factors appeared. The first
seemed to be an English language factor receiving its strongest loadings
from Reading Vocabulary (.992), Cloze (.651), Reading Comprehension
(.565, and Language Expression (.560). The second factor also got a
substantial loading from Cloze (.542), but received its heaviest contributions from Language Mechanics (.748) and Language Expression (.697).

The third factor received its primary loadings from Math Computation (.638) and Math Concepts (.538). However, Math Applications distributed its modest loadings primarily on factors one (.477) and two (.358). It would appear that factors one and two are substantially dependent on English language skills while factor three is dominated by computational abilities. At this grade level, the tests with the largest communalities were Reading Vocabulary (.999), Language Expression (.804) and Cloze (.731). Spelling had the lowest communality with the three factors extracted (.188).

**TABLE 10.12**

Principal Factor Analysis with Iterations (Varimax Rotation) for a Cloze Test and the *Comprehensive Tests of Basic Skills* Fifth Graders at Rock Point in 1978-79, N > 21 < 24

| Tests | Factor One | Factor Two | Factor Three | $h^2$ |
|---|---|---|---|---|
| Cloze | .651 | .542 | .115 | .731 |
| *Comprehensive Tests of Basic Skills* | | | | |
| Reading Vocabulary | .992 | -.127 | .004 | .999 |
| Reading Comp | .565 | .371 | .071 | .463 |
| Language Mechanics | .216 | .748 | .049 | .608 |
| Language Expression | .560 | .696 | .074 | .804 |
| Spelling | -.002 | .430 | -.047 | .188 |
| Math Computation | -.021 | -.083 | .639 | .415 |
| Math Concepts | .447 | .263 | .538 | .558 |
| Math Applications | .477 | .358 | .112 | .368 |

**TABLE 10.13**

Principal Factor Analysis with Iterations (Varimax Rotation) for a Cloze Test and the *Comprehensive Tests of Basic Skills*: Sixth Graders at Rock Point in 1978-79, N > 36 < 40

| Tests | Factor One | Factor Two | Factor Three | $h^2$ |
|---|---|---|---|---|
| Cloze .561 | .483 | .112 | .562 | |
| *Comprehensive Tests of Basic Skills* | | | | |
| Reading Vocabulary | .032 | .470 | .197 | .261 |
| Reading Comp | .148 | .659 | .236 | .511 |
| Language Mechanics | .393 | .538 | .066 | .448 |
| Language Expression | .070 | .754 | -.065 | .577 |
| Spelling | .207 | .302 | .684 | .602 |
| Math Computation | .550 | .289 | -.353 | .511 |
| Math Concepts | .968 | .015 | .125 | .952 |
| Math Applications | .502 | .072 | .247 | .318 |

*TABLE 10.14*

Principal Factor Analysis with Iterations (Varimax Rotation) for a Cloze
Test and the *Comprehensive Tests of Basic Skills*: Seventh
Graders at Rock Point in 1978-79, N > 18 < 23

| Tests | Factor One | Factor Two | $h^2$ |
|---|---|---|---|
| Cloze | .754 | -.117 | .582 |
| *Comprehensive Tests of Basic Skills* | | | |
| Reading Vocabulary | .522 | .116 | .286 |
| Reading Comprehension | .731 | .113 | .633 |
| Language Mechanics | .126 | .437 | .207 |
| Language Expression | .829 | .109 | .698 |
| Spelling | .439 | .124 | .208 |
| Math Computation | -.238 | .964 | .986 |
| Math Concepts | .666 | .035 | .445 |
| Math Applications | .329 | .658 | .541 |

*TABLE 10.15*

Principal Factor Analysis with Iterations (Varimax Rotation) for a
Cloze Test and the *Comprehensive Tests of Basic Skills*: Eighth
Graders at Rock Point in 1978-79, N > 20 < 23

| Tests | Factor One | Factor Two | $h^2$ |
|---|---|---|---|
| Cloze | .701 | .523 | .765 |
| *Comprehensive Tests of Basic Skills* | | | |
| Reading Vocabulary | .036 | .811 | .659 |
| Reading Comprehension | .461 | .755 | .782 |
| Language Mechanics | .523 | .314 | .373 |
| Language Expression | .576 | .696 | .816 |
| Spelling | .838 | .070 | .708 |
| Math Computation | .717 | .154 | .538 |
| Math Concepts | .214 | .591 | .395 |
| Math Applications | .723 | .451 | .726 |

At grade six, where there was a somewhat larger number of cases
(N > 36 < 40), again three factors appeared. Factor one might have
been judged to be dominated by mathematical abilities except that it
received a substantial loading (. 561) from Cloze. Its heaviest contribution was from Math Concepts (.968) followed by Cloze, then Math
Computation (.550), and Math Applications (.502). The second factor,
however, was more clearly dominated by language tests--Language

Expression (.754), Reading Comprehension (.659), Language Mechanics (.538), Cloze (.484) and Reading Vocabulary (.470). The tests with the largest communalities for the sixth graders were Math Concepts (.952), Language Expression (.577), and Cloze (.562).

**TABLE 10.16**

Principal Factor Analysis with Iterations (Varimax Rotation) for a Cloze Test and the *Comprehensive Tests of Basic Skills*: Ninth Graders at Rock Point in 1978-79, N > 14 < 18

| Tests | Factor One | Factor Two | $h^2$ |
|---|---|---|---|
| Cloze | .518 | .215 | .314 |
| *Comprehensive Tests of Basic Skills* | | | |
| Reading Vocabulary | .937 | .148 | .900 |
| Reading Comprehension | .847 | .322 | .821 |
| Language Mechanics | .501 | .219 | .299 |
| Language Expression | .628 | .378 | .537 |
| Spelling | .782 | .127 | .627 |
| Math Computation | .337 | .870 | .871 |
| Math Concepts | .303 | .940 | .975 |
| Math Applications | .003 | .781 | .610 |

For the seventh grade sample only two significant factors were found. The first received substantial loadings from Language Expression (.829), Cloze (.754), Reading Comprehension (.731), Math Concepts (.666), and Reading Vocabulary (.522). The second factor was best defined by Math Computation (.991), and Math Applications (.658). It also received a modest positive loading from Language Mechanics (.379), and a weak but negative loading from Cloze (-.339). In this data sample, the tests with the largest communalities were Math Computation (.986), Language Expression (.698), Reading Comprehension (.633), Cloze (.582), and Math Applications (.542).

In the eighth grade sample, there were two factors again. The first was defined primarily by the Spelling test (.838) followed by Math Applications (.723), Math Computation (.717), Cloze (.701), Language Expression (.576), and Language Mechanics (.523). The second also received a significant loading from the Cloze test (.523) but got its primary loadings from Reading Vocabulary (.811), and Reading Comprehension (.755). It also received substantial loadings from Language Expression (.696) and Math Concepts (.591). Math Applications also loaded modestly on this factor (.477). The tests with the largest communalities at this grade level were Language Expression (.816), Reading Comprehension (.782), Cloze (.765), Math Applications (.726), and Spelling (.708). All of the tests, however, showed substantial communalities with the two factors extracted.

Two factors also appeared in the ninth grade sample. Factor one received substantial loadings from what would appear to be mainly language based tasks while the second factor received its primary loadings from the math tests. The heaviest loaders on factor one were Reading Vocabulary (.937), Reading Comprehension (.847), Spelling (.781), Language Expression (.628), Cloze (.518), and Language Mechanics (.501). Weak loadings also appeared from Math Computation (.337) and Math Concepts (.303). The second factor received its heaviest loadings from Math Concepts (.940), Math Computation (.870), and Math Applications (.781). It also received weak loadings from Language Expression (.378) and Reading Comprehension (.322). The tests with the largest communalities in this data set were Math Concepts (.975), Reading Vocabulary (.900), Math Computation (.871), and Reading Comprehension (.821).

**TABLE 10.17**

Specificities and Error Terms for Grades 3 to 9 at Rock Point on the *Comprehensive Tests of Basic Skills* and Written Cloze Tests

| Tests | $r_{ii}$ | Grade 3 N = 30 $h^2$ | $b^2$ | $e^2$ | $r_{ii}$ | Grade 4 N = 27 $h^2$ | $b^2$ | $e^2$ | $r_{ii}$ | Grade 5 N = 23 $h^2$ | $b^2$ | $e^2$ |
|---|---|---|---|---|---|---|---|---|---|---|---|---|
| Cloze | .95 | .661 | .289 | .05 | .95 | .380 | .570 | .05 | .92 | .731 | .189 | .08 |
| *Comprehensive Tests of Basic Skills* | | | | | | | | | | | | |
| Read Voc | .92 | .529 | .391 | .08 | .93 | .994 | .000 | .07 | .92 | .999 | .000 | .08 |
| Read Comp | .94 | .842 | .098 | .06 | .94 | .313 | .627 | .06 | .92 | .463 | .457 | .08 |
| Lang Mech | .85 | .755 | .095 | .15 | .86 | .466 | .394 | .14 | .82 | .608 | .212 | .18 |
| Lang Expr | .90 | .200 | .700 | .10 | .91 | .594 | .316 | .09 | .88 | .804 | .076 | .12 |
| Spelling | .89 | .498 | .392 | .11 | .91 | .473 | .705 | .09 | .89 | .188 | .702 | .11 |
| Math Comp | .95 | .316 | .634 | .05 | .95 | .204 | .746 | .05 | .92 | .415 | .505 | .08 |
| Math Con | .89 | .546 | .344 | .11 | .89 | .530 | .360 | .11 | .82 | .558 | .262 | .18 |
| Math Ap | .91 | .415 | .495 | .09 | .92 | .407 | .513 | .08 | .89 | .368 | .522 | .11 |
| Col Means $b^2$ & $e^2$ | | | .382 | .09 | | | .470 | .08 | | | .325 | .11 |
| Grand Means for $h^2$, $b^2$, & $e^2$ | | | | | | | | | | | | |

The final step in the analysis was to examine the specificities of all the tests. These are given by grade in Table 10.17. As in previous chapters, wherever negative specificities would appear they are recorded as zeroes. There were only five occasions where specificity estimates would have been negative. Presumably these are due to unreliabilities attributable to the relatively small sample sizes.

In every case but one (Language Mechanics, a surface oriented test), the mean specificity across all seven grades (see the right most portion of Table 10.17, column two under the heading Row Means) was more than twice as large as the mean error term (column three under Row Means). On the whole, the subscales on the *Comprehensive Tests of Basic Skills* had an average communality of .585 while the Cloze test had a communality of .571. Those subscales had an average speci-

138   *Language and Bilingualism: More Tests of Tests*

ficity of .348 against .359 for the Cloze test. Given the lapse of time between the administration of the *Comprehensive Tests of Basic Skills* and the Cloze, the amount of variance shared by them may be regarded as substantial. The test which had the lowest overall communality with the other tests on the average was Spelling (.472). The one with the greatest communality was Reading Vocabulary (.661).

TABLE 10.17
(continued)

| Tests | Grade 6 N = 40 | | | | Grade 7 N = 22 | | | | Grade 8 N = 22 | | | |
|---|---|---|---|---|---|---|---|---|---|---|---|---|
| | $r_{ii}$ | $h^2$ | $b^2$ | $e^2$ | $r_{ii}$ | $h^2$ | $b^2$ | $e^2$ | $r_{ii}$ | $h^2$ | $b^2$ | $e^2$ |
| Cloze | .91 | .562 | .348 | .09 | .93 | .582 | .348 | .07 | .93 | .765 | .165 | .07 |
| *Comprehensive Tests of Basic Skills* | | | | | | | | | | | | |
| Read Voc | .94 | .261 | .679 | .06 | .93 | .286 | .644 | .07 | .94 | .659 | .281 | .06 |
| Read Comp | .93 | .511 | .419 | .07 | .92 | .633 | .287 | .08 | .93 | .782 | .148 | .07 |
| Lang Mech | .82 | .448 | .372 | .18 | .77 | .207 | .563 | .23 | .80 | .373 | .427 | .20 |
| Lang Expr | .89 | .577 | .313 | .11 | .89 | .698 | .192 | .11 | .90 | .816 | .084 | .10 |
| Spelling | .90 | .602 | .298 | .10 | .88 | .208 | .672 | .12 | .89 | .709 | .181 | .11 |
| Math Comp | .94 | .511 | .429 | .06 | .94 | .986 | .000 | .06 | .95 | .538 | .412 | .05 |
| Math Con | .85 | .952 | .000 | .15 | .85 | .445 | .405 | .15 | .89 | .395 | .531 | .11 |
| Math Ap | .90 | .318 | .582 | .10 | .89 | .542 | .348 | .11 | .91 | .726 | .184 | .09 |
| Col Means $b^2$ & $e^2$ | | | .382 | .10 | | | .384 | .11 | | | .268 | .10 |
| Grand Means $h^2$, $b^2$, and $e^2$ | | | | | | | | | | | | |

TABLE 10.17
(continued)

| Tests | Grade 9 N = 17 | | | | Row Means | | |
|---|---|---|---|---|---|---|---|
| | $r_{ii}$ | $h^2$ | $b^2$ | $e^2$ | $h^2$ | $b^2$ | $e^2$ |
| Cloze | .93 | .314 | .602 | .07 | .660 | .272 | .07 |
| *Comprehensive Tests of Basic Skills* | | | | | | | |
| Read Voc | .91 | .900 | .010 | .09 | .520 | .414 | .07 |
| Read Comp | .91 | .821 | .089 | .09 | .465 | .467 | .07 |
| Lang Mech | .78 | .299 | .481 | .22 | .532 | .310 | .19 |
| Lang Expr | .85 | .537 | .313 | .15 | .432 | .473 | .11 |
| Spelling | .88 | .627 | .253 | .12 | .617 | .290 | .11 |
| Math Comp | .94 | .871 | .069 | .06 | .495 | .450 | .05 |
| Math Con | .86 | .975 | .000 | .14 | .464 | .402 | .12 |
| Math Ap | .87 | .610 | .260 | .13 | .425 | .473 | .10 |
| Col Means $b^2$ & $e^2$ | | | .231 | .12 | | | |
| Grand Means $h^2$, $b^2$, and $e^2$ | | | | | .583 | .349 | .10 |

CONCLUSION

It would seem that semiotic skills play a large part in the variance generated by the *Comprehensive Tests of Basic Skills*. Although two or three factors emerged at each grade level, English language proficiency was an important element underlying nearly all the factors extracted. It seems on the basis of the samples examined here that there may be a trend toward decreasing specificities and increasing communalities as children progress upward through the grades. This finding, incidentally, is consistent with research by Oltman, Stricker, and Barrows (1990) showing a similar trend in an extensive analysis of the *Test of English as a Foreign Language*. They observe that as subjects become more competent in English, the various dimensions (or factors if viewed from a different angle) of the *TOEFL* tend to converge toward greater unity. With respect to school achievement a similar phenomenon might be expected in language maturation which would subsequently blossom into a greater variety of achievement dimensions as specialized knowledge would become increasingly accessible as a result of growth in language abilities.

# Part IV: Achievement and Bilingualism

# Chapter 11
# Language and Achievement of Choctaw-English Bilinguals in Kindergarten

## with Robert Scott
## Texas Education Agency; Austin, Texas

The population sampled for the pilot study reported in this chapter consisted of Choctaw-English bilingual children in Mississippi. They were all at the kindergarten level. In this case, objective scores and subjective ratings were obtained in the primary language (Choctaw) as well as in the secondary language (English) and were regressed onto a measure aimed at assessing readiness for instruction. The purpose was to investigate the importance of primary language development to school performance.

## WHAT ABOUT THE PRIMARY LANGUAGE?
Common sense suggests that understanding the language used at school will help in all sorts of school performances. This assumption seems plausible even prior to any research evidence. But what about development of the primary language of the child when it is different from the language of instruction? Will a child who has advanced farther in the primary language perform better on achievement tests in another language than a child who has developed less skill in the primary language?

Cummins (1978, 1984, 1986) has argued persuasively that in fact the child who has a better foundation in the native language should advance more rapidly. Indeed, he has claimed that unless a certain threshold level of development has been attained before the problem of learning an additional language is confronted, the child will face a severe handicap and may very well fail at schoolwork. This last expectation, however, could turn out to be true only in extreme cases (or not at all), and the weaker claim that development in the primary language is correlated with school performance might still be true. In fact, Skutnabb-Kangas and Toukomaa (1976) found evidence that children whose mother tongue was better developed when they entered school performed significantly better than those whose first language was less well developed at the time they were introduced to instruction in a second language. They argued that sufficient development of the native language is especially important to the acquisition of "the conceptual operations connected with mathematics" (p. 69). Additional evidence along the same lines, and supporting the threshold hypothesis, has been reviewed by Cummins (1984, pp. 107-108).

The theory of a deep factor of semiotic capacity, presented above in Chapter 2, would also suggest a positive relationship between development of skill in the first language and school achievement. Moreover, there is evidence that first and second language skills tend to be substantially correlated (see Oller and Perkins 1978, p. 118, and Cummins, 1979). Therefore, it is plausible that scores in the primary language will be substantially correlated with achievement scores (or in this case, "readiness" scores) in a second language.

## SUBJECTS

The 32 subjects employed in this study represented a population which has not (so far as is known) previously been discussed in published research on language testing. Also, the children studied were somewhat younger than subjects included in previous samples in this volume and elsewhere. The vast majority, approximately 90% of them, came from homes where Choctaw was the main language of communication (parents reported that they used Choctaw 95% of the time). In fact, as shown by the measures discussed below, the reports of parents were quite accurate. The vast majority of the children actually *were* mostly dominant in Choctaw and some appeared to be virtually monolingual in Choctaw when they started kindergarten. From the beginning of the program, they were taught subject matter in Choctaw by paraprofessionals who spoke Choctaw natively, and they were exposed to English as a second language by the regular teachers who spoke English natively.

## TESTS

As the achievement criterion, the *Metropolitan Readiness Test*, Form A (1970) was selected. This test was administered in English by the regular classroom teacher. The instructions given by the publisher were carefully adhered to. Tasks included sound-letter matching, visual figure matching, and listening comprehension, as well as problem-solving with quantitative concepts and operations.

In addition to the criterion for achievement, there were several predictor measures. Among them was the *Test of Basic Experiences* (*TOBE*), Form K. Both the Math and Science subtests from this battery were selected. They were chosen because of their brevity and ease of administration. Each was first interpreted into Choctaw by Choctaw-English bilinguals and reviewed for bias by tribal elders. Afterwards, they were pre-tested, item analyzed, revised, and finally used in the present study.[16]

The tests were administered by the Choctaw-speaking paraprofessionals. The modified version of the *TOBE* Math consisted of 28 items where subjects heard a sentence or question and then made a

---

[16]See Scott (1976a, 1976b, and 1977) for detailed discussion of the procedures employed for adapting the *TOBE* subtests into Choctaw. The items were not merely translated, but were culturally adapted.

selection from one of four pictures. The *TOBE* Science test also contained 28 items in a multiple choice format with four alternatives for each item.

The third predictor test was the *South Western Cooperative Educational Laboratory Test of Oral English Production*. It contains three subtests--Vocabulary, Pronunciation, and Structure. In the *SWCEL* Vocabulary subtest, the examinee names 24 objects. The responses in this portion are analyzed to obtain the *SWCEL* Pronunciation score as well. Phonological elements examined include consonant clusters and vowels--these were apparently derived from a contrastive analysis of English and Spanish. The *SWCEL* Structure subtest is an oral interview in which examinees answer questions about pictures. Responses are scored for surface morphology and syntax.

In addition to the two *TOBE* scores, and the three *SWCEL* scores, ratings of English and Choctaw skills were obtained from the regular teachers and from the paraprofessionals. These ratings provided four additional predictors of the achievement criterion--Teacher Rating of English Skill, Aide Rating of English Skill, Teacher Rating of Choctaw Skill, and Aide Rating of Choctaw Skill.

Also, measures in English and in Choctaw were obtained from the *Bilingual Syntax Measure* (for a review of this test, see Oller, 1976b). The Spanish version of this test was interpreted into Choctaw. The English version, of course, was used without modification.

The predictor measures were administered in February and March of 1976. The criterion measure, the *Metropolitan Readiness Test*, was given in April of the same year. Hence, all the 1976 data were collected over a three month span during the second half of the school year. Under the supervision of the staff of the Bilingual Project, the Choctaw instruments were administered by teacher aides who spoke Choctaw natively while the English instruments were given by the regular classroom teachers. The *Bilingual Syntax Measure* was an exception since it was administered by Scott who served as the linguist on the staff of the Bilingual Project.

## RESULTS AND DISCUSSION

The means and standard deviations are given in Table 11.1 along with the correlations between each of the predictor variables and the criterion, the *Metropolitan Readiness Test*. The language scores and ratings consistently showed a marked advantage in Choctaw over English. In all cases the contrast between assessed skill in Choctaw and English was greater than a full average standard deviation of the two measures in question. For instance, on the *Bilingual Syntax Measure* (assuming a rough equivalence between the Choctaw and English versions of the test), the contrast favored Choctaw by 2.1 average standard deviations. On the teacher ratings, similarly, the advantage went to Choctaw by a margin of 1.4 average standard deviations, and for the teacher aide ratings by 1.7. This consistent contrast and its correspondence to the perceptions of the project staff concerning the relative skill in the two languages suggests that the measures had some validity.

Interestingly, the best predictors of scores on the *Metropolitan Readiness Test* were *TOBE* Science (.69), *TOBE* Math (.67), *SWCEL* Vocabulary (.63), and the English version of the *Bilingual Syntax Measure* (.57). Here it is important to remember that the *TOBE* subtests were obtained through conversations in Choctaw. Another factor which may be at play here is the relatively greater need for attention to content in the *TOBE* tests. Could this factor account for their being somewhat stronger predictors of the criterion? Unfortunately, there were no language measures included in the study that would qualify as fully pragmatic tests.

**TABLE 11.1**

Means and Standard Deviations on the *Metropolitan Readiness Test* and Selected Predictor Measures: 1976 Sample, N = 32

| Tests | m | s | r |
|---|---|---|---|
| *Metropolitan Readiness Test* | 54.96 | 16.44 | ---- |
| PREDICTORS | | | |
| *Test of Basic Experiences*, Math | 15.25 | 4.07 | .67* |
| *Test of Basic Experiences*, Science | 14.84 | 4.62 | .69* |
| *SWCEL* Vocabulary | 14.78 | 5.20 | .63* |
| *SWCEL* Pronunciation | 22.42 | 4.02 | .48* |
| *SWCEL* Structure | 35.28 | 10.66 | .00 |
| Teacher Rating of English Skill | 2.03 | 1.03 | .43* |
| Aide Rating of English Skill | 2.21 | .79 | .47* |
| Teacher Rating of Choctaw Skill | 3.31 | .86 | -.38* |
| Aide Rating of Choctaw Skill | 3.56 | .84 | -.21 |
| *Bilingual Syntax Measure* (English) | 21.06 | 7.44 | .57* |
| *Bilingual Syntax Measure* (Choctaw) | 37.21 | 7.97 | .28 |

*$p < .01$ (one-tailed test)

As in other studies (see especially Chapters 9, 10, and 12 of this volume), the scores assigned on the rating scales seemed to influence each other markedly. This can be seen in the fact that the English ratings by teachers and aides both correlated positively with the readiness criterion (.43 and .47, respectively) while the Choctaw ratings correlated negatively in both cases (-.38 and -.21). Therefore, it may be inferred that when the teachers or aides were inclined to judge a child *higher* in one language they generally judged the same child *lower* in the other language. However, objective scores obtained from the *Bilingual Syntax Measure* tended to correlate positively with the readiness criterion (.57 for English and .28 for Choctaw). The discrepancy between the objective scores and the ratings in this respect can probably be understood as a result of a halo effect in the ratings (cf. Yorozuya and Oller, 1980).

The problem arises due to the mutual influence of scales on which the same subject is rated. This influence is absent from the objective scores both in Choctaw and in English and perhaps this is why they correlate positively (though not always significantly) with the readiness criterion in nearly every case. An exception is the *SWCEL* Structure test which does not correlate at all with the criterion: perhaps this is due to a lack of validity in that test.

Although the *Bilingual Syntax Measure* in Choctaw was not as good a predictor of the readiness criterion ($r = .28$) as the English version of the same test ($r = .57$), the Choctaw versions of the two subscales from the *Test of Basic Experiences* were the best predictors of all ($r = .67$ and $.69$, respectively for Math and Science). Also, the *SWCEL* Vocabulary score was a fairly good predictor ($r = .63$).

A step-wise multiple regression analysis showed that the score on the *TOBE* Science subtest (in Choctaw) and the *SWCEL* Vocabulary score taken together accounted for no less than 63% of the total variance in the *Metropolitan Readiness Test*. By itself, the *TOBE* Science score predicted 48% of the variance and an additional 15% was explained when the *SWCEL* Vocabulary score was added into the equation.

### CONCLUSION

As predicted by the theory discussed above in Chapter 2, both English and Choctaw measures were substantially related to the criterion. This result is consistent with the view that intellectual development (insofar as it is measured by the *Metropolitan Readiness Test* as employed here) is dependent on the development of propositional capabilities. More importantly, there is some evidence here to suggest that skill in the primary language may be an even more important predictor than skill in the language of instruction.

# Chapter 12
# Language and Achievement of Spanish-English Bilinguals, Grades 3-5[17]

In Chapters 8-11, bilingual populations were examined. However, in those studies it was not possible to obtain actual measures of proficiency in English and the primary language of the bilinguals tested. For instance, in Chapter 8 all of the test scores ostensibly represented proficiency in English, achievement, or non-verbal intelligence; in Chapter 10, all of the testing was actually done in English though many of the children had learned Navajo as their first language; in Chapter 11, it was possible to get a measure of proficiency in Choctaw in addition to the scores on English-based achievement tests, but there was no measure aimed explicitly at proficiency in English (only subjective ratings of English ability by teachers and aides were obtained). Here, in Chapter 12, therefore, it may be interesting to examine the relative predictive power of measures of Spanish and English proficiency in relation to achievement scores of Spanish-English bilinguals. Another unique aspect of the present study is that here it was possible to compare a widely used set of procedures for assessing bilingual competencies in Spanish and English, namely, the DeAvila and Duncan *Language Assessment Scales* (often referred to by the abbreviation *LAS*) with a more or less standard application of cloze procedure (also see Laesch and Van Kleeck, 1987).

## PROCEDURE

### SUBJECTS
Seventy-one children from Spanish-English bilingual backgrounds in the San Antonio area were selected (more or less randomly) from school records. There were 23 third graders, 23 fourth graders, and 25 fifth graders. They were characterized as "low in socio-economic status". All of them attended school in an inner city bilingual program. A criterion for inclusion in the data sample was that the child had to have begun school with Spanish as the stronger language. This information was obtained from school records and supplemented in some cases by school personnel.

According to their teachers, on the average, the children at the third grade received approximately 20 minutes of subject matter instruction four times a week in Spanish. The fourth graders got the

---

[17]The data for the present chapter were supplied thanks to help from V. Streiff and Armando Ibarra of the University of Texas at San Antonio. However, what is said here and the conclusions drawn are the sole responsibility of the author.

same type of exposure for 20 minutes each time but only three times per week, and in the fifth grade, instruction conducted in Spanish occurred only four times a week for 15 minutes on each occasion.

TABLE 12.1
Dominance Ratings by Grade Level for Spanish-English Bilinguals in San Antonio, Texas, N = 70

| Grade | N | Only Spanish (1) | Mainly Span. (2) | Equal (3) | Mainly Engl. (4) | Only English (5) | Mean |
|---|---|---|---|---|---|---|---|
| 3 | 22 | 0 | 7 | 7 | 7 | 1 | 3.091 |
| 4 | 23 | 1 | 2 | 14 | 5 | 1 | 3.130 |
| 5 | 25 | 0 | 4 | 10 | 6 | 5 | 3.480 |
| Column Totals | | 1 | 13 | 31 | 18 | 7 | |
| Grand Mean | | | | | | | 3.234 |

TABLE 12.2
Fluency Ratings in English and Spanish

| Grade Language | N | 1 Low | 2 | 3 Mid | 4 | 5 High | Mean Rating |
|---|---|---|---|---|---|---|---|
| 3 English | 22 | 0 | 3 | 7 | 7 | 5 | 3.636 |
| Spanish | 22 | 1 | 3 | 9 | 3 | 6 | 3.455 |
| 4 English | 23 | 4 | 1 | 8 | 8 | 2 | 3.130 |
| Spanish | 23 | 0 | 6 | 9 | 6 | 2 | 3.174 |
| 5 English | 25 | 0 | 2 | 7 | 6 | 10 | 3.960 |
| Spanish | 25 | 2 | 1 | 8 | 9 | 5 | 3.560 |
| Column Totals | | | | | | | |
| English | 70 | 4 | 6 | 22 | 21 | 17 | |
| Spanish | 70 | 3 | 10 | 26 | 18 | 13 | |
| Grand Means | | | | | | | |
| English | | | | | | | 3.575 |
| Spanish | | | | | | | 3.396 |

Dominance and fluency ratings of the type discussed in Chapters 9 and 10 were also obtained for these subjects. (For a more detailed description of the measures, see the discussion of tests below.) The distributions on the Dominance Scale are given in Table 12.1 and on the fluency scales 12.2--in each case, by grade level.

The judgment that all of the children began school as monolingual speakers of Spanish may or may not have been correct since 7 of the children were judged by their teachers to be monolingual in English. Be that as it may, in view of the meager exposure to Spanish during time at school, it is not surprising that dominance was viewed by the teachers as shifting toward English.

According to school administrators, the third graders had experienced the most consistent participation in bilingual schooling in prior grades, but the ratings on the dominance scale do not show any marked difference between children at grade 3 and those at grades 4 and 5. On the whole, the children were rated as slightly dominant in English even at grade 3 (3.09). By grade 5 they were leaning more definitely toward English (3.48).

# TESTS

## CLOZE

Both the Spanish and the English Cloze tests were based on texts used by Streiff (1978). An every-fifth-word deletion ratio was used. The English texts were carefully translated into Spanish following the procedure outlined by Oller, Bowen, Dien, and Mason (1973). The intent was to arrive at texts of roughly equivalent difficulty in Spanish and English. Therefore, the translator tried to use the same register in Spanish that the original writers had used in English. The translations, therefore, were not word for word but rather text for text. Moreover, wherever the local Spanish (the variety known to the children) required a lexical item different from standard Mexican Spanish, the local term was preferred by the translator (Ibarra).

The purpose of the Cloze tests was to allow a comparison to be made between relative skills in English and Spanish on the written task as well as on the subjective ratings (see Tables 12.1 and 12.2 above; also see the more detailed descriptions of the scales themselves which follow.) It was believed that this comparison would also facilitate the interpretation of relationships between language proficiency measures and achievement scores.

## DOMINANCE RATINGS

As in Chapters 9 and 10, a five-point Likert-type scale in the tradition of Spolsky and colleagues was used. A rating of 1 indicated that the teacher thought that the subject was monolingual in Spanish. A rating of 2 meant stronger in Spanish than in English; 3, equally skilled in the two languages; 4, stronger in English than in Spanish; and 5, monolingual in English. (The distributions of subjects by grade are given in Table 12.1 above along with mean ratings for each grade and the grand mean.)

FLUENCY RATINGS

As in Chapters 9 and 10, also, fluency scales were used. As before, a rating of 1 indicated that the subject had low ability in the language, while a rating of 5 indicated high ability. Both Spanish and English ratings were recorded. (See Table 12.2 above for the distribution of subjects by grade and language along with mean scores by grade as well as means averaged across grades.)

*LANGUAGE ASSESSMENT SCALES*

Scores from the *LAS* I for grades K-5 (second edition, developed by DeAvila and Duncan, 1975, 1977) were also obtained. This battery of tests represents an interesting mix of integrative and discrete-point philosophies. These scales were designed to measure bilingual proficiencies in Spanish and English. They consist of five subscales each of which contributes to the overall *LAS* Level score.

SOUND DISCRIMINATION (MINIMAL PAIRS)

This 30 item subtest requires subjects to indicate whether two auditorily presented elements are the same or different. The items are recorded on audio tape.

LEXICAL ITEMS

This part consists of 20 items where the child is asked to name a pictured object, e.g., a "chicken" or a "banana", etc.

PHONEMES

There are 35 items in this section. It is a discrete-point elicited imitation task. The examinee is asked to repeat a word or sequence. In scoring each item, attention is focussed on a certain phonemic element. The problem is to correctly produce the phoneme in question.

SENTENCE COMPREHENSION

In this part, 9 sentences are presented one at a time and the examinee is asked to indicate the picture to which the sentence applies in each case.

PRODUCTION (STORY-TELLING)

A taped story titled "The Silly Old Monster" is presented twice through and then the child is asked to retell the story on the basis of the pictures which accompany the recording. The monster likes pink lemonade, but ends up very sick from drinking pink ink. His friends bring him gifts to ease his distress.

*LAS* LEVEL SCORE

This score is in fact a rating on a scale from 1 to 5 which gives a rough indication of overall ability in either Spanish or English based on the subject's performance on the composite of scales. The scale is positively oriented so that a higher score represents higher skill in the language.

### THE *METROPOLITAN ACHIEVEMENT TESTS*

All of the children were also tested on several parts of the *Metropolitan Achievement Tests*. This battery of tests is quite similar to the *Comprehensive Tests of Basic Skills* (discussed in Chapter 10) and also to the *California Achievement Tests* (Chapter 9), although there are some differences. The third graders took the tests at the Primer II level. This battery of tests is judged appropriate, according to the user's manual, for grades 2.5 to 3.4. The fourth and fifth graders, however, took the battery of tests at the elementary level. The tests at this level are supposed to be appropriate for grades 3.5 to 4.9. Brief descriptions of each part follow:

#### WORD KNOWLEDGE

This subtest contains 40 items at the Primer II level and 50 at the Elementary level. Some of the items require the selection of synonyms, and antonyms. Others require decisions about word classification, e.g., a "grape" is a "fruit".

#### WORD ANALYSIS

This part is not used in the Elementary battery, but does appear in the Primer II inventory. It contains 35 items and is intended to assess knowledge of sound-letter correspondences. The examiner actually says each example word three times. The word is first given once in isolation, then in the context of a sentence, and then again in isolation. The examinee must choose from four alternatives the word that the examiner has said. Each of the distractors is phonetically and/or orthographically similar to the correct word.

#### READING

There are 44 items at the Primer II level and 45 at the Elementary level for this subtest. Two basic types of items are used. About one third of the items require the child to select from a field of alternatives the one statement that best describes a given picture. The remaining two thirds are based on short paragraphs where questions are put in a sentence-completion format. For each item there are four possible choices.

#### LANGUAGE

This subtest is not used at the Primer II level. At the Elementary level there are 50 items. About a fourth of the items in this section purport to assess ability to distinguish questions from statements, and sentences from non-sentences. The other three fourths are aimed at the assessment of punctuation, capitalization, and surface grammar (i.e., "usage"). For instance, the examinee must identify such forms as "*have ate", "*you is" and "*me and Tom" as "errors". (For children who are exposed to non-standard varieties of English, this subtest offers some special problems.)

### MATH CONCEPTS

In this part there are 40 items for both levels. They focus on counting, place values, sets, and measurement. An interesting aspect of this test is that the stem is read aloud by the teacher and may sometimes be fairly complex. Thus, this part may present a listening comprehension problem though it is supposed to be a test of mathematical concepts.

### MATH COMPUTATION

This part contains 33 items at the Primer II level and 40 at the Elementary level. It focusses on the basic arithmetic operations of addition, subtraction, multiplication, and division.

### SPELLING

The teacher dictates a list of words one by one. The task is to spell each word correctly. There are 30 items for the Primer II level and 40 for the Elementary level.

### RESULTS AND DISCUSSION

In the SUBJECTS section above, results have already been presented on the subjective rating scales completed by the teachers. However, for ease of comparison, those scales are also included in Table 12.3 which presents by grade level the means, standard deviations, and estimated reliabilities (wherever reliabilities could be obtained) for each of the measures included in the study.

The scores reported for the Cloze tests in this study, as in Chapters 9 and 10, are based on the criterion of contextual appropriateness. As before, the purpose was to use the maximum amount of reliable variance in the Cloze scores. Although it was observed that the correlations between scores obtained by the exact-word method and the criterion of contextual appropriateness were strong, ranging from .850 to .978 (not tabled), as expected, the scores based on the contextual appropriateness criterion generated slightly higher reliabilities. (This finding is consistent with previous research; Oller, 1979; and Brown, 1983.) For the Spanish Cloze tests the reliabilities of the exact scores across the three grades ranged from .870 to .958 (not tabled) while the reliabilities of the contextually appropriate scores ranged from .947 to .969 (these are KR-21 estimates adjusted for full length tests). On the English Cloze tests the respective ranges were .901 to .947 (not tabled) for exact scores and .953 to .969 for contextually appropriate scores.

From Table 12.3, it is apparent that the children had a substantial advantage in English over Spanish on the Cloze tests at all three grade levels. This tendency was obscured in the *LAS* scores due to the fact that the samples on which the English *LAS* scores and the

Spanish *LAS* scores are based were somewhat different. Also, it must be noted that the *LAS* scores were obtained in the fall semester while the Cloze scores were obtained in the spring. Nonetheless, in grade 5, the English *LAS* mean surpasses the Spanish mean. On the *Metropolitan Achievement Tests*, a consistent pattern of growth is observed.

### TABLE 12.3
Means, Standard Deviations, and Reliabilities for Grades 3, 4, and 5 in a San Antonio Inner City School on English and Spanish Cloze Scores, Dominance and Fluency Ratings, the *Language Assessment Scales*, and the *Metropolitan Achievement Tests*

| Tests | Grade 3 | | | | Grade 4 | | | | Grade 5 | | | |
|---|---|---|---|---|---|---|---|---|---|---|---|---|
| | N | *m* | *s* | $r_{ii}$ | N | *m* | *s* | $r_{ii}$ | N | *m* | *s* | $r_{ii}$ |
| English Cloze | 23 | 27.17 | 14.09 | .969 | 23 | 20.96 | 11.89 | .953 | 25 | 28.84 | 12.13 | .958 |
| Spanish Cloze | 23 | 15.13 | 13.07 | .969 | 23 | 10.43 | 8.89 | .947 | 25 | 14.96 | 10.04 | .947 |
| Dominance | 22 | 3.09 | .92 | ---- | 23 | 3.13 | .81 | ---- | 25 | 3.48 | 1.00 | ---- |
| Eng Fluency | 22 | 3.64 | 1.00 | ---- | 23 | 3.13 | 1.22 | ---- | 25 | 3.96 | 1.02 | ---- |
| Span Fluency | 22 | 3.45 | 1.18 | ---- | 23 | 3.17 | .94 | ---- | 25 | 3.56 | 1.12 | ---- |
| *Language Assessment Scales* | | | | | | | | | | | | |
| Eng Min Pairs | 19 | 21.58 | 4.49 | .840 | 19 | 24.84 | 5.95 | .670 | 23 | 25.26 | 2.96 | .720 |
| Span Min Pairs | 16 | 25.75 | 2.79 | .840 | 11 | 24.18 | 4.12 | .670 | 9 | 27.00 | 1.87 | .720 |
| Eng Lexicon | 19 | 16.79 | 2.80 | .521 | 19 | 18.68 | 2.13 | .830 | 23 | 18.65 | 1.64 | .370 |
| Span Lexicon | 16 | 13.00 | 4.19 | .520 | 11 | 14.27 | 2.69 | .830 | 9 | 14.78 | 2.05 | .370 |
| Eng Phonology | 19 | 29.47 | 6.34 | .840 | 19 | 31.37 | 5.59 | .910 | 23 | 32.34 | 5.19 | .880 |
| Span Phonology | 16 | 33.62 | 3.42 | .840 | 11 | 32.82 | 4.26 | .910 | 9 | 33.56 | 2.30 | .880 |
| Eng Sentences | 19 | 7.26 | 1.69 | .620 | 19 | 8.10 | 1.49 | .540 | 23 | 8.17 | 1.47 | .720 |
| Span Sentences | 16 | 8.25 | 1.18 | .620 | 11 | 8.27 | 1.49 | .540 | 9 | 8.78 | 1.30 | .720 |
| Eng Production | 19 | 2.68 | .95 | ---- | 19 | 3.37 | .95 | ---- | 23 | 3.56 | .73 | ---- |
| Span Production | 16 | 2.94 | .77 | ---- | 11 | 3.18 | .98 | ---- | 9 | 3.56 | .88 | ---- |
| English Total | 19 | 65.63 | 13.20 | ---- | 19 | 76.68 | 13.40 | ---- | 22 | 78.18 | 8.06 | ---- |
| Spanish Total | 16 | 70.38 | 10.31 | ---- | 11 | 72.54 | 13.47 | ---- | 9 | 77.11 | 11.47 | ---- |
| *Metropolitan Achievement Tests* | | | | | | | | | | | | |
| Words | 19 | 2.71 | .59 | .950 | 23 | 3.32 | 1.18 | .950 | 25 | 4.84 | 1.48 | .950 |
| Reading | 19 | 2.52 | .60 | .950 | 23 | 3.37 | .98 | .930 | 25 | 3.85 | 1.02 | .930 |
| Word Analysis | 19 | 3.23 | .77 | .93 | | | | | | | | |
| Language | | | | | 23 | 3.74 | 1.58 | .930 | 25 | 4.67 | 1.32 | .930 |
| Math Concepts | 19 | 3.11 | 1.22 | .890 | 23 | 3.48 | 1.28 | .910 | 24 | 5.33 | 1.11 | .910 |
| Math Comp | 19 | 3.16 | .87 | .910 | 22 | 4.57 | .96 | .910 | 24 | 5.44 | .83 | .910 |
| Spelling | 19 | 3.18 | .99 | .960 | 23 | 3.91 | 1.56 | .970 | 25 | 5.59 | 1.23 | .970 |

As in previous studies, all of the measures, with the exception of some of the subscales on the *LAS* (notably the Lexical Items subtests in Spanish and English), had substantial reliability. For the *LAS* subtests the reliability estimates were taken from the manual by DeAvila and Duncan (1977). The authors of that manual did not indicate what type of reliability estimates these were.

The estimates for the *Metropolitan Achievement Tests* were taken from the user's manual for that test as well. They were designated as approximations to KR-20 estimates adjusted to full length tests.

The next step in the analysis was to examine the correlations between the various measures of language proficiency and the *Metropolitan Achievement Tests*. To begin with three total scores were computed for the achievement tests. First there was an unweighted overall total computed from all common subtests (Word Knowledge, Reading, Math Concepts, and Math Computation). Second, there was a subtotal for the common subtests aimed at reading skills (Word Knowledge and Reading), and third, there was a subtotal for the common subtests aimed at math (Math Concepts and Math Computation). Then, the entire matrix of all correlations between all measures was computed. Here there were two basic questions: for one, how would cloze scores compare with the subtests and overall scores on the *Language Assessment Scales* as predictors of the achievement scores? And for another, what would the factorial structure of the achievement tests turn out to be relative to the measures aimed at language proficiency in Spanish and English?

### TABLE 12.4

Correlations between English and Spanish Cloze Tests, the *Language Assessment Scales*, and Three Composite Scores from the *Metropolitan Achievement Tests*

| Tests | Grade 3 N > 15 < 20 | | | Grade 4 N > 10 < 24 | | | Grade 5 N > 8 < 26 | | | Row Means | | |
|---|---|---|---|---|---|---|---|---|---|---|---|---|
| | Total | Reading | Math | Total | Reading | Math | Total | Reading | Math | Total | Read | Math |
| English Cloze | .690 | .606 | .653 | .712 | .712 | .664 | .689 | .650 | .604 | .697 | .656 | .640 |
| Spanish Cloze | -.048 | .089 | -.124 | .512 | .335 | .597 | .307 | .326 | .230 | .257 | .250 | .234 |
| *Language Assessment Scales* | | | | | | | | | | | | |
| Eng Min Pairs | .149 | .570 | -.137 | .305 | .305 | .258 | .518 | .481 | .387 | .324 | .452 | .169 |
| Span Min Pairs | -.033 | .175 | -.145 | .412 | .248 | .437 | .461 | .251 | .614 | .280 | .225 | .302 |
| Eng Lexicon | .239 | .404 | .092 | .581 | .426 | .604 | .524 | .532 | .412 | .448 | .454 | .369 |
| Span Lexicon | -.164 | .058 | -.260 | .043 | .002 | .065 | .073 | .036 | .102 | -.016 | .032 | -.031 |
| Eng Phonology | .383 | .295 | .364 | .592 | .325 | .697 | -.085 | -.111 | -.037 | .297 | .170 | .341 |
| Span Phonology | -.223 | -.208 | -.192 | .190 | -.140 | .412 | .165 | .069 | .245 | .044 | -.093 | .155 |
| Eng Sentences | .493 | .705 | .270 | .490 | .505 | .404 | .558 | .468 | .596 | .514 | .559 | .423 |
| Span Sentences | .308 | .144 | .346 | .384 | .060 | .548 | .283 | .269 | .244 | .325 | .158 | .379 |
| Eng Production | .495 | .327 | .504 | .435 | .262 | .494 | .644 | .654 | .517 | .525 | .414 | .505 |
| Span Production | .343 | .077 | .432 | -.292 | -.370 | -.151 | -.378 | -.220 | -.485 | -.109 | -.171 | -.068 |
| Eng *LAS* Total | .563 | .564 | .455 | .570 | .401 | .612 | .637 | .651 | .459 | .590 | .539 | .509 |
| Span *LAS* Total | .224 | .080 | .265 | -.077 | -.239 | -.077 | -.235 | -.167 | -.269 | -.029 | -.109 | -.027 |
| Eng *LAS* Level | .487 | .494 | .391 | .600 | .406 | .650 | .612 | .678 | .419 | .566 | .526 | .487 |
| Span *LAS* Level | .191 | .090 | .215 | -.063 | -.243 | .102 | -.065 | .021 | -.151 | .021 | -.044 | .055 |
| Column Means for *LAS* (totals and composite scores excluded) | | | | | | | | | | | | |
| Eng *LAS* Means | .352 | .460 | .219 | .481 | .365 | .491 | .432 | .405 | .375 | | | |
| Sp *LAS* Means | .046 | .049 | .036 | .147 | -.040 | .262 | .121 | .081 | .144 | | | |
| Grand Means for *LAS* (totals and composite scores excluded) | | | | | | | | | | | | |
| English Grand Means | | | | | | | | | | .422 | .410 | .361 |
| Spanish Grand Means | | | | | | | | | | .105 | .030 | .147 |

Since there were insufficient cases on the *Language Assessment Scales* to do factor analyses over all the correlations, and also because of the fact that the *LAS* scores were obtained in the fall while the other scores were from spring testing, only the simple correlations of *LAS* and Cloze scores with the three computed totals for the *Metropolitan Achievement Tests* are examined. As a result, in subsequent steps only the correlations between cloze scores, fluency ratings, and achievement scores can legitimately be analyzed with exploratory factoring methods.

Table 12.4 gives the relevant correlations pertinent to the comparison of the Cloze scores with the *Language Assessment Scales*. While the differences are not great, the Cloze tests correlate more strongly with the three composite scores from the *Metropolitan Achievement Tests* than do the *LAS* scores. This was anticipated because the *LAS* scores were obtained in the fall while the Cloze tests were administered in the spring nearer the time when the achievement tests were given. On the average, somewhat contrary to the usual expectations, the English Cloze test correlated about as well with the Math subtotal as with the Reading subtotal. This was true also for the Spanish Cloze, though the correlations there were weak in the latter case. With the *LAS* scores, however, on the average the Spanish scores do not correlate much with the achievement totals though the English scores do seem to show a positive relationship.

Reading across the rows, and examining the Row Means, we get a rough impression of the effectiveness of the various subtests of *LAS* in predicting the achievement totals. For instance, English Phonology and English Minimal Pairs were both weak predictors, while English Sentences, English Production, and English Lexicon in that order were somewhat better. As pragmatic testing theory predicts (Oller and Streiff, 1975; Oller, 1979), the more integrative tasks in the *LAS* battery were the better predictors. However, none of the *LAS* scales was very strongly correlated with the achievement scores.

### TABLE 12.5
Correlations between Spanish and English Cloze Tests, Fluency Ratings, and the *Metropolitan Achievement Tests* for a Sample of Spanish and English Bilinguals in San Antonio at Grade 3, N > 18 < 23

| Tests | 1 | 2 | 3 | 4 | 5 | 6 | 7 | 8 | 9 | 10 |
|---|---|---|---|---|---|---|---|---|---|---|
| 1 English Cloze | 1.000 | .074 | .274 | -.105 | .635 | .516 | .548 | .577 | .619 | .668 |
| 2 Spanish Cloze | | 1.000 | .115 | .416 | .229 | -.057 | .428 | -.200 | .010 | .158 |
| 3 English Fluency Rating | | | 1.000 | -.576 | .260 | .304 | -.022 | .201 | .074 | .150 |
| 4 Spanish Fluency Rating | | | | 1.000 | .021 | -.194 | .151 | .090 | .137 | .022 |
| *Metropolitan Achievement Tests* | | | | | | | | | | |
| 5 Word Knowledge | | | | | 1.000 | .803 | .735 | .649 | .407 | .617 |
| 6 Reading | | | | | | 1.000 | .593 | .660 | .551 | .414 |
| 7 Word Analysis | | | | | | | 1.000 | .422 | .605 | .762 |
| 8 Math Concepts | | | | | | | | 1.000 | .649 | .401 |
| 9 Math Computation | | | | | | | | | 1.000 | .543 |
| 10 Spelling | | | | | | | | | | 1.000 |

**TABLE 12.6**

Correlations between Spanish and English Cloze Tests, Fluency Ratings, and the *Metropolitan Achievement Tests* for a Sample of Spanish and English Bilinguals in San Antonio at Grade 4, N > 21 < 24

| Tests | 1 | 2 | 3 | 4 | 5 | 6 | 7 | 8 | 9 | 10 |
|---|---|---|---|---|---|---|---|---|---|---|
| 1 English Cloze | 1.000 | .416 | .537 | -.212 | .638 | .718 | .632 | .616 | .566 | .877 |
| 2 Spanish Cloze | | 1.000 | .339 | -.293 | .326 | .306 | .342 | .572 | .573 | .560 |
| 3 English Fluency Rating | | | 1.000 | -.380 | .410 | .308 | .373 | .507 | .204 | .565 |
| 4 Spanish Fluency Rating | | | | 1.000 | -.266 | -.357 | -.420 | -.436 | -.351 | -.285 |
| *Metropolitan Achievement Tests* | | | | | | | | | | |
| 5 Word Knowledge | | | | | 1.000 | .789 | .902 | .864 | .611 | .766 |
| 6 Reading | | | | | | 1.000 | .839 | .694 | .672 | .787 |
| 7 Word Analysis | | | | | | | 1.000 | .838 | .676 | .799 |
| 8 Math Concepts | | | | | | | | 1.000 | .741 | .767 |
| 9 Math Computation | | | | | | | | | 1.000 | .695 |
| 10 Spelling | | | | | | | | | | 1.000 |

**TABLE 12.7**

Correlations between Spanish and English Cloze Tests, Fluency Ratings, and the *Metropolitan Achievement Tests* for a Sample of Spanish and English Bilinguals in San Antonio at Grade 5, N > 23 < 26

| Tests | 1 | 2 | 3 | 4 | 5 | 6 | 7 | 8 | 9 | 10 |
|---|---|---|---|---|---|---|---|---|---|---|
| 1 English Cloze | 1.000 | .540 | .430 | -.064 | .593 | .551 | .580 | .546 | .365 | .513 |
| 2 Spanish Cloze | | 1.000 | .154 | .187 | .247 | .350 | .442 | .255 | .076 | .541 |
| 3 English Fluency Rating | | | 1.000 | .020 | .364 | .114 | .330 | .314 | .306 | .289 |
| 4 Spanish Fluency Rating | | | | 1.000 | -.183 | -.266 | -.121 | -.364 | -.207 | -.092 |
| *Metropolitan Achievement Tests* | | | | | | | | | | |
| 5 Word Knowledge | | | | | 1.000 | .557 | .724 | .553 | .562 | .588 |
| 6 Reading | | | | | | 1.000 | .542 | .617 | .319 | .440 |
| 7 Word Analysis | | | | | | | 1.000 | .532 | .572 | .623 |
| 8 Math Concepts | | | | | | | | 1.000 | .190 | .583 |
| 9 Math Computation | | | | | | | | | 1.000 | .310 |
| 10 Spelling | | | | | | | | | | 1.000 |

The second question about language and achievement scores concerned their factorial structure. In order to form some tentative hypotheses about the relationship between these complex variables in the San Antonio data, the submatrices for which there were sufficient numbers of subjects to justify factoring were used. These are given

158    *Language and Bilingualism: More Tests of Tests*

(above) as Tables 12.5, 12.6, and 12.7--one for each grade level. The variables included were the Spanish and English Cloze tests scored by the criterion of contextual appropriateness, the subjective fluency ratings, and the subscores of the *Metropolitan Achievement Tests.*

Before going on to the factor analyses, there are some points to be noted about the correlation matrices themselves. For instance, the correlation between the English Cloze and Spanish Cloze scores was nil at grade 3, $r = .074$, but at grade 4 the correlation was significant at $p < .024$, $r = .416$, and at grade 5 it was still higher, $r = .540$, and was significant at $p < .003$. Only for children at grade 3 did the Spanish Fluency Rating correlate significantly with the Spanish Cloze ($r = .416$, $p < .027$), and only at grades 4 and 5 did the English Fluency Rating correlate significantly with the English Cloze ($r = .537$ and .430, respectively). Also, it is noteworthy that the English Cloze scores consistently correlated positively with the *Metropolitan Achievement Tests* (unadjusted mean $r = .598$) while the Spanish Cloze scores correlated weakly with those tests (unadjusted mean $r = .287$). This pattern is perhaps what should be expected since the *Metropolitan Achievement Tests* are all largely dependent on English. However, the fluency ratings are less clearly related to the *Metropolitan Achievement Tests.* On the whole the English Fluency Ratings are somewhat positively correlated with the achievement scores (unadjusted mean $r = .281$) while the Spanish Fluency Ratings appear to be somewhat negatively correlated with achievement (unadjusted mean $r = -.190$). Also as expected, the achievement scores are substantially correlated with each other--more so for grades 3 and 4 than for 5 in this sample.

*TABLE 12.8*

Principal Factor Analysis with Iterations (Varimax Rotation) for Spanish and English Cloze Tests, Ratings of Spanish and English Fluency, and the *Metropolitan Achievement Tests* for a Sample of Spanish and English Bilinguals in San Antonio at Grade 3, $N > 18 < 24$

| Tests | Factor One | Factor Two | Factor Three | $h^2$ |
|---|---|---|---|---|
| English Cloze | .726 | -.188 | .170 | .592 |
| Spanish Cloze | .008 | .262 | .624 | .457 |
| English Fluency Rating | .200 | -.587 | -.076 | .390 |
| Spanish Fluency Rating | .076 | .979 | .168 | .991 |
| *Metropolitan Achievement Tests* | | | | |
| Word Knowledge | .789 | -.144 | .305 | .737 |
| Reading | .766 | -.258 | .030 | .655 |
| Word Analysis | .716 | .049 | .648 | .935 |
| Math Concepts | .907 | .063 | -.356 | .955 |
| Math Computation | .735 | .081 | .037 | .548 |
| Spelling | .648 | -.095 | .405 | .593 |

Factor analyses using iteratively determined estimates of communalities on the diagonals of each of the foregoing matrices were also computed. The results of these analyses are reported in Tables 12.8, 12.9, and 12.10.

For the data from the third graders (Table 12.8, below), three factors emerged. The first could probably be defined as an achievement or language proficiency factor. It received its heaviest loadings from Math Concepts (.907), Word Knowledge (.789), Reading (.766), Math Computation (.735), the English Cloze (.726), Word Analysis (.716) and Spelling (.648). The second factor received its heaviest loadings from the fluency scales--especially the Spanish Fluency Rating (.979) with a secondary loading from the English Fluency Rating (-.587). This is no doubt due in part to the halo (or spillover) effect commented on in Chapter 9. Otherwise, the scales ought to be positively correlated with each other, and presumably with the same factor or factors. The third factor was defined mainly by Word Analysis (.648), and Spanish Cloze (.624). The fact that the Spanish Cloze test loads on a factor orthogonal to the one receiving its heaviest loadings from the fluency scales suggests caution in interpreting those scales.

*TABLE 12.9*

Principal Factor Analysis with Iterations (Unrotated Solution) for Spanish and English Cloze Tests, Ratings of Spanish and English Fluency, and the *Metropolitan Achievement Tests* for a Sample of Spanish and English Bilinguals in San Antonio at Grade 4,
N > 22 < 24

| Tests | Factor One | Factor Two | $h^2$ |
|---|---|---|---|
| English Cloze | .779 | .050 | .609 |
| Spanish Cloze | .557 | .564 | .627 |
| English Fluency Rating | .509 | .203 | .301 |
| Spanish Fluency Rating | -.412 | -.112 | .185 |
| *Metropolitan Achievement Tests* | | | |
| Word Knowledge | .877 | -.287 | .851 |
| Reading | .849 | -.263 | .790 |
| Language | .911 | -.293 | .916 |
| Math Concepts | .907 | .072 | .827 |
| Math Computation | .758 | .106 | .586 |
| Spelling | .928 | .096 | .871 |

For the fourth grade data (Table 12.9), two factors emerged. Here, there is a departure from standard practice by using the unrotated solution which seemed to give a more interpretable differentiation of factors. The first factor, as in the case of the third graders, would appear to be a general language or achievement variable. It even received modest loadings from the fluency ratings (English Fluency Rating, .509, and Spanish Fluency Rating, -.412). It is interesting that the Spanish Cloze loaded positively on this factor (.557) while the Spanish Fluency Rating loaded negatively. This suggests, again, the same sort of halo effect associated with the rating scales here as observed earlier for ratings in Hopi and English in Chapter 9 above. That is, if the teachers assigned a high rating in English, they tended to assign a low rating in Spanish somewhat irrespective (it would seem) of the child's actual ability to use Spanish as indicated by the Spanish Cloze scores.

The second factor in the fourth grade data was best defined as a factor of proficiency in written Spanish as indicated by the Spanish Cloze scores. However, it is interesting that the Spanish Cloze scores loaded about equally on the first factor which appeared to be a general factor of achievement--or perhaps deep language proficiency. All of the measures except for the fluency scales showed substantial communalities with one or both factors.

In the fifth grade data (Table 12.10, below) three factors appeared. Again, the unrotated factor solution was somewhat more interpretable than the varimax rotation. The first factor seems to be a general achievement or language proficiency factor having received its strongest loadings from Language (.831), Word Knowledge (.814), Math Concepts (.764), and English Cloze (.760). Again their is a significant correlation with Spanish Cloze (.533), and, encouragingly this time, a positive loading from the English Fluency Rating (.406).

**TABLE 12.10**

Principal Factor Analysis with Iterations (Unrotated Solution) for Spanish and English Cloze Tests, Ratings of Spanish and English Fluency, and the *Metropolitan Achievement Tests* for a Sample of Spanish and English Bilinguals in San Antonio at Grade 5, N > 23 < 26

| Tests | Factor One | Factor Two | Factor Three | $h^2$ |
|---|---|---|---|---|
| English Cloze | .760 | .170 | -.011 | .607 |
| Spanish Cloze | .533 | .711 | .039 | .792 |
| English Fluency Rating | .406 | .004 | -.149 | .187 |
| Spanish Fluency Rating | -.207 | .461 | -.217 | .303 |
| *Metropolitan Achievement Tests* | | | | |
| Word Knowledge | .814 | -.188 | -.174 | .729 |
| Reading | .680 | -.081 | .195 | .507 |
| Language | .831 | .007 | -.200 | .731 |
| Math Concepts | .764 | -.201 | .530 | .905 |
| Math Computation | .548 | -.311 | -.492 | .640 |
| Spelling | .729 | .170 | .058 | .564 |

The second factor is clearly a Spanish proficiency measure. It got its heaviest loadings from Spanish Cloze (.711) and from the Spanish Fluency Rating (.461). The latter is interesting since it suggests that the teachers at this grade level may have had a closer acquaintance with the actual proficiencies of the children than those at the previous grades.

Oddly the third factor appears to be a weak composite of a positive loading from Math Concepts (.530) and a negative loading from Math Computation (-.492; which also loaded somewhat negatively on the second factor, -.311).

The final step in the factor analyses was to examine the specificities and error terms of each of the data samples. Since reliability estimates were not available for the fluency scales, they were excluded from this part of the analysis. The relevant figures for all of the other measures, however, are given in Table 12.11. On the average, the variance of the various tests could be partitioned into .708 communality, .232 specificity, and .061 error variance. It is interesting that the achievement test which tended to have the least specificity was Math Concepts (.029, averaged without adjustments for variations in sample size over the three grades). Perhaps this is because of the nature of that test. It seems to rely heavily on language abilities since the items are presented orally, and it requires some computational operations as well. Possibly it is because of these aspects of the test that it appears to contain almost no specific variance. By contrast, the tests with the greatest specificities were the English Cloze test (.357), the Spanish Cloze test (.329), Math Computation (.319), Spelling (.291), and Reading (.286), in that order. In this case, all of the tests showed large communalities.

**TABLE 12.11**

Specificities and Error Terms on Spanish and English Cloze Tests, Fluency Scales, and the *Metropolitan Achievement Tests*

| Test | Grade 3 $r_{ii}$ | $h^2$ | $b^2$ | $e^2$ | Grade 4 $r_{ii}$ | $h^2$ | $b^2$ | $e^2$ | Grade 5 $r_{ii}$ | $h^2$ | $b^2$ | $e^2$ | Row Means $h^2$ | b2 | $e^2$ |
|---|---|---|---|---|---|---|---|---|---|---|---|---|---|---|---|
| | N > 18 < 31 | | | | N > 21 < 24 | | | | N > 22 < 25 | | | | | | |
| Eng Cloze | .969 | .592 | .377 | .031 | .953 | .609 | .344 | .047 | .958 | .607 | .351 | .042 | .603 | .357 | .040 |
| Span Cloze | .969 | .457 | .512 | .031 | .947 | .627 | .320 | .053 | .947 | .792 | .155 | .053 | .625 | .329 | .046 |
| *Metropolitan Achievement Tests* | | | | | | | | | | | | | | | |
| Word Knowl | .950 | .737 | .213 | .050 | .950 | .851 | .099 | .050 | .950 | .729 | .221 | .050 | .772 | .178 | .050 |
| Reading | .950 | .655 | .295 | .050 | .930 | .790 | .140 | .070 | .930 | .507 | .423 | .070 | .651 | .286 | .063 |
| Word Anal | .930 | .935 | .000 | .070 | | | | | | | | | .935 | .000 | .070 |
| Language | | | | | .930 | .916 | .014 | .070 | .930 | .731 | .199 | .070 | .814 | .107 | .070 |
| Math Con | .890 | .955 | .000 | .110 | .910 | .827 | .083 | .090 | .910 | .905 | .005 | .090 | .896 | .029 | .097 |
| Math Comput | .910 | .548 | .362 | .090 | .910 | .586 | .324 | .090 | .910 | .640 | .270 | .090 | .591 | .319 | .090 |
| Spelling | .960 | .593 | .367 | .040 | .970 | .871 | .099 | .030 | .970 | .564 | .406 | .030 | .676 | .291 | .083 |
| Column Means | | .684 | .266 | .059 | | .760 | .178 | .062 | | .684 | .254 | .062 | | | |
| Grand Means | | | | | | | | | | | | | .708 | .232 | .061 |

CONCLUSION

As in previous chapters, it seems that semiotic factors play the sort of role in the achievement tests examined here predicted by the semiotic model proposed in Chapter 2 above. The picture is not monochromatic, and the factors observed are complex. However, it seems clear that both primary and non-primary language skills are important to performance on achievement tests. An implication of this finding is that Cummins' threshold hypothesis (esp. Cummins, 1984) is worth closer scrutiny than it has received so far. Also, from an educational viewpoint, it would make sense to look at the potential impact of instructional strategies designed to improve discourse and reasoning skills in one or both languages of bilingual students. Monolinguals too should be studied with a view to determining the extent of the impact of acquiring another language. The expectation, on the basis of the research reported here and the theory presented in Chapters 2-4 above, is that becoming thoroughly bilingual can be expected to have a significantly positive impact on cognitive abilities in general (cf. Hakuta, 1986, and Hakuta and Diaz, 1984).

# References

Asher, James J. and Garcia, Robert. 1969. The optimal age to learn a foreign language. *Modern Language Journal* 53, 334-341.

Asher, James J. and Price, B. S. 1967. The learning strategy of the total physical response: some age differences. *Child Development* 38, 1219-1227.

Bachman, Lyle F., and Palmer, Adrian S. 1981. The construct validation of the FSI Oral Interview. *Language Learning* 31, 67-86. Reprinted in Oller (1983b), 154-169.

Bachman, Lyle F., and Palmer, Adrian S. 1982. The construct validation of some components of communicative proficiency. *TESOL Quarterly* 16, 449-465.

Bloom, Benjamin J. 1976. *Human characteristics and school learning.* New York: McGraw Hill.

Bobrow, D. and Collins, A., eds., 1975. *Representation and understanding.* New York: Academic.

Boldt, Robert F. 1989. Latent structure analysis of the *Test of English as a Foreign Language. Language Testing* 6, 123-142.

Bower, T. G. R. 1971. The object in the world of the infant. *Scientific American* 225, 30-38.

Bower, T. G. R. 1974. *Development in infancy.* San Francisco: Freeman.

Boyle, Joseph P. 1987. Intelligence, reasoning, and language proficiency. *Modern Language Journal* 71, 277-288.

Brown, H. Douglas. 1973. Affective variables in second language acquisition. *Language Learning* 23, 231-244.

Brown, James Dean. 1983. A closer look at cloze: validity and reliability. In Oller (1983b), 237-250.

Brown, James Dean. 1988a. *Understanding research in second language acquisition: a teacher's guide to statistics and research design.* Cambridge, England and New York: Cambridge University.

Brown, James Dean. 1988b. Tailored cloze: improved with classical item analysis techniques. *Language Testing* 5, pp. 19-31.

Carroll, John B. 1983a. Psychometric theory and language testing. In Oller (1983b), 80-107.

Carroll, John B. 1983b. Studying individual differences in cognitive abilities: through and beyond factor analysis. In Dillon, R. and Schneck, R., eds., *Individual differences in cognition.* New York: Academic, 1-28.

Cattell, R. B. n. d. *An introduction to IPAT (Cattell's) Culture Fair Intelligence Testing.* Champaign, Illinois: Institute for Personality and Ability Testing.

Cattell, Raymond B. and A. K. S. Cattell. 1960. *Handbook for the Individual or Group Culture Fair Intelligence Test: a Measure of "g" Scale 2: Forms A and B, Children 8-13 years.* Champaign, Illinois: Institute for Personality and Ability Testing.

Chase, A. 1977. *The legacy of Malthus: the social costs of the new scientific racism.* New York: Knopf.

Chomsky, Noam. 1965. *Aspects of the theory of syntax.* Cambridge, Massachusetts: MIT.

Chomsky, Noam. 1972. *Language and mind.* New York: Harcourt, Brace, and Jovanovich.

163

Church, A. 1951. The need for abstract entities in a semantic analysis. *Daedalus* 80, 100-112.
Clark, Brian F. C. 1977. *The genetic code*. London: E. Arnold.
Clifford, Ray T. 1981. Convergent and discriminant validation of integrated and unitary language skills: the need for a research model. In Palmer, Groot, and Trosper (1981), 62-70.
Coles, Gerald S. 1978. The learning disabilities test battery: empirical and social issues. *Harvard Educational Review* 48, 313-340.
Condon, W. S. and Ogston, W. D. 1971. Speech and body-motion synchrony of the speaker-hearer. In Horton, D. L. and Jenkins, J. J., eds., *The perception of language*. Columbus, Ohio: Merrill, 150-173.
Critchley, M. 1955. *The parietal lobes*. London: E. Arnold.
Cummins, Jim. 1976. The influence of bilingualism on cognitive growth: a synthesis of the research findings and explanatory hypotheses. *Working Papers on Bilingualism* No. 9, 1-43.
Cummins, Jim. 1979. Linguistic interdependence and the educational development of bilingual children. *Review of Educational Research* 49, 222-251.
Cummins, Jim. 1981. Wanted: a theoretical framework for relating language proficiency to academic achievement among bilingual students. Presented at the InterAmerica Language Proficiency Assessment Symposium, Arlie House, Virginia, March. In Rivera, Charlene, ed., *Communicative competence approaches to language proficiency assessment: research and application* Clevedon, England: Multilingual Matters, pp. 2-19.
Cummins, Jim. 1983a. Functional language proficiency in context: classroom participation as an interactive process. In Tikunoff, W. J., ed., *Compatibility of the SBIS features with other research on instruction for LEP students*. San Francisco: Far West Laboratory, pp. 109-131.
Cummins, Jim. 1983b. *Heritage language education: a literature review*. Toronto, Canada: Ministry of Education.
Cummins, Jim. 1983c. Language proficiency and academic achievement. In Oller (1983b), 108-130.
Cummins, Jim. 1984. *Bilingualism and special education: issues in assessment and pedagogy* Clevedon, England: Multilingual Matters.
Cummins, Jim. 1986. Empowering minority students: a framework for intervention. *Harvard Educational Review* 56, 18-35.
Cummins, Jim. 1989. "Teachers are not miracle workers": Lloyd Dunn's call for Hispanic activism. *Hispanic Journal of Behavioral Science* 10, pp. 263-272.
Cummins, Jim. and Mulcahy, Robert. 1978. Orientation to language in Ukrainian-English bilingual children. *Child Development* 49, 1239-1242.
Dale, E. and Chall, Jean S. 1948. A formula for predicting readability. *Educational Research Bulletin* 27, 11-20, 28.
Damico, Jack S. 1985. *The effectiveness of direct observation*. Doctoral dissertation, University of New Mexico, Albuquerque.
Damico, Jack S., Oller, John W., Jr., and Storey, Mary E. 1983. The diagnosis of language disorders in bilingual children: pragmatic and surface-oriented criteria *Journal of Speech and Hearing Disorders* 48, 285-294.
DeAvila, E. A. and S. E. Duncan. 1975. *Language Assessment Scales: English/Spanish, technical notes*. Rio Piedras , California: Linguametrics.
DeAvila, Edward A. and Duncan, Sharon E. 1977. *Language Assessment Scales: Level I, examiner's manual*. Corte Madera, California: Linguametrics.
Denton, Michael. 1986. *Evolution: a theory in crisis*. Bethesda, Maryland: Adler and Adler.
Dewey, John. 1938. *Logic: the theory of Inquiry*. New York: Holt.

Dulay, Heidi, Burt, Marina K., and Hernandez-Chavez, Eduardo. 1973. *Bilingual Syntax Measure: technical manual*. New York: Harcourt.

Duncan, Sharon E. and DeAvila, Edward A. 1979. Bilingualism and cognition: some recent findings. *NABE Journal* 4, 15-50.

Dunn, Lloyd. 1965. *Peabody Picture Vocabulary Test: manual* . Circle Pines, Minnesota: American Guidance Service.

Dunn, Lloyd, and Markwardt, Frederick C. Jr. 1970. *Peabody Individual Achievement Test: manual*. Circle Pines, Minnesota: American Guidance Service.

Einstein, Albert. 1941. The common language of science. In *Out of my later years*, author. Secaucus, New Jersey: Citadel, 111-113. Also in Oller (1989b), 61-65.

Einstein, Albert. 1944. Remarks on Bertrand Russell's theory of knowledge. In Schilpp, Paul A., ed., *The philosophy of Bertrand Russell*. New York: Tudor Library of Living Philosophers, 277-291. Also in Oller (1989b), 21-29.

Farhady, Hossein. 1983. On the plausibility of the unitary language proficiency factor. In Oller (1983b), 11-28.

Findley, 1978. Review of the *Comprehensive Tests of Basic Skills*. In Buros, Oscar K., ed., *Mental measurements yearbook*.

Flahive, Douglas E. 1980. Separating the *g* factor from reading comprehension. In Oller and Perkins (1980), 34-46.

Gartner, A., Greer, C., and Reissman, F., eds. 1974. *The new assault on equality: IQ and social stratification*. New York: Harper and Row.

Gregg, Kevin. 1985. Krashen's monitor and Occam's razor. *Applied Linguistics* 5, 79-100.

Gregg, Kevin. 1988. Epistemology without knowledge: Schwartz on Chomsky, Fodor, and Krashen. *Second Language Research* 4, 66-76.

Guilford, Joy P. and B. Fruchter. 1978. *Fundamental statistics in psychology and education*. New York: McGraw Hill.

Guilford, Joy P. 1967. *The nature of human intelligence*. New York: McGraw Hill.

Gunnarsson, B. 1978. A look at the content similarities of between intelligence, achievement, personality and language tests. In Oller and Perkins (1978), 17-35.

Hakuta, Kenji, and Diaz, Rafael. 1984. The relationship between bilingualism and cognitive ability: a critical discussion and some new longitudinal data. In Nelson, Kathy, ed., *Children's language*, Vol. 5, Hillsdale, New Jersey: Lawrence Erlbaum.

Hakuta, Kenji. 1986. *Mirror of language: the debate on bilingualism*. New York: Basic Books.

Hale, Gordon A., Stansfield, Charles W., Rock, Donald A., Hicks, Marilyn M., Butler, Frances A., and Oller, John W., Jr. 1988. *Multiple-choice cloze items and the Test of English as a Foreign Language: Research Report 26*. Princeton, New Jersey: Educational Testing Service.

Hamayan, Else, and Damico, Jack S., eds., in press. *Non-biased assessment of limited English proficient special education students*. Austin, Texas: PRO-ED.

Hanzeli, Victor. 1977. The effectiveness of cloze tests in measuring the competency of students in French in an academic setting. *French Review* 50, 8 65-874.

Hartshorne, Charles, and Weiss, Paul, eds., 1931-1935. *Collected writings of Charles S. Peirce*, Volumes I and VI. Cambridge, Massachusetts: Harvard University.

Herrnstein, Richard J. 1973. *IQ in the meritocracy*. Boston: Little Brown.

Herrnstein, Richard J. and Wagner, A. R. 1981. *Quantitative analysis of behavior*. Cambridge, Massachusetts: Ballinger.

Hieronymus, A. N. 1972. Review of the Tests of Adult Basic Education. In Buros, Oscar K., ed., *Seventh mental measurements yearbook.* New Jersey: Gryphon.

Hinegardner, R. T. and Engelberg, J. 1963. Rationale for a universal genetic code. *Science* 142, 1083-1085.

Hinegardner, R. T. and Engelberg, J. 1964. Comment on a criticism by Woese. *Science* 144, 1031.

Hinofotis, F. B. and B. Snow. 1980. An alternative cloze testing procedure. In Oller and Perkins (1980), 129-133.

Hoyle, Fred. 1983. *The intelligent universe.* London: Michael Joseph.

Jakobson, Roman. 1980. *The framework of language.* Ann Arbor: University of Michigan.

Jensen, Arthur R. 1969. How much can we boost IQ and scholastic achievement? *Harvard Educational Review* 39, 1-23.

Jensen, Arthur R. 1973. *Educability and group differences.* New York: Harper and Row.

Jensen, Arthur R. 1980. *Bias in mental testing.* New York: Free Press.

Jerison, Harry J. 1977. *Evolution of the brain.* In Wittrock, et al, 39-62.

Kant, Immanuel. 1783. *Prolegomena to any future metaphysics.* New York: Liberal Arts, 1950.

Kaufman, Alan S. 1079. *Intelligent testing with the WISC-R.* New York: Wiley.

Kessler, Carolyn, and Quinn, Mary Ellen. 1980. Positive effects of bilingualism on science problem-solving abilities. In Alatis, James E., ed., *Georgetown University Roundtable on Languages and Linguistics.* Washington, D.C.: Georgetown University.

Kieslar, Evan and McNeil, J. 1962. Teaching science and mathematics by auto-instruction in the primary grades: an experimental strategy in curriculum development. In Coulson, J. F., ed., *Programmed learning and computer based instruction.* New York: Wiley.

Kirk, Samuel A., McCarthy, J. J., and Kirk, W. D. 1968. *Illinois Test of Psycholinguistic Abilities.* Urbana: University of Illinois.

Krashen, Stephen D. 1982. *Principles and practice in second language acquisition.* Oxford: Pergamon.

Krashen, Stephen D. 1985. *The input hypothesis: issues and implications.* London and New York: Longman.

Kretschmer, Robert E. in press. Exceptionality and the limited English proficient student: historical and practical contexts. In Hamayan and Damico (in press).

Labov, William. 1970. Systematically misleading data from test questions. Paper presented at the University of Michigan. Also in *The Urban Review* 9, 1976, 146-171.

Laesch, Kelley B. and van Kleeck, Anne. 1987. The cloze test as an alternative measure of language proficiency of children considered for exit from bilingual education programs. *Language Learning* 37, 171-189.

Lambert, Wallace E. 1975. Culture and language as factors in learning and education. In Wolfgang, A., ed., *Education of immigrant students.* Toronto: Ontario Institute for Studies in Education.

Lane, Harlan. 1984. *When the mind hears.* New York: Random House.

Lane, Harlan. 1988. Educating the American Sign Language minority of the United States: a paper for the Commission on the Education of the Deaf. In Wilcox (1988), 221-230.

Lenneberg, Eric. 1967. *Biological foundations of language.* New York: Wiley.

Lotz, John 1951. Natural and scientific languages. *Daedalus* 80, 87-88.

Luria, Alexander R. 1961. *The role of speech in the regulation of normal and abnormal behavior.* New York: Irvington.

Luria, Alexander R. 1973. *The working brain: an introduction to neuropsychology*. Tr. B. Haigh. New York: Penguin.

Luria, Alexander R., and Yudovich, F. A. 1959. *Speech development and the mental processes of the child*. London: Staples.

Macnamara, John 1973. The cognitive strategies of language learning. In Oller, John W., Jr. and Richards, Jack C., eds., *Focus on the learner*. Rowley, Massachusetts: Newbury House, 57-65.

Macnamara, John 1982. *Names for things: a study of human learning*. Cambridge, Massachusetts: MIT.

Matthews, G. H. 1976. Bilingual education at Crow Agency. *Studies in Language Learning* 1 , 265- 287.

McClelland, David. 1971. Testing for competence rather than for intelligence. Public lecture at Educational Testing Service, Princeton, New Jersey. Also in *American Psychologist* 28, 1973, 1-14.

Moore, Edward C., et al., eds., 1984. *Writings of Charles S. Peirce: a chronological edition*. Volume 2. Indianapolis: Indiana University.

Nagel, Ernest. 1959. Charles Sanders Peirce: a prodigious but little known American philosopher. *Scientific American* 200, 185-192.

Naismith, A. 1962. *1200 notes quotes and anecdotes*. Moody: Chicago.

Newmark, Leonard. 1966. How not to interfere with language learning. *International Journal of American Linguistics* 32. Also in Najam, Edward W. and Hodge, Carlton T., eds., *Language learning: the individual and the process*. Bloomington, Indiana: Indiana University, and in Oller, John W., Jr. and Richard-Amato, Patricia, eds., *Methods that work: a smorgasbord of ideas for language teachers*. Rowley, Massachusetts: Newbury House, 49-58.

Oller, John W., Jr. 1972. Scoring methods and difficulty levels for cloze tests of proficiency in English as a second language. *Modern Language Journal* 56, 151-158.

Oller, John W., Jr. 1976a. Evidence for a general language proficiency factor: an expectancy grammar. *Die Neuren Sprachen* 76, 165-174. Also in Oller (1983b), 3-10.

Oller, John W., Jr. 1976b. Review essay: the measurement of bilingualism. *Modern Language Journal* 60, 399-400.

Oller, John W., Jr. 1979. *Language tests at school*. London: Longman.

Oller, John W., Jr. 1981. Language as Intelligence? *Language Learning* 31, 465- 492.

Oller, John W., Jr. 1983a. A consensus for the 80's? In Oller (1983b), 351-356.

Oller, John W., Jr., ed., 1983b. *Issues in language testing research*. Rowley, Massachusetts: Newbury House.

Oller, John W., Jr. 1986. Communication theory and testing: what and how? In Stansfield, Charles W., ed., *Proceedings of the second international invitational Conference on the Test of English as a Foreign Language*. Princeton, New Jersey: Educational Testing Service, 99-179.

Oller, John W., Jr. 1988. *The input hypothesis: issues and implications* by Stephen D. Krashen 1985 London and New York: Longman. *Language* 64, 171-173.

Oller, John W., Jr. 1989a. Conclusions toward a rational pragmatism. In Oller (1989b), 223-250.

Oller, John W., Jr., ed., 1989b. *Language and experience: classic pragmatism*. Lanham, Maryland: University Press of America.

Oller, John W., Jr., Bowen, D., Dien, T. T., and Mason, V. 1972. Cloze tests in English, Thai, and Vietnamese. *Language Learning* 22, 1-15.

Oller, John W.,Jr. and Damico, Jack S. In press. Theoretical considerations in the assessment of LEP students. In Hamayan and Damico (in press).

Oller, John W.,Jr. and Hinofotis, Frances B. 1980. Paper presented at the Annual Meeting of the Linguistic Society of America, 1976, Philadelphia. Reprinted with some changes in Oller and Perkins (1980), 13-23.

Oller, John W., Jr. and Perkins, Kyle, eds., 1978. *Language in education: testing the tests.* Rowley, Massachusetts: Newbury House.

Oller, John W., Jr. and Perkins, Kyle, eds., 1980. *Research in language testing.* Rowley, Massachusetts: Newbury House.

Oller, John W., Jr., and Streiff, Virginia. 1975. Dictation: a test of grammar-based expectancies. *English Language Teaching.* 30, 25-36. Also in Jones, Randall L. and Spolsky, Bernard, eds., *Testing language proficiency*, Arlington, Virginia: Center for Applied Linguistics, 71-88.

Olson, David. 1977. From utterance to text: the bias of language in speech and writing. *Harvard Educational Review* 47, 257-281.

Oltman, Philip K., Stricker, Lawrence J., and Barrows, Thomas S. 1990. Analyzing test structure by multidimensional scaling. *Journal of Applied Psychology* 75, 21-27.

Ortiz, Alba A. and Yates, James R. 1983. Incidence of exceptionality among hispanics: implications for manpower planning. *NABE Journal* 7, 41-54.

Osgood, Charles E. 1957a. A behavioristic analysis of perception. In de Sola Pool, Ithiel, ed., *Contemporary approaches to cognition.* Cambridge, Massachusetts: Harvard.

Osgood, Charles E. 1957b. Motivational dynamics and language behavior. In *Nebraska symposium on motivation.* Lincoln: University of Nebraska.

Paraskevopoulos, J. N. and Samuel A. Kirk. 1969. *The development and psychometric characteristics of the Revised Illinois Test of Psycholinguistic Abilities.* Urbana, Illinois: University of Illinois.

Palmer, Adrian S., de Groot, Peter J. M. and Trosper, George. *The construct validation of oral proficiency tests.* Washington: D. C., TESOL.

Palmer, Leslie and Spolsky, Bernard. 1975. *Papers on language testing 1967-1974.* Washington: D. C., TESOL.

Piaget, Jean. 1947. *The psychology of intelligence.* Totowa, New Jersey: Littlefield Adams.

Piatelli-Palmarini, Massimo, ed., 1980. *Language and learning: the debate between Jean Piaget and Noam Chomsky.* Cambridge, Massachusetts: Harvard.

Pribram, Karl. 1971. *Languages of the brain.* Englewood Cliffs, New Jersey: Prentice-Hall.

Purcell, Edward T. 1983. Models of pronunciation accuracy. In Oller (1983b), 133-153.

Raven, J. C. 1965. *Guide to using the Colored Progressive Matrices, Sets A, AB, and B.* London: H. K. Lewis.

Roth, D. 1978. *Raven's Progressive Matrices as cultural artifacts.* In Hall, W. S. and Cole, Michael, eds., *Quarterly Newsletter of the Laboratory of Comparative Human Psychology* 1, 1-15.

Rumelhart, D. 1975. Notes on a schema for stories. In Bobrow and Collins (1975), 211-236.

Russell, B. 1919. *Introduction to mathematical logic.* London: Allen and Unwin.

Sagan, Carl. 1978. *The dragons of Eden: speculations on the evolution of human intelligence.* New York: Ballantine.

Schank, Roger. 1975. The structure of episodes in memory. In Bobrow and Collins (1975), 237-272.

Schank, Roger. 1980. Language and memory. *Cognitive Science* 4, 243-284.

Schank, Rover, and Abelson, Robert P. 1977. *Scripts, plans, goals, and understanding.* Hillsdale, New Jersey: Erlbaum.

Schumann, John. 1975. Affective factors and the problem of age in second language acquisition. *Language Learning* 25, 209-235.

Schumann, John. 1986. Research on the acculturation model for second language acquisition. *Journal of Multilingual and Multicultural Development* 7, 379-392.

Scott, J. Robert. 1976a. *Annual evaluation report: bilingual education for Choctaws of Mississippi*. Unpublished manuscript. Philadelphia, Mississippi.

Scott, J. Robert. 1976b. *Test development in the native language*. Unpublished manuscript. Philadelphia, Mississippi.

Scott, J. Robert. 1977. *Annual evaluation report: bilingual education for Choctaws of Mississippi*. Unpublished manuscript. Philadelphia, Mississippi.

Scovel, Thomas. 1988. *A time to speak: a psycholinguistic inquiry into the critical period for human speech*. Cambridge, Massachusetts: Newbury House.

Selinker, Larry. 1972. Interlanguage. *International Review of Applied Linguistics* 10, 209-231.

Shuy, Roger W. 1978. Problems in assessing language ability in bilingual education. In Lafontaine, H., Persky, H., and Golubchick, L., eds., *Bilingual education*. Wayne, New Jersey: Avery.

Shuy, Roger W. 1981. Conditions affecting language learning and maintenance among Hispanics in the United States. *NABE Journal* 6, 1-18.

Skutnabb-Kangas, T. and Toukomaa, P. 1976. *Teaching migrant children's mother tongue and learning the language of the host country in the context of the socio-cultural situation of the migrant family*. Helsinki: The Finnish National Commission for UNESCO.

Spearman, Charles E. 1904. "General intelligence" objectively determined and measured. *American Journal of Psychology* 15, 201-293.

Spearman, Charles E. and Jones, L. Wynn 1950. *Human ability*. London: Macmillan.

Spener, David. 1988. Transitional bilingual education and the socialization of immigrants. *Harvard Educational Review* 58, 133-153.

Spolsky, Bernard. 1985. A critical review of Krashen. Lecture presented at the University of New Mexico.

Spolsky, Bernard. 1988. Review: Rod Ellis, *Understanding second language acquisition*. Oxford University Press, 1986. Robert C. Gardner, *Social psychology and second language learning: the role of attitudes and motivation*. Edward Arnold, 1985. *Applied Linguistics*, 9, 100-110.

Spolsky, Bernard, Murphy, Penny, Holm, Wayne, and Ferrel, Allen. 1972. Three functional tests of oral proficiency. *TESOL Quarterly* 6, 221-235. Also in Palmer and Spolsky (1975), 76-90.

Sternberg, Robert J. 1982. *Handbook of human intelligence*. New York: Academic.

Streiff, Virginia A. 1978. Relationships among oral and written cloze scores and achievement test scores in a bilingual setting. In Oller and Perkins (1978), 65-102.

Streiff, Virginia A. 1983. The roles of language in educational testing. In Oller (1983b), 343-350.

Stump, Thomas A. 1978. Cloze and dictation tasks as predictors of intelligence and achievement. In Oller and Perkins (1978), 36-64.

Swanson, Henry L. 1988. Toward a metatheory of learning disabilities. *Journal of Learning Disabilities* 21, 196-209.

Teitelbaum, H. 1976. *Testing bilinguality in elementary school children*. Unpublished doctoral dissertation, University of New Mexico, Albuquerque.

Thorndike, E. L. 1921. Intelligence and its measurement. *Journal of Educational Psychology* 12, 124-127.

Tucker, G. Richard, and Gray, Tracy C. 1980. The pursuit of equal opportunity. *Language and Society* 2, 5-8.

Upshur, John A. and Homburg, Taco J. 1983. Some relations among language tests at successive ability levels. In Oller (1983b), 188-202.

Vigil, Neddy, and Oller, John W. Jr. 1976. Rule fossilization: a tentative model. *Language Learning* 26, 281-295.

Vollmer, Helmut J. and Sang, Fritz. 1983. Competing hypotheses about second language ability: a plea for caution. In Oller (1983b), 29-79.

Von Neumann, John. 1966. *Theory of self-reproducing automata*. Urbana-Champaign, Illinois: University of Illinois.

Vygotsky, Lev Semenovich. n.d. *Mind in society: the development of higher psychological processes*. Edited by Michael Cole, Vera John-Steiner, Sylvia Scribner, and Ellen Souberman, 1978. Cambridge, Massachusetts: Harvard University.

Vygotsky, Lev Semenovich. 1934. *Thought and language*. Moscow-Leningrad: Sozekgiz. Tr. by E. Hanfmann and G. Vakar and printed in English 1962, Cambridge, Massachusetts: MIT.

Wesman, A. G. 1968. Intelligent testing. *American Psychologist* 23, 267-274.

Wilcox, Sherman, ed., 1988. *Academic acceptance of American Sign Language: Sign Language Studies, Special Issue*. 59. Silver Spring, Maryland: Linstok.

Wittrock, M. C. 1963. Response mode in the programming of kinetic molecular theory concepts. *Journal of Educational Psychology* 54, 89-93.

Wittrock, M. C. 1977. The generative process of memory. In Wittrock, et al. 153-184.

Wittrock, M. C., Beatty, Jackson, Bogen, Joseph E., Gazzaniga, Michael S., Jerison, Harry J., Krashen, Stephen D., Nebes, Robert, and Teyler, Timothy J. 1977. *The human brain*. Englewood Cliffs, New Jersey: Prentice Hall.

Woese, Carl R. 1967. *The genetic code: the molecular basis for genetic expression*. New York: Harper and Row.

Wolfram, W. and Christian, D. 1977. On the application of sociolinguistic information: test evaluation and dialect differences in Appalachia. In Shopen, Timothy, ed., *Variation in the structure and use of English*. New York: Winthrop.

Wolpert, Gordon. 1978. Pattern formation in biological development. *Scientific American* 239, 154-164.

Yorozuya, Ryuichi, and Oller, John W., Jr. 1980. Oral proficiency scales: construct validity and the halo effect. *Language Learning* 30, 135-153.

Young, J. Z. 1978. *Programs of the brain*. Oxford, England: Oxford University.

# Tests, Manuals, and Reports

*Adult Performance Level Manual.* n. d. Austin: University of Texas.
*Bilingual Syntax Measure.* 1973. (Heidi Dulay, Marina K. Burt, and Eduardo Hernandez-Chavez) New York: Harcourt.
*California Achievement Tests.* 1970. Monterey, California: McGraw Hill (CTB).
*California Achievement Tests: Technical Bulletin 1.* 1970. Monterey, California: McGraw Hill (CTB).
*Cattell's Culture Fair Intelligence Tests, Scale 2, Forms A and B.* 1938-56. (Raymond B. Cattell)
*Colored Progressive Matrices.* 1956, 1962. (J. C. Raven) Essex, England: E. T . Heron, and New York: Psychological Corporation.
*Comprehensive Tests of Basic Skills.* Monterey, California: McGraw Hill (CTB).
*Illinois Test of Psycholinguistic Abilities: Examiner's Manual, Experimental Edition.* 1961. (James J. McCarthy and Samuel A. Kirk) Urbana, Illinois: University of Illinois.
*Illinois Test of Psycholinguistic Abilities.* 1963. (James J. McCarthy and Samuel A. Kirk) The construction, standardization, and statistical characteristics of the *Illinois Test of Psycholinguistic Abilities.* Urbana, Illinois: University of Illinois.
*Illinois Test of Psycholinguistic Abilities.* 1961. (James J. McCarthy and Samuel A. Kirk) Urbana, Illinois: University of Illinois.
*Language Assessment Scales: English/Spanish, LAS I for Grades K-5.* 1975, 1977. Second edition. (E. A. DeAvila and S. E. Duncan) Rio Piedras, California: Linguametrics.
*Metropolitan Readiness Test.* 1970. New York: Harcourt.
*Peabody Individual Achievement Test: Volumes I and II.* 1970. (Lloyd M. Dunn and Frederick C. Markwardt, Jr.) Circle Pines, Minnesota: American Guidance Service.
*Peabody Picture Vocabulary Test.* 1965. (Lloyd M. Dunn) Circle Pines, Minnesota: American Guidance Service.
*Peabody Picture Vocabulary Test: Manual.* 1965. (Lloyd M. Dunn) Circle Pines, Minnesota: American Guidance Service.
*Raven's Progressive Matrices.* 1938-1965. (J. C. Raven and H. K. Lewis) New York: Psychological Corporation.
*Southwestern Cooperative Educational Laboratory Test of Oral English Production.* 1970. SWCEL: Albuquerque, New Mexico.
*Test of Basic Experiences.* 1971. (Del Monte Research Park) Monterey, California: McGraw Hill.
*Tests of Adult Basic Education: Publisher's Manual.* 1976. Monterey, California: McGraw Hill.
*Tests of Adult Basic Education: Technical Report.* 1976. Monterey, California: McGraw Hill.
*Test of Non-Verbal Reasoning.* 1963. Washington, D. C.: Richardson, Bellows, and Henry.
*Test of Non-Verbal Reasoning: Directions for Administering and Scoring.* 1963. Washington, D. C.: Richardson, Bellows, and Henry.
*Wechsler Intelligence Scales for Children.* 1949-1974. (David Wechsler) New York: Psychological Corporation.

# Index

abductive 6
Abelson, Robert P. 57, 169
acquisition 17, 20-23, 29, 45, 59, 85, 143, 163, 166, 169, 170
Adult Performance Level xi, 65, 69-73
Alatis, James E. 166
American Sign Language (ASL) 16, 22, 167, 170
APL (Adult Performance Level) xi, 65, 69-73
Asher, James J. 20, 163
ASL 22
auditory xii, xiii, 29, 95, 99, 100, 105-112
Bachman, Lyle F. 5, 163
Balbiani 41
Basic Interpersonal Communicative Skills (from Cummins) 25-27
Barrows, Thomas S. 4, 50, 139, 168
Beatty, Jackson 171
Bellugi, Ursula xii, xiii, 9, 95, 101, 106-108, 110, 111, 112
Berk, Virginia v, 8, 9, 75, 85
BICS (Basic Interpersonal Communicative Skills, from Cummins) 25-27
bilingual iii, ix, 7, 9-11, 24, 25, 29, 93, 95, 113, 125, 143, 145-148, 150, 151, 162, 164, 165, 167, 169-171
bilingualism i, ix, 24, 29, 126, 141, 164-167
bilinguality 170
Blanco, George 11
Bloom, Benjamin 127, 163
Bobrow, D. 163, 169
Bogen, Joseph E. 171
Boldt, Robert F. 4, 50, 163
Bowen, J. Donald 150, 168
Bower, T. G. R. 17, 19, 163
Boyle, Joseph P. iv, 3, 5, 6, 8, 163
Brown, H. Douglas 21, 163
Brown, James Dean 70, 88, 113, 153, 163
Buros, Oscar K. 165, 166
Burt, Marina K. 165, 171
Butler, Frances (also known as Frances Butler Hinofotis) 165
CALP (Cognitive Academic Language Proficiency, from Cummins) 25-27
Carroll, John B. 3, 4, 49, 50, 163
Cattell, Raymond B. xii, xiii, 9, 51-53, 95, 100, 102, 103, 106, 107, 108, 110-112, 163, 171
Chall, Jean S. 87, 126, 164
Chase, A. 30, 163

Chavez-Oller, Mary Anne 165, 171
Chesarek, Steve i, v, 9, 95
Chomsky, Noam A. 12, 14, 17, 19, 29, 32, 45, 164, 165, 169
Chomskyan 27
Christian, D. 64, 171
Church, Alonzo 22, 104, 164
Clark, Brian F. C. 37, 39, 43, 164
Clarke, Mark A. 11
Clifford, Ray T. 49, 164
cloze xii, xiii, xiv, xv, xvi, 9, 10, 87-91, 113, 114, 116-138, 148, 150, 153-161, 163, 165, 166, 167, 168, 170
Cognitive Academic Language Proficiency (from Cummins) 25-27
Cole, Michael 169, 170
Coles, Gerald S. 27, 30, 63, 74, 164
Comprehensive Test of Basic Skills 128ff
Collins, A. 163, 169
communality 8, 9, 49, 69, 71, 72, 82-84, 90, 91, 111, 123, 131, 132, 134, 137, 138, 161
Condon, W. S. 16, 164
correlation 4, 49, 66-68, 71, 86, 87, 106, 117-120, 129, 158, 160
Coulson, J. F. 166
Critchley, M. 43, 164
CTBS (Comprehensive Test of Basic Skills) 128
Cummins, Jim 5, 24-27, 29, 30, 63, 74, 143, 144, 162, 164
Dale, E. 87, 126, 164
Damico, Jack S. 11, 27, 30, 74, 164, 166, 168
de Sola Pool, Ithiel 168
DeAvila, E. A. 10, 24, 148, 151, 154, 165, 171
Defense Language Institute 76, 78, 85, 86
deictic 15
deixis 27
Delisle, Helga 11
Denton, Michael J. 37, 38, 41-46, 165
Dewey, John iv, 4, 6, 29, 35, 36, 38, 165
Diaz, Rafael 24, 29, 162, 165
Dien, Ton That 150, 168
Dillon, R. 163
DLI (Defense Language Institute) 76, 78, 85, 86
Dulay, Heidi 165, 171
Duncan, Sharon 24, 148, 151, 154, 165, 171
Dunn, Lloyd 105, 106, 164, 165, 171

172

ECL (English Comprehension Level) 75, 78, 80, 81, 87-89
eigenvalue 90
Einstein, Albert iv, 4, 11, 12, 14, 22, 26, 29, 34, 165
Ellis, Rod 170
English Comprehension Level 75, 78, 80, 81, 87-89
Engelberg, J. 37, 166
ESL ix, 9, 61, 75, 85-87, 89, 90
Farhady, Hossein 3, 4, 50, 165
Ferrel, Allen 170
Findley, Charles A. 127, 165
Flahive, Douglas 79, 85, 165
Fodor, Jerry A. 45, 165
Foreign Service Institute 163
Fruchter, B. 70, 165
FSI (Foreign Service Institute) 163
Garcia, Robert 20, 163
Gardner, Robert C. 170
Gartner, A. 63, 64, 165
Gazzaniga, Michael 171
giftedness 30
Golubchick, L. 169
Grammatic Closure 95, 99, 100, 105-110, 112
graphemic 115
Gray, Tracy 73, 170
Greer, C. 63, 165
Gregg, Kevin 20, 21, 23, 165
Groot, Peter J. M. 164, 168
Guilford, Joy P. 70, 165
Gunnarsson, Bjarni 3, 5, 55, 64, 96, 165
Haigh, B. 167
Hakuta, Kenji 24, 29, 162, 165
Hale, Gordon A. 89, 165
Hamayan, Else 11, 74, 166, 168
Hanfmann, E. 170
Hanzeli, Victor 88, 166
Hartshorne, Charles 22, 166
Haskell, John 11
Hernandez-Chavez, Eduardo 165, 171
Herrnstein, Richard 56, 63, 166
Hicks, Marilyn 165
Hieronymus, A. N. 76, 166
Hinegardner, R. T. 37, 166
Hinofotis, Frances Butler 5, 89, 166, 168
Hodge, Carlton 167
Holm, Wayne 114, 170
Horton, D. L. 164
Hoyle, Sir Fred 37, 166
Ibarra, Armando v, 10, 148, 150
iconic 14, 15, 60
Illinois Test of Psycholinguistic Abilities xvii, 52, 163
index ix, 14, 15, 67, 68, 77, 172
inductive 6
intellect 11, 12, 19, 29-31, 49
intelligence iv, ix, xii, xiii, 4-12, 21, 26, 29, 30, 31, 32, 35-40, 47, 49-52, 59, 60, 63, 64, 65, 85-87, 95, 100, 102, 103, 107, 108, 109, 111, 112, 148, 163, 165, 167, 168, 169-171
intelligent 35, 37-40, 86, 87, 166, 170
interlanguage 169
intertranslatability 19, 23
ITPA (Illinois Test of Psycholinguistic Abilities) xii, xiii, 107-112
Jakobson, Roman 26, 60, 166
Jenkins, J. J. 164
Jensen, Arthur Robert iii, 50, 51, 56, 63, 85, 102, 166
Jerison, Harry 49, 166, 171
John-Steiner, Vera 170
Jones, L. Wynn 170
Kant, Immanuel 29, 38, 166
Kaufman, Alan S. 49, 50, 90, 104, 111, 112, 166
Kepler, Johannes 46
Kessler, Carolyn 24, 166
Kieslar, Evan 60, 166
kinesic 8, 11, 14-17, 19, 20, 25-27, 30, 32, 33
Kirk, Samuel A. 99, 100, 106, 166, 168, 171
Kirk, W. D. 166
Kleeck, Anne van 148, 167
Krashen, Stephen D. 5, 23, 165, 166, 168, 170, 171
Kretschmer, Robert E. 22, 166
Krueger, Anne v, 9, 85
Labov, William 64, 167
Lackland Air Force Base 76, 85, 87
Laesch, Kelley 148, 167
Lafontaine, H. 169
Lambert, Wallace E. 24, 167
Lane, Harlan 22, 167
langue 32
Lau-scales 114, 125, 126
Leibnitz, Gottfried Wilhelm von 6
Lenneberg, Eric 43, 167
LEP (Limited English Proficiency) 164, 168
Lewis, H. K. 41, 169, 171
Likert scale 114, 150
Lotz, John 22, 104, 167
Luria, A. R. 22, 167
Macnamara, John 23, 167
Markwardt, Frederick C., Jr. 105, 165, 171
Mason, Victor 150, 168
Matthews, P. H. 95, 167
McCarthy, J. J. 99, 100, 166, 171
McClelland, David 64, 65, 76, 167
Mcneil, J. 60, 166
metalinguistic awareness 24, 27
monolinguals ix, 9, 27, 29, 61, 63, 162
Moore, Edward C. 14, 167
Mueller, H. J. 11
Mulcahy, Robert 24, 164
multicultural v, 169
multilingualism 24
multilinguals 7, 27
Murphy, Penny 114, 170

NABE (National Association of Bilingual Education) 165, 168, 169
Nagel, Ernst 6, 167
Naismith, A. 46, 167
Najam, Edward W. 167
Nebes, Robert 171
Newmark, Leonard 22, 167
Ogston, W. D. 16, 164
Oller, John W., Jr. i, iv, 3-7, 11, 12, 14, 21, 23, 25-27, 29, 30, 33, 35, 56, 74, 88, 113, 114, 128, 144, 145, 147, 150, 153, 156, 163-171
Olson, David 25-27, 168
Oltman, Philip K. 4, 50, 139, 168
orthogonal 159
Ortiz, Alba 30, 73, 168
Osborn, Joyce v, 9, 85
Osgood, Charles E. 99, 168
Paivio, Alan 59, 60
Palmer, Adrian S. 5, 163, 164, 168
Palmer, Leslie 168, 170
Paraskevopoulos, J. N. 106, 168
parole 32
Peabody tests xii, xiii, 9, 95, 96, 100, 103-112, 165, 171
Pearson, Karl 67
Peirce, Charles S. iv, 4, 6, 8, 12, 14-16, 22, 26, 29, 34, 35, 60, 104, 166, 167
Peircean 6, 25, 26
Perkins, Kyle v, 3, 7, 56, 144, 165, 166, 168, 170
persKy, H. 169
physico-chemical 41
Piaget, Jean 17, 22, 29, 31, 169
PIAT (Peabody Individual Achievement Test) xvii, 96-98, 107-112
Piatelli-Palmarini, Massimo 17, 45, 169
pragmatic iv, xvii, 12, 13, 17, 18, 26, 27, 37, 38, 55, 58, 60, 101, 146, 156, 164
pragmatic mapping xvii, 12, 13, 17, 18, 27, 38, 58, 60
pragmatics 28, 99
Pribram, Karl 42, 169
Price, B. S. 20, 163
proposition 15, 33-35, 37, 52, 53, 55, 57, 58
propositional 8, 19, 31, 33, 39, 40, 43, 51-60, 85, 86, 103, 104, 123, 147
psycholinguistic xii, xiii, 9, 95, 99, 104-110, 112, 166, 168, 169, 171
psychometricians 8, 49
Purcell, E. 5, 169
Quinn, Mary Ellen 24, 166
Quinzio, Sandra di v, 9, 85
Raven, J. C. xii, xiii, xvii, 9, 51, 53, 64, 85, 95, 100-103, 105-112, 169, 171
reactionally degenerate 15, 30

reasoning iv, xii, 5, 6, 8, 21, 23, 27, 29, 57, 59, 68, 69, 85, 87, 89-91, 104, 110, 112, 162, 163, 171
Reissman, F. 63, 165
reliabilities xi, xii, xiii, xv, 70, 79, 80, 88-91, 105-107, 113, 116, 117, 122, 128, 153, 154
reliability iv, 50, 67-71, 78, 82, 88, 89, 101, 105, 106, 111, 154, 161, 163
Richard-Amato, Patricia 167
Rivera, Charlene 164
Rock, Donald A. xiv, xv, 128-137, 165
Roth, David 50, 54, 64, 85, 169
Rumelhart, David 57, 169
Russell, Bertrand 22, 165, 169
Sagan, Carl 36, 169
Sang, Fritz 3, 4, 170
Saussure, Ferdinand de 4, 12, 32
Schank, Roger 57, 169
schema 169
Schilpp, Paul A. 165
Schneck, R. 163
Schumann, John 21, 169
Scott, Rober J. i, v, 10, 39, 143-145, 169
Scovel, Thomas 21, 169
Scribner, Sylvia 170
Searle, John 14
Selinker, Larry 21, 169
semantics 28
semiosis ix, 6, 11, 30-32, 34, 35, 37, 85
semiotic iv, xvii, 4-8, 11-13, 16-21, 23, 24, 26, 27, 30-33, 35, 36, 38, 39, 42, 47, 55, 59, 60, 79, 81, 85-87, 90, 95, 103, 104, 123, 125, 138, 144, 162
sensory-motor 8, 11, 14-17, 19, 20, 23, 25-27, 30
Shopen, Timothy 171
Shuy, Roger 25, 169
Skutnabb-Kangas, T. 27, 143, 169
Smith, Frank 11
Snow, Becky 14, 89, 166
Souberman, Ellen 170
spatio-temporal 34
Spearman, Charles E. 7, 49, 70, 88, 102, 169, 170
specificity xi, xiii, xiv, 49, 69, 71, 82-84, 90, 91, 111, 112, 123, 124, 137, 138, 161
Spener, David 63, 170
Spolsky, Bernard 23, 114, 115, 150, 168, 170
Stansfield, Charles 165, 168
Stephenson 49
Sternberg, Robert J. 5, 170
Storey, Mary Ellen 27, 30, 164
Streiff, Virginia v, 3, 5, 7-10, 35, 75, 85, 88, 113, 115, 125, 126, 148, 150, 156, 168, 170
Stricker, Lawrence J. 4, 50, 139, 168
Stump, Thomas 3, 5, 170
superordinate 38, 55
superordination 39, 43

Swanson, Henry L. 27, 170
SWCEL (South West Cooperative Educational Laboratory) 145-147, 171
syntax xii, xiii, 9, 22, 28, 36, 95, 99, 101, 106, 107, 108, 110-112, 145-147, 164, 165, 171
TABE (Test of Adult Basic Education) 75-82, 84
Teitelbaum, Herta 114, 126, 170
TESOL (Teachers of English to Speakers of Other Languages) 11, 163, 168, 170
Teyler, Timothy 171
Thorndike, Robert L. 8, 170
Tikunoff, W. J. 164
TOBE (Test of Basic Experiences 144-147
TOEFL (Test of English as a Foreign Language) 139
Toukomaa, P. 27, 143, 169
Trosper, George 164, 168
Tucker, G. Richard 11, 73, 170
unreliability 68, 69
unrotated factor solutions xvi, 159, 160
Upshur, John A. 49, 170
Vakar, G. 170

validity iii, iv, 5-8, 10, 15, 16, 67-69, 75, 86, 87, 88, 89, 103, 111-113, 128, 146, 147, 163, 171
van Kleeck, Anne 148, 167
varimax rotated solutions xi, xiii, xiv, xv, xvi, 6, 83, 84, 109, 110, 111, 120-123, 133-136, 158, 160
Vigil, Neddy 21, 170
Vollmer, , Helmut 3, 4, 170
Von Neumann, John 45, 170
Vygotsky, Lev Semenovich 22, 29, 35-37, 170
Wechsler, David (or Wechsler tests) 49, 171
Weiss, Paul 22, 166
Wesman, A. G. 7, 170
Wilcox, Sherman 22, 32, 167, 170
WISC (Wechsler Intelligence Scale for Children) 49, 50, 166
Wittrock, M. C. 59, 60, 166, 170, 171
Woese, Carl R. 36, 39, 43, 166, 171
Wolfgang, A. 167
Wolfram, W. 64, 171
Wolpert, Gordon 41, 171
Yates, James R. 30, 74, 168
Yorozuya, Ryiuichi 114, 147, 171
Young, J. Z. 42, 171
Yudovich, F. A. 22, 167